The eleventh commandment

THE ELEVENTH COMMANDMENT

Church and mission today

Peter Cotterell

Inter-Varsity Press

Inter-Varsity Press
38 De Montfort Street, Leicester LE1 7GP, England

© Peter Cotterell 1981

All rights reserved. No part of this publication may be reproduced, stored in a retrieval system, or transmitted, in any form or by any means, electronic, mechanical, photocopying, recording or otherwise, without the prior permission of Inter-Varsity Press.

Unless otherwise stated, quotations from the Bible are from the Revised Standard Version, copyrighted 1956, 1952, © 1971, 1973, by the Division of Christian Education, National Council of the Churches of Christ in the USA, and used by permission.

First published 1981

British Library Cataloguing in Publication Data
Cotterell, Peter
   The eleventh commandment.
   1. Missions
   I. Title
   266   BV2061

ISBN 0-851100-705-2

Nov. 81

Set in Times Roman 10/11pt
Typeset in Cyprus by Memo Typography Ltd.
Printed in Great Britain by Billing and Sons Ltd,
Guildford, London and Worcester

Inter-Varsity Press is the publishing division of the Universities and Colleges Christian Fellowship (formerly the Inter-Varsity Fellowship), a student movement linking Christian Unions in universities and colleges throughout the British Isles, and a member movement of the International Fellowship of Evangelical Students. For information about local and national activities in Great Britain write to UCCF, 38 De Montford Street, Leicester LE1 7GP.

Contents

Abbreviations	7
1. Defining mission	9
1.1 What mission is not: Rahner's theses	9
1.2 What mission is: elenctics	16
1.3 Six missiological principles	18
2. The church	22
2.1 The origin of the church	24
2.2 The nature of the church	26
2.3 The function of the church	34
2.4 The identity of the church	38
3. The task of the church	42
3.1 What is man?	42
3.2 Witnessing and discipling	47
3.3 Power for mission	52
3.4 Proclamation and persuasion	59
3.5 Liberation theology	61
3.6 Categories of mission	69
4. The end of an era	75
4.1 The history of Christian mission	76
4.2 The modern missionary movement	79
4.3 The new world for world mission	85
5. The Church Growth movement	93
5.1 Introduction	93
5.2 Some axioms of the Church Growth movement	95
5.3 Effective Church Growth investigation	109
5.4 Types of growth	116
5.5 Church Growth: an assessment	122

6. Confrontation	124
6.1 Introduction	124
6.2 The impact of Marxism	126
6.3 The impact of Islam	134
6.4 Confrontation with world religions	142
7. The way ahead	149
7.1 The task unchanged	149
7.2 The new situation	151
7.3 Missionary societies	156
7.4 Theological training	157
7.5 Repentance and renewal	164
Bibliography	166
Index	172

Abbreviations

AV	Authorized (King James') Version of the Bible
EMQ	*Evangelical Missions Quarterly*
ET	*Expository Times*
IRM	*International Review of Mission(s)*
JB	Jerusalem Bible
JTS	*Journal of Theological Studies*
NEB	New English Bible
RSV	Revised Standard Version of the Bible
RV	Revised Version of the Bible
TDNT	*Theological Dictionary of the New Testament,* ed. G. W. Bromiley (Eerdmans, Grand Rapids, 1964-76).

Someone once described the Great Commission of Matthew 28:19 as the eleventh commandment:

> *Go, therefore and make disciples of all nations.*

This surely is more than a 'commission'. It is a command. This book is about this 'eleventh commandment'.

1
Defining mission

This book is about mission. Christian mission to the people next door and to the nations a thousand and more miles away. Mission carried on in the hope and expectation that it will lead to people putting their faith in God through Jesus Christ, finding meaning for life in Jesus Christ. Mission that would openly expect people to leave Buddhism or Hinduism or Islam in response to Jesus' imperative 'Follow me.'

I begin with this rather blunt and non-academic introduction to the concept of mission because, certainly in Britain and almost certainly in most of the traditionally mission-sending countries, the modern heresy is religious relativism: 'All religions are basically the same. We're all seeking God. We should leave the Jew to his Judaism and the Muslim to Islam. What makes you think that Christianity is any better than Buddhism?'

Religious relativism begins from the assumption that God has *not* spoken, that there is *no* ultimately authoritative revelation available to us from God, and that I am therefore free to make up my own mind, to use my own intellect, to weigh up the competing claims of the world's religions, and then to decide for myself which, or perhaps which mixture, I should opt for — rather like a theological Woolworth's pick-'n'mix.

Such a viewpoint ought not to be merely assumed. It does need some justification, especially as Christianity does *not* pretend to be a humanly concocted philosophy which provides answers to humanly conceived questions, but claims to be a divine revelation which shows us the significance of life and offers us an otherwise unobtainable quality of life through Christ.

1.1 WHAT MISSION IS NOT: RAHNER'S THESES

Any thinking person eventually becomes aware of the plurality of religions on offer today. Any thinking Christian eventually faces the question of the relationship between Christianity and these religions. More humanly, every Christian faces the question not of the status of the religions so much as the position of their adherents: how should the Christian relate to the Muslim or the Jew? Does their religion meet their religious needs? Ultimately the question becomes one of their standing before God. Does God know them? Are they in his family? Christian mission is concerned with the answer to these and related questions.

In an attempt to make clear what, to me, mission is *not*, I take the missiology of the Roman Catholic theologian and philosopher, Karl Rahner. I choose Rahner because he has propounded a concept which has found rather widespread favour, the concept of the *anonymous Christian*. Rahner's is, however, only one of many unbiblical options for an understanding of Christian mission, and chapter 3 looks at a second, the option offered in liberation theology.

Fundamental to Rahner's thinking is the concept of the anonymous Christian, the individual who has made no overt commitment to Christ, who may, indeed, be a member of a non-Christian religion and even expressly opposed to Christianity. Rahner would see such an individual as one who stands under the saving grace and forgiveness of God, needing only to be *told* his position as an anonymous Christian, but not to be converted either from his own religion or to the Christian faith. Following the relativity of Roman Catholic soteriology,[2] Rahner would not suggest that the anonymous Christian is 'saved', but that he is *likely* to be saved (although the overt, practising Christian is *more likely* to be saved). Even before the anonymous Christian is met with the proclaimed word of Christ, say through a missionary, he *is* a Christian.

Rahner's ideas are neatly embodied in four theses. The first of these theses is superficially orthodox: *'Christianity understands itself as the absolute religion, intended for all men, which cannot recognize any other religion beside itself as of equal right.'*[3]

While this statement appears orthodox, an important qualification is added to it. The historical events of the Bible, for example God's revelation of himself to Moses, the incarnation, or the passion, do not necessarily invalidate world religions until those religions are meaningfully confronted by Christianity:

> Christianity can recognize itself as the true and lawful religion for all men only where and when it enters with existential power and

---

[1]For Karl Rahner's missiology see chapter 6 of volume 5 of his *Theological Investigations* (Darton, Longman and Todd, London, 1954 and onwards). A useful collection of readings on the Christian approach to the peoples of other religions is in John Hick and Brian Hebblethwaite (eds.), *Christianity and Other Religions* (Collins, Glasgow, 1980). This book includes Rahner's theses.

[2]Obviously, Roman Catholic soteriology would avoid the categorical assertion than anyone was 'saved'.

[3]Rahner, *op.cit.*, p. 118.

demanding force into the realm of another religion and ... puts it in question.[4]

The concept appears to develop from Rahner's drawing of a radical distinction between Old Testament and New Testament, and between the 'religion' of the Old Testament, and Christianity, the 'religion' of the New Testament. Rahner is here almost dispensational: the Old Testament covenant is seen by him as having been valid (although in some sense inadequate) until it was confronted by Christ, when it at once lost its validity.[5]

But Christ explicitly did *not* come to begin something new, but rather to demonstrate the true meaning of the old (Mt. 5:17). The foundation of later Judaism cannot seriously be taken back beyond Moses and the law-giving (or at best Abraham). These events, however, form part of a continuum which reaches back to Noah, Enoch and Abel (Heb. 11:4-7) and forward to the church. And this continuing people of God, throughout its history, has always constituted a judgment on the alternative *religions* of the nations. Long before Christ, the religion of the Canaanites was put under judgment by the Hebrews, the idolatry of Babylon by Isaiah, and the perversions of Nineveh by Jonah. There is, in fact, no point discernible in the biblical record where the world's religions are accorded any kind of legitimacy. The violence of the language of Deuteronomy 13, which deals with the action to be taken against individuals who might try to lead Israel into following such religions, is typical of the consistent attitude of the Bible record to other religions. They are *always* illegitimate.

It would appear to me that a fundamental error in Rahner's reasoning is that of assigning a starting point for Christianity at the passion, ignoring the real continuity that Christianity has with Judaism properly understood. There is no suggestion that apostate, nationalistic, Pharisaic Judaism was ever valid. The attempt to make a corrupt form of Judaism legitimate until the confrontation with Christ in the passion fails, and with it the attempt to establish legitimacy for other religions until some parallel confrontation takes place in them.

The second thesis recognizes the presence in non-Christian religions of *'supernatural elements arising out of the grace which is given to men as a gratuitous gift on account of Christ'*.[6] This would suggest that within, say, Hinduism, there are elements given by God as a kind of *charismata*, grace-gifts. The position is reached as follows:

---

[4]*Ibid.*
[5]Which prompts the question: are Jews, then, excluded from being anonymous Christians? If this is so (and it would appear to follow from Rahner's thinking), it produces the curious result that an adherent of, say, African traditional religion, who has never heard of Christ and has never encountered the Bible, is an anonymous Christian, while a Jew, whose God is the God of the Old Testament and who accepts as authoritative 78% of the Christian Scriptures, is not.
[6]Rahner, *op.cit.*, p. 121.

If God wills all men to be saved
and
if the majority of mankind is allied to the non-Christian religions
and
if salvation is only to be found in Christ
then
Christ must somehow be at work in these religions, by grace.

Evidence for the activity of Christ within the non-Christian religions is found by Rahner in the 'religious' acts of their adherents, acts which are interpreted as *moral* acts, which then become morally *right* acts, and finally, because they are morally *right, Christian* acts. And so Christ is at work even in the non-Christian religions.

Against such a theory there is the undeniable evidence of the opposition of the Old Testament prophets to the religions of the surrounding nations. There is no suggestion that these religions are legitimate alternatives to Yahwism or that Yahweh is somehow present in them. Rahner deals with this problem by denying the legitimacy of the criticisms levelled at, for example, the Canaanite religions, by the prophets. The Old Testament has no ultimate authority until the New Testament legitimizes it:

> Since the infallible delimitation of the canon of the Old Testament is again to be found only in the New Testament, the exact and final differentiation between the lawful and the unlawful in the Old Testament religion is again possible only by making use of the New Testament as something eschatologically final.[7]

In response to the second thesis we comment, firstly, that the New Testament does not *legitimize* the Old Testament, but *confirms* the Old Testament in that it presents precisely the same attitude to world religions. Before their conversion the Christians of Ephesus were 'without hope and without God' (Eph. 2:12). The Colossian Christians were 'dead in trespasses' (Col. 2:13). Paul takes up Isaiah 52:15 and announces:

> They shall see who have never been told of him,
> and they shall understand who have never heard of him (Rom. 15:21).

There is no suggestion here that already, before the proclamation of Christ reached them, these people had somehow had Christ in their own religions.

Secondly, it does not appear that these religions, within which Christ

[7]*Ibid.*, pp. 126f.

is supposed to have distributed certain grace-gifts, actually dispose their adherents to follow Christ. How, for example, are we to find Christ's grace-gifts in Islam, which has consistently denied the essence of Christianity, the death of Christ on the cross? Those who have actually lived and witnessed amongst Muslims and Hindus and Buddhists seem uniformly to have found that these religions predispose man to reject Christ.

Thirdly, the argument is not logically coherent. The conclusion does not necessarily follow from the three premises. The majority of people *are* to be found in the other religions, and there *is* no salvation apart from Christ, but the divine response to this situation is twofold: the testimony of creation (Rom. 1:20) and the witness of the church. We shall see more of this later in chapter 2.

The third thesis introduces the concept of the anonymous Christian: *'Christianity does not simply confront the member of an extra-Christian religion as a mere non-Christian but as someone who can and must already be recognized in this or that respect as an anonymous Christian.'*[8]

It is here that Rahner betrays the fact that he writes as a philosopher-theologian and not as one who has engaged in practical mission. He supposes that the 'pagan' has had an experience of the grace of God in his own religion and suggests that if he has 'already accepted this grace as the ultimate, unfathomable entelechy of his existence by accepting the immeasurableness of his dying existence as opening out into infinity', then he has already been given revelation 'in a true sense', even before he has been affected by missionary preaching.

If we unravel the syntax and interpret the vocabulary, Rahner seems to be saying that if a pagan is able to see that death is not the end of life but its fulfilment, and that the proper fulfilment of this life in the afterlife is made available to man by the grace of God, then this measure of perception is actually divine revelation. God has shown it to him. But there are too many 'ifs' here. Pagan man, non-Christian man, does not see life and death in terms of entelechy ('unfolding') or grace, but in terms of dread, fear. Death *is*, universally, the last enemy.

Again it must be said that from the New Testament record, the approach of the Christian to the pagan religions was not of the kind envisaged by Rahner. Far from identifying pagans as anonymous Christians, Paul is at pains to announce the inherent invalidity of their religions. Acts 14:8-18 probably represents the first 'uncontaminated' contact between Christianity and a non-Jewish religion, the worship of Zeus and Hermes. But Paul tells the worshippers:

> Turn from *these vain things (mataioi,* ineffective, ungrounded, useless, unprofitable) to a living God (Acts 14:15).

[8]*Ibid.,* p. 131.

At Athens Paul deliberately refrains from building on to the Athenians' named gods and denies the validity of their philosophy: God does *not* live in shrines and *cannot* be served by human hands, and Paul decries their thought forms: we ought *not* to think that the Deity is like gold (Acts 17:16-34).

Again, when Paul was at Ephesus, complaint was made against him that he had 'persuaded and turned away' many people, 'saying that gods made with hands are not gods' (Acts 19:26).

And finally, it is not clear what can be meant by accounting a person a Christian 'in this or that respect'. Rahner's concept of the Christian is existential, not biblical. God is, for Rahner, 'the comprehensive, though never comprehended ground and presupposition of our *experience* and of the objects of that experience.'[9] Similarly Rahner's concept of the Spirit owes more to existentialism than to Scripture; for him it is apparent that the Spirit is experienced wherever and however man surrenders to ultimate mystery,[10] a viewpoint which Buddhists like Christmas Humphreys might find more congenial than would the orthodox Christian. This reinterpretation of trinitarian Christianity would presumably make any person who surrenders himself to mysticism or even, to use one of Rahner's own examples, anyone who freely forgives someone who has harmed him, a possessor of the Spirit and therefore a Christian 'in this or that respect'.

Positively, however, it must be commented that Rahner is surely right in rejecting the idea that the 'pagan' is entirely abandoned by God. God sends the rain on the just and the unjust. The option is not a simple choice between the Christian in the favoured family of God and the pagan altogether abandoned to his fate. We must allow for the reality of the pagan actively sought by God (Is. 42:6-8), even though perversely the religion he has created for himself leaves him godless (*atheos,* Eph. 2:12).

The fourth thesis defines the missionary task as being *'to bring to explicit consciousness' what is already present implicitly.*[11] The missionary is confronted by enormous numbers of people in a plurality of non-Christian religions. How is he to respond to them? Rahner recognizes that this religious pluralism may well not wither away as had once been confidently expected, but 'it is nevertheless absolutely permissible for the Christian himself to interpret this non-Christianity as Christianity of an anonymous kind'.[12]

Here is a peculiar combination of ruthless religious imperialism and outdated mission triumphalism. The church, through its mission, suggests Rahner, should expect to triumph, and yet appearances are to the contrary. What then?

[9]*The Spirit in the Church* (Burns and Oates, London, 1979), p. 14.
[10]*Ibid.,* pp. 19-22.
[11]*Theological Investigations* 5, chapter 6, p. 133.
[12]*Ibid.*

DEFINING MISSION

Those who oppose 'are merely those who have not yet recognised what they nevertheless really already are (or can be) even when, on the surface of existence, they are in opposition; they are already anonymous Christians'.[13] Man, it appears, loses all his humanness. He cannot choose, cannot oppose, but is merely manipulated. Bishop Lesslie Newbigin recently characterized this absurdity of the anonymous Christian as being like 'conferring an *aégrotat* degree *in absentia* upon a non-matriculant who does not even believe in tertiary education'. Newbigin comments on Rahner's theses in his *The Open Secret*; his generally negative assessment is succinctly summarized in his comment: 'The scheme is vulnerable at many points.'[14]

Of course Rahner's concept of the anonymous Christian is only one attempt to deal with the problems raised by the concept of a unique vehicle of salvation, the Christian faith. These problems must be taken seriously. It is a fact that in general one's religion is dependent on the accident of birth. An Indian is likely to be a Hindu, an Arab a Muslim, a Japanese a Buddhist, a Chinese a Communist, and an American a Christian. If Christianity alone is the vehicle of salvation, this seems unfair to those born in, for example, Asia.

A second problem is that one's salvation appears to depend on someone else — not on myself; not even on God, but on the willingness of the Christians to come and tell me about Christ. Why should I be penalized for someone else's disobedience?

Thirdly, and arising out of the second problem, it appears that the expressed love of God and his desire that all men should be saved have in the church a very inadequate vehicle. Surely we should expect something more reliable than the Model T Ford which the church often appears to be.

And, fourthly, there is the problem raised by the recognition that many so-called Christians have very poor moral standards, while many of the adherents of other religions have clearly higher moral standards.

It is in battling with these and many related problems that some have felt it necessary to abandon the concept of a unique vehicle of salvation for the world, and to open the gates of the church even to those who have to be, as it were, carried in screaming, struggling and protesting that they are *not* Christians. Over against such solutions the biblical picture is simple and uncompromising:

1. Christianity is the absolute vehicle of life which is available to all men, and recognizes no religion as possessing eternal validity.

2. Non-Christian beliefs include within themselves genuine human insights into the nature of the world, of man and of God, but with such an admixture of error as to make them incapable of leading

[13]*Ibid.*, p. 134.
[14]Lesslie Newbigin, *The Open Secret* (SPCK, London, 1978), pp. 195-197.

THE ELEVENTH COMMANDMENT

their adherents to God.

3. The Christian mission is urgent in that it confronts members of the world's religions with the claims of Christ, and with Christ himself, who alone is the way to God.

4. Religious and irreligious pluralism will continue to the end of time, representing always the spiritual conflict of the two kingdoms, the kingdom of God and the kingdom of darkness. The Christian mission is to be effected in this context of spiritual conflict.

1.2 WHAT MISSION IS: ELENCTICS[15]

The Christian mission is not concerned with an attempt to reach some kind of mutual understanding with world religions, nor is it particularly concerned with the reformation of religious *systems*. Systems of theology or philosophy cannot repent. The Christian mission is *elenctic* in the New Testament sense of that word, rebuking, refuting, confuting and calling to repentance the *peoples* of the world.

The verb *elenchein* occurs eighteen times in the New Testament. In nine of these occurrences the word is used in direct relation to sin. For example, Jesus asks: 'Which of you *convicts* me of sin?' (Jn. 8:46); and Paul tells Timothy: 'As for those who persist in sin, *rebuke* them in the presence of all' (1 Tim. 5:20). Again, James comments on the person who discriminates against the poor: 'You commit sin, and are *convicted* by the law' (Jas. 2:9).

The Revised Standard Version uses eight words to translate the one Greek verb: reveal, expose, reprove, rebuke, convince, convict, confute, and exhort.[16] These words effectively map the domain of meaning of the Greek word. In missiological terms an elenchus is *a confrontation with error in which error is exposed for what it is, the one guilty of error feels rebuked and compelled to admit his error and, one hopes, is led to repentance.*[17]

There is, of course, a church elenctic, a situation within the church which calls for a confrontation with error and its refutation. In Titus

[15]On elenctics see John R. W. Stott's discussion, 'The Place of Elenctics' in *Christian Mission in the Modern World* (CPAS, London, ²1977), pp. 69-71; and, in great detail, J. H. Bavinck's *An Introduction to the Science of Missions* (originally published in Dutch; English translation by D. H. Freeman, Presbyterian and Reformed Publishing Company, Philadelphia, 1960), Part II, pp. 221-272. David Hesselgrave, *Communicating Christ Cross-culturally* (Zondervan, Grand Rapids, 1978), devotes chapter 42 to the subject of elenctics.

[16]'Exhort', Heb. 12:14. This translation owes more to the translator's cultural prejudice concerning the appropriate relationship between father and son than to the actual meaning of the text. The suggestion is *not* that the father exhorts the son to do well, but that he rebukes his son for doing wrong.

[17]Friedrich Büchsel comments: 'The word does not mean only "to blame" or "to reprove", nor "to convince" in the sense of proof, nor "to reveal" or "expose", but "to set right", namely "to point away from sin to repentance" *(TDNT,* article *elenchō).*

16

this is seen as the responsibility of the bishop:

> A bishop ... must hold firm to the sure word as taught, so that he may be able to give instruction in sound doctrine and also to *confute* those who contradict it (Tit. 1:9).

1.2.1 The elenchus of the Spirit

The predominant subject of the verb *elenchein* is the Holy Spirit. It is the responsibility of the Christian to be a witness about Christ, but it is not his responsibility to argue his listener through to the experience of conversion. We may witness, but it is the Holy Spirit who reveals, exposes, reproves, rebukes, convinces and convicts. Jesus makes this clear in his clarification of the role of the Paraclete in mission:

> When he comes, he will *convince* the world concerning sin and righteousness and judgment: concerning sin, because they do not believe in me; concerning righteousness, because I go to the Father, and you will see me no more; concerning judgment, because the ruler of this world is judged (Jn. 16:8-11).

The word 'paraclete' has a forensic background and might be related to the modern concept of a counsel either for the defence or for the prosecution. The noun is used only by John. In 1 John 2:1 the 'advocate' is Jesus who stands on the side of the believer. In John 14-16 the 'advocate' is the Holy Spirit who convicts the prisoner of his guilt and forces him to admit that what is being said by the Christian witness is true.

This elenctic ministry of the Spirit is vital to mission, because it is naturally impossible for man to respond appropriately to the preached word of God. As William Temple comments:

> The Comforter will bring evidence to prove the world wrong in certain respects ... the three matters most important to man's life: sin, righteousness and judgement ... the world has to learn that its very conception of these things is all wrong. If it tries to avoid sin or to seek righteousness, it does not avoid or seek the right things; if it fears or prepares for judgement, it does not fear or prepare for the right thing.[18]

The Christian mission, then, is not discussion aimed at reaching a consensus, nor dialectic whose outcome is some unpredictable synthesis, nor a proclamation to anonymous Christians. It is the Christian confronting error and proclaiming the good news about Jesus Christ in the power of the Holy Spirit, in the hope that the hearer will be con-

---

[18] *Readings in St John's Gospel* (Macmillan, London, 1953), pp. 282-283.

victed, confuted and rebuked concerning his sin and will repent and turn to faith in God through Christ.

1.3 SIX MISSIOLOGICAL PRINCIPLES

It would be comforting to suppose that theological investigation could be carried out with complete objectivity. Even the scientists have long since given up the attempt to maintain the fiction of objective study. The following six principles determine what I say in this book.

1.3.1 Missiology is trinitarian

It seems to be the case that man is always attracted by the reduction of all forms of complexity, all types of compound, to a mathematical unity. To take physics as an example, there is the continuing search for a unified field theory to combine the field theories dealing with electromagnetism and gravity and light and so on. And there is the irritation felt by some over the wave/particle duality in light. This same feeling of the innate rightness of mathematical unity plagues the theologian. Despite this pressure, however, the Christian is left with a trinitarian theology as the only theology adequate to cope with the biblical data concerning the Godhead.

The same is true as we study the teaching of the Bible regarding mission. Mission takes its origin from God the Father who so loved the world that he gave his only Son, sending him into the world to live and ultimately to die for its sins. It is, again, God the Father who, at the request of the risen Son, sends his Spirit into the world to the church, empowering the church for mission, and convincing the world concerning its sin, concerning righteousness and judgment. It is the Spirit who leads the church into truth.

The Son is first of all Saviour; but he is also head of the church, alive in the church and interceding for the church.

1.3.2 Missiology is biblical

This is, of course, easier to assert than it is to substantiate. Most of the competing Christian theologies would say they were biblical. I can claim only to have attempted to take biblical evidence seriously. So far as I am aware I have not begun with some preconceived idea about mission and then clothed the idea with appropriate biblical proof texts, but have attempted a *canonical* understanding of mission, starting with the Bible, and, what is more, starting with the *whole* Bible.

There is no intention here of relativizing or reinterpreting Scripture in the interests of a preconceived systematic theology. If the results of taking the biblical text seriously are unacceptable to 'modern man' or (worse) to 'modern thinking', so much the worse for modern man and modern thinking. I have a distinct advantage here over many of my colleagues, since I have been a working missionary for most of my life, and have crept into academic life very late and somewhat unwillingly. Thus I do not stand in any particular awe of the theologians.

But how is Scripture to be interpreted? For me, hermeneutics begins with a recognition that the Bible is inspired and that the total biblical revelation was given because of its on-going importance to the people of God. As a linguist, however, I recognize that the biblical text exhibits many *forms*, including poetry, biography, parable and so on. The *form* is significant in understanding the *message*. So also is the observation of the context within which the message is formed.

Interpretation also necessarily involves contextualization: the ability to relate the biblical message and contemporary society properly.[19] The temptation to wrench Scripture out of its own context in the interest of current or cultural relevance is as much to be resisted as the unthinking assumption that certain parts of the biblical text are irrelevant simply because the immediate context is unfamiliar.

I would distinguish between what is *prescriptive* in the Bible and what is *descriptive*. The distinction is not always easy to make, but, to take an example, Paul's missionary methodology seems to me to be described in Acts but nowhere prescribed as the right one for all subsequent missionaries.

Biblical revelation focuses on salvation history. This is not *Heilsgeschichte* in the sense sometimes employed, where salvation history has no relationship to real events in real history. Rather the historical events selectively included in the Bible are there not because of their intrinsic importance to human history, but because of their bearing on the unfolding plan of redemption. Thus Omri, humanly speaking a very important king in Israel, is all but ignored in the Old Testament (1 Ki. 16:21-28), while Ahab is given six chapters (1 Ki. 17-22).

The Bible supposes a real fall, sets out a way of salvation, and commissions the people of God as his witnesses, heralds of his salvation.

1.3.3 Missiology is also ecclesiology

Mission is a task committed to the church, and missiology cannot be developed adequately without clear reference to ecclesiology. The Latin American theologian Orlando Costas criticizes the missiology of the Church Growth writers such as Donald McGavran because it concentrates too much attention on the church:

> When church growth theorists affirm that the aim of evangelism is *the* multiplication of churches, they are advocating a theology that makes the church the end of God's mission.[20]

---

[19]See particularly Bruce J. Nicholls, *Contextualization: a Theology of Gospel and Culture* (IVP, Downers Grove, and Paternoster Press, London, 1979).
[20]*The Church and its Mission* (Tyndale House, Wheaton, 1974), p. 135.

But it is precisely the weakness of Costas' own ecclesiology that drives him to this incorrect and illogical statement. Certainly missionaries expect Christian communities, churches, to result from their proclamation, but that is not the goal of proclamation, still less the ultimate goal. The goal is to proclaim Christ, whether there is a response to that proclamation or not. The ultimate expectation is the return of the King and the inauguration of the kingdom.

Mission, however, *starts* from the church, so that missiology must also be ecclesiology. But the church is to be seen in its twentieth-century form as the world-wide church. Mission is the concern of all churches and not the preserve of the so-called North Atlantic churches. Mission is in all continents, it is from all continents and it is to all continents. Since the church-body is one, we should recognize that the resources of the world-wide church are common resources: a common asset and a common responsibility.

1.3.4 Mission is evangelism

On biblical grounds it is difficult to justify the separation of evangelism from mission. It does not appear possible to indicate just where evangelism ceases to be evangelism and becomes instead mission. Moreover, there is no special biblical category of *missionary* which corresponds to the modern English usage of that word. Every Christian is constituted a witness, and some are given a particular gift of evangelism (Eph. 4:11), but there is no mention of a distinct category of evangelist labelled missionary.

Obviously there are quantitative differences between pioneer missionary outreach in a new language to people of a different culture who have never heard the good news previously, and sharing that same good news with a neighbour. But the differences are quantitative only. The language barriers may be higher, the cultural differences more apparent, the sheer physical demands more intense, but in all evangelism the same problems are present in some measure.

1.3.5 Mission is holistic

The church follows Jesus in being concerned for the whole person. It ought not to be possible to preach the good news without at the same time identifying with the poverty and the oppression and the hunger and the fear of those to whom we speak.

And yet there have been times when missions have tried to do just that—artificially to separate spirit from body and to minister to the one as though it had no connection with the other. It is doubtful whether mission in Christ's name can be carried on where the element of human compassion is absent. It is even arguable that the Christian who lacks such compassion is cut off from communion with God. At Corinth the church was divided on many issues, not least on the issue of rich and

DEFINING MISSION

poor. The rich ate their meat and drank their wine and grew merry in the process. The poor sat in the same room and 'had nothing' (1 Cor. 11:22). And in that context the church essayed to have communion. Paul retorted, 'It is not the Lord's supper that you eat.' They broke the bread and passed it round, they filled the cup and they sipped the wine. But Paul insisted that it was not communion. Where the people gathered around the table were not recognized as constituting the body of Christ, there could be no communion. The body of the Lord could not be shared. The ritual was observed at Corinth, but there was no communion.

Where mission is attempted without compassion, communion with God is lost. And without that, mission is not mission. But while mission will always be holistic, there *is* a biblical priority. As John Stott has said, 'the word "mission" cannot be used to cover everything God is doing in the world'.[21] The Lausanne Covenant comments: 'In the church's mission of sacrificial service, evangelism is primary.'[22]

God is at work in the world in many ways. He is at work in his church in many ways. But not all that the church does is to be equated with mission. It is right that the church should be involved in feeding the hungry, but when the hungry have been fed they have not thereby been evangelized; the good news has not necessarily been preached to them. Good works may be practised for many reasons, not all of them glorifying to God.

1.3.6 Mission implies exclusivism

Mission implies lostness and foundness, that all are initially lost but that some will be found. Fundamentally there is the recognition that man is spiritually lost, spiritually dead[23] and unable to find his own way back to God. The Bible lends no support to the naive notion that man is somehow maturing and that he will one day be able to conquer his limitations, transform his environment, synthesize God and escape from his humiliating need for revelation.

Where revelation and salvation are refused an eternally significant separation takes place. Potentially, mission enfolds people into the family of God, but mission also defines unmistakably the category, not of those who are being excluded, but of those who choose exclusion.

---

[21] *Christian Mission in the Modern World*, p. 19.
[22] *Let the Earth Hear His Voice* (World Wide Publications, Minneapolis, 1975), p. 5.
[23] See my *Salvation* (Kingsway Press, 1980), chapter 2.

2
The church

In 1789 the French Revolution ushered in a storm which, for Europe, ended an era of ecclesiastical and political magnificence matched only, perhaps, by its irrelevance to the needs of the labouring masses.

Only three years later, while French émigrés were still daily fleeing to the coasts of Britain with no assurance whatever that the Terror would not shortly follow them to their temporary refuge,[1] William Carey (1761-1834) initiated a theological revolution in England with the publication of his treatise *An Enquiry into the Obligation of Christians to Use Means for the Conversion of the Heathen.*

But the church in England at the end of the eighteenth century was ill prepared for this particular revolution. Protestant theology was in one of its periodic surrenders to hyper-Calvinism. Mission had become *missio Dei,* God's mission. When Carey presented the matter of mission as a subject for discussion at the Ministers' Fraternal in Northampton, Dr John Ryland silenced him:

> Young man, sit down, sit down. You're an enthusiast. When God pleases to convert the heathen, He'll do it without consulting you or me.[2]

In spite of the opposition, Carey's revolution could not be held back. At Nottingham, on May 1792, the Northampton Baptist Association began the day with prayer at six o'clock in the morning. At ten o'clock Carey preached from Isaiah 54. F.W. Gotch later commented:

> I call that sermon of Carey's wonderful, because there has, perhaps, been no sermon preached in modern days, which has had so distinct and traceable an effect on Protestant Christianity throughout the world.[3]

[1] See Arthur Bryant, *The Years of Endurance, 1793-1802* (Collins, Fontana Books, London and Glasgow, (1942) 1961) for a graphic account of England in Carey's day.
[2] A. H. Oussoren, *William Carey* (Suthoff, Leiden, 1945), p. 29.
[3] Quoted in S. Pearce Carey's *William Carey* (Hodder and Stoughton, London, 1924), p. 78. Gotch

THE CHURCH

Carey was unashamedly emotional:

> Find larger canvas, stouter and taller poles, stronger tent-pegs. Catch wider visions. Dare bolder programmes. Dwell in an ampler world.

At the close of the Association meetings it was resolved to form 'a Baptist Society for propagating the gospel among the heathens'. On 2 October 1792 the Society was formed. In November of 1793 Carey reached India.

The situation today is unimaginably different from that which confronted Carey. At the end of the eighteenth century the world church was only a dream, a dream shared by only a few. When Carey reached India there were few ecclesiastical structures for him to relate to.[4] The Thomas Christians had established a *modus vivendi* with their Hindu neighbours and had then busied themselves with converting the church into an institution. Carey's revolution was irresistible. In under two centuries the situation in India has been radically transformed. The determined pessimism of the statistician records that 'only' some 2.8% of the people of India are Christians. The pessimism conceals the reality of a church of some seventeen million members.

When the South American Missionary Society reached Chile in 1860, the indigenous population was almost untouched by the church. In the larger cities of the sub-continent the Roman Catholic Church flourished but the vast areas of the hinterland were largely ignored. By 1980 the Protestant church in South America numbered perhaps fifteen million in what was then the fastest-growing Christian community in the world.

When Livingstone reached Africa in 1841, mission societies had already been active for some thirty-seven years. To the north-east of the continent was the ancient but moribund church of Ethiopia. Still further to the north lay the Coptic churches of Egypt. To the south were the principally expatriate churches of the Cape. Livingstone's restless spirit led him into the heart of Africa, blazing the way for later missionaries—and for commerce. Here, again the revolution would not be denied. Just a century after Livingstone we find an Africa-wide church numbering 150 millions. At Kinshasa in 1971 the All Africa Conference of Churches declared:

---

was related to one of the Fuller Baptist church deacons.

[4]There were the Roman Catholic churches, of course, and the Mar Thoma church. There had been missionary work in India before Carey's arrival and there had even been something of a people movement in Tinnevelly: Stephen Neill, *A History of Christian Missions* (Pelican, Harmondsworth, 1964), p. 235, and his *The Story of the Christian Church in India and Pakistan* (Eerdmans, Grand Rapids, 1970), p. 61. Such movements were localized and did not become continuing channels of the divine activity.

We have hope that by the year 2,000, out of a total African population of 800 million, there will be an estimated Christian population of 350 million.[5]

Today, wherever we turn, we find that a transformation has taken place in our world. At his enthronement as Archbishop of Canterbury in 1942, William Temple referred to the existence of the world-wide church as 'the great new fact of our time'. When all the criticisms of the missionaries have been made, when all their failings have been catalogued and all their sins confessed, still the one fact remains: they went out to plant the church, and here, today, is the church.

2.1 THE ORIGIN OF THE CHURCH

But now we must ask: What *is* this world-wide church, planted at such a cost, and growing at such a rate? What are the origins of the church?

2.1.1 The human contribution

In a spirit of human triumphalism it would be fatally easy to suppose that the missionaries planted the church. That would be incorrect both historically and theologically. Historically, the missionaries have been primarily catalysts, in situations where there was no church. Once the church has been planted they have usually become, rightly or wrongly, teachers and trainers rather than evangelists. Practical mission has tended to become the responsibility of the new Christians.[6]

We would still be in error, however, even if we supposed that the world church has its origins in the church members themselves. It is true that throughout the world significant growth has tended to come when ordinary men and women have found the gospel such genuinely *good* news that they have been irresistibly impelled to gossip the gospel, without benefit of mission structures, wherever they have found themselves. Acts 8:4 describes this kind of spontaneity in witnessing, in this instance set in the context of persecution, although there is no evidence to suggest that persecution is a *necessary* adjunct to spontaneous witness.[7]

The true origin of the church, however, is to be found neither in the missionary nor in the activity of spontaneously witnessing church members.

---

[5]The Kinshasa Declaration, in the *International Review of Mission*, LXI, 242, April 1972, pp. 115-116. David Barrett's Unit of Research at Nairobi more conservatively suggests a total of 300 millions (quoted in Stephen Neill, *Salvation Tomorrow*, Lutterworth, London, 1976, p.128).

[6]Certainly of the nearly 3,000 churches in Ethiopia related to the work of the Sudan Interior Mission only some 2% trace their origins *directly* to a missionary.

[7]But see my article 'An Indigenous Church in Southern Ethiopia', *The Bulletin of the Society for African Church History*, III, 1-2, 1969-70, especially pp. 94-96.

2.1.2 The creation purpose of God

We come closer to the mark when we note the sense in which the church is seen to originate in creation. The church is, here and now, a worshipping community, and it is as a worshipping community that the church is presented in the final chapter of Revelation:

> There shall no more be anything accursed, but the throne of God and of the Lamb shall be in it, and his servants shall worship him; they shall see his face, and his name shall be on their foreheads (Rev. 22:3-4).

Since this is the end product of the entire process of creation and redemption it is surely reasonable to assume that it was at least part of the original purpose of God: to establish a worshipping community.

Certainly the first human couple are presented to us as enjoying fellowship with God, but the primal condition is abruptly terminated by the fall. The perfect worshipping community would include within itself all mankind, but such an all-inclusive community has not existed at any point in human history and cannot in present circumstances be brought into existence. Cain was the first of many to be overtly excluded from the community and so to suggest one of the distinguishing features of that community, its exclusiveness. While some are in the church, in the community, others are outside. It is a bounded community. The act of creation was presumably intended to lead into the establishment of a worshipping human community which we today label the church.

2.1.3 The apostolic church

The Nicene creed points to a further view of the origin of the church, in the apostles: the church is 'holy, catholic and apostolic'. The Roman Catholic theologian Hans Küng takes the third element here as determinative of the others:

> What is in question is not *any* kind of unity, holiness and catholicity, but that which is founded on the apostles and in that sense is apostolic.[8]

But what is meant by 'apostolic'? It is possible to reduce the concept to a mere theory of physical succession, but Küng offers an alternative, and more biblical, interpretation:

> Everything the church does must be directed toward fulfilling its

[8]*The Church* (Search Press, London 1968), p. 344. Küng goes on to consider the meaning of the term 'apostle' in the New Testament and in secular Greek, concluding that in many respects the New Testament concept is derived from the Old Testament šālīaḥ, 'envoy' (p. 346). But see also Thomas Wieser, 'Notes on the Meaning of the Apostolate', *IRM*, LXIV, 254, April 1975.

apostolic mission to the outside world ... To be itself, the church must follow the apostles in continually recognizing and demonstrating that it has been sent out into the world ... This makes it clear that apostolicity, like unity, holiness and catholicity, is not a static attribute of the church. Like them it is an historical dimension, a dimension which has constantly to be fulfilled anew in history.[9]

Of course Küng is speaking of the *church*, God's community whose history lies subsequent to the cross. It is well to recognize that the church so identified is historically and theologically related to the Old Testament community, which was not strictly speaking *apostolic*, although it had its own charismatic leadership which might arguably correspond to the New Testament apostolate.

For Küng, however, the church is apostolic, and the apostles are seen not as the ultimate *progenitors* of the church, but as the *archtypes*, people by whose activities the church is, through the centuries, to be judged. To apostolic *doctrine* there must be added apostolic *praxis*, apostolic action, if the church is to be allowed the title 'apostolic'. Precisely as 'not all who are descended from Israel belong to Israel', so not all who are descended from the apostles are apostolic. The apostolic church must *live* apostolically. In this, Küng is certainly pointing to a biblically based concept of apostolicity.

2.2 THE NATURE OF THE CHURCH

The church, then, is not *simply* a continuation of the Old Testament congregation. Certainly there is continuity between the worshipping community of the Old Testament and that of the New Testament. But continuity must not be confused with identity. As we shall see in the next chapter, Pentecost introduces a new element into the life of the individual worshipper and into the communal life of the community.

The *nature* of the church is most conveniently investigated through a study of the various biblical designations for God's people. Paul Minear examined some eighty such designations,[10] and we turn now to look at the most important of these.

2.2.1 The Old Testament *qāhāl*, 'congregation'

The concept of Israel as the *qāhāl*, the congregation, first appears in Genesis 28:3, in Isaac's *b^{e}rāḵâ*: 'God Almighty bless you and make you fruitful and multiply you, that you may become a company *(qāhāl)* of peoples.' In this application of the word there is, of course, no institutional element supposed of the *qāhāl*, although the fact that this par-

---
[9] Küng, *op. cit.*, p. 358.
[10] Paul S. Minear, *Images of the Church in the New Testament* (Lutterworth Press, London, 1961).

THE CHURCH

ticular 'company of peoples' has its origin in a particular prophecy distinguishes the company from a mere crowd.

The word occurs four times in 1 Kings 8, in the context of the dedication of the temple. In verse 14 it occurs twice: 'Then the king faced about, and blessed all the *assembly* of Israel, while all the *assembly* of Israel stood.' It occurs again in verse 22: 'Then Solomon stood before the altar of the Lord in the presence of all the *assembly* of Israel', and again in verse 65: 'So Solomon held a feast at that time, and all Israel with him, a great *assembly*, from the entrance of Hamath to the Brook of Egypt.'

Historically we have here the high point in the development of the *qāhāl*. The Solomonic empire has reached its greatest extent, peace reigns in the land, and the temple has now been built in Jerusalem, counterpart on earth of the Eternal City. At the same time the Bible's account of the period makes it evident that theologically the *qāhāl* has so far departed from the divine pattern that its ultimate collapse is already assured.

The nature of the step which disqualified Israel from faithfully representing God is significant for our study of the nature of the church. Something like sixty years before the dedication of the temple a decision had been taken by the assembly to conform to the pattern of kingship which they saw in the nations around them:

> We will have a king over us, that we also may be like all the nations, and that our king may govern us and go out before us and fight our battles (1 Sa. 8:19-20).[11]

God is here dethroned as peremptorily as Samuel had been dismissed. Yahweh observes: 'They have rejected me from being king over them' (1 Sa. 8:7).

Yet even the establishment of the monarchy could not entirely efface the concept of a theocratic state. The king ruled for Yahweh, and when he forgot that, the continuing line of prophets might be relied upon to remind him of it.[12] It is interesting to note here that even the aberrant political structure of the kingdom could not disqualify Israel from her role: the socio-political structure was not the decisive factor that it proved to be in the history of other nations. Vriezen comments:

> Israel was really preserved when its existence as a people was destroyed. In spite of their popular religion the ancient Eastern nations could not survive; their gods perished together with the

---

[11] A king who would fight their battles was, ironically, what they did *not* get: Saul fails to take up the challenge to single combat made by the Philistine champion, Goliath (1 Sa. 17).
[12] 1 Sa. 15:16ff.; 2 Sa. 12; 24:11-14; 1 Ki. 13:1-10; 17:1; 2 Ki. 20:12-19; 1 Ch. 11:1-3.

people. Israel, which was doomed to destruction as a people ... could keep on functioning as a religious community. That it did survive in this sense is due to the preaching of the prophets who, predicting the downfall of the state and the destruction of the national existence as being the will of God, made Israel preserve its communion with God. In this way Israel could become a congregation, denoted as *qāhāl* ('men called up' in the Deuteronomist works and in Chronicles) ... Israel considers itself the congregation of those who have been called up by the Word of God.[13]

There is certainly a great deal of difference between the *qāhāl* prophesied by Isaac (Gn. 28:3) and the *qāhāl* of Solomon's time. It was not the visible structures, however, but the rule of God which in fact constituted the congregation.

If we are right in tracing some measure of continuity between the Old Testament people of God and the New Testament people of God, we may draw comfort from this observation as we look at the enormous variety of structures within the modern church. A great diversity of patterns of church government has emerged, but this need not conflict with the real existence of the congregation. The structures do not *necessarily* determine the function of the church, although it is conceivable that some structures may seriously interfere with the expression of the sovereignty of God.

2.2.2 The New Testament congregation, the *ekklēsia*

The New Testament church, the *ekklēsia*, may be seen as a continuation of the Old Testament congregation or *qāhāl* in its corporate sense, just as the New Testament congregation must be seen as a continuation of the synagogue. In the Septuagint the word *ekklēsia* occurs about 100 times, almost always standing for Hebrew *qāhāl*.

Costas would like to restrict the usage of *ekklēsia* to the church gathered for worship:

> Far from using this word in a sociological or judicial sense (as a political assembly), the New Testament uses *ecclēsia* as a liturgical term, ie in reference to the assembly of the faithful coming together for worship.[14]

---

[13]Th. C. Vriezen, *An Outline of Old Testament Theology* 2 (Blackwell, Oxford, 1958, ²1970), p. 373. For the word *qāhāl*, see also *TDNT*, article *ekklēsia*. There is, of course, a sense in which neither the word *qāhāl* nor the word *ekklēsia* is used consistently and consciously as a technical word with a clearly defined meaning. But the meaning being assigned to each word becomes clear when the usage in parallel context is examined. R. de Vaux deals with the subject of the *qāhāl* in some detail in *Ancient Israel: its Life and Institutions* (Darton, Longman and Todd, London, 1961).

[14]Orlando Costas, *The Church and its Mission* (Tyndale House, Wheaton, 1974), p. 43. Alan Richardson notes that in later parts of the Septuagint a distinction is made between '*edhah*, translated *synagogē*, and *qāhāl*, translated *ekklēsia*: *A Theological Word Book of the Bible* (SCM, London, 1957), entry 'Church'.

But the church is still the church even when it is not gathered together, just as the *qāhāl* remained the congregation even in exile. In Jesus' important reference to the *ekklēsia* in Matthew 18:17 his followers are invited to pass judgment on a dispute within the congregation, and this is scarcely a liturgical activity. In Acts 9:31 the word is used absolutely of the whole body of believers, enjoying peace, being built up, walking in the fear of the Lord, being comforted by the Spirit, and being multiplied.

In fact, as in the case of the *qāhāl*, it is the presence of the Lord that truly identifies the people of God. Jesus, it would appear, expanded the rabbinic dictum that where two or three gathered for the study of the *Torah* then the Presence (*šᵉḵînâ*) was with them.[15] The presence of Jesus is not restricted to formal gatherings of a local congregation, but is to be relied upon even in the encounter of two of his followers.

So far so good. There is a good measure of continuity between Old Testament *qāhāl* and New Testament *ekklēsia*. But there is a new urgency and a new universality in the commission given to the church. In contrast even to the followers of the Messiah ('Go nowhere among the Gentiles, and enter no town of the Samaritans, but go rather to the lost sheep of the house of Israel,' Mt. 10:5-6) the church is called out in order to be sent out.

2.2.3 The body of Christ

The two New Testament passages which may be taken as normative of the body of Christ motif are 1 Corinthians 11 – 14 and Colossians 1 – 3. These passages are sacramental, missiological and Christological in their emphases. In 1 Corinthians the doctrine of the body develops out of the confusion in the church's attempt to observe the Lord's supper. The church is divided: socially divided into rich and poor; practically divided into those who demonstrate certain *charismata* and those who do not; theologically divided into those who believed that the resurrection was past, applying only to Christ, and those who accepted the reality of the resurrection for all believers; and personally divided into followers of Paul, of Apollos, of Peter and simply of Christ. The people gathered together, broke bread and drank from the one cup, but failed to discern the body of Christ in the elements because they failed to discern the body of Christ in the total membership of the church.

This passage shows a clear progression from 11:24, where Jesus breaks bread and says 'This is my body', to 11:27, where those Christians who break bread in 'an unworthy manner' (presumably in the divided state then prevailing in the church) are 'guilty of profaning the body', to 11:29, where those who eat and drink 'without discerning the body' eat and drink judgment on themselves, to 12:27 and the simple statement 'You are the body of Christ'. The use of the word *sōma*,

---

[15] *Pirqe abōth*, iii, 3.

'body', in this passage, passes from the unambiguous reference to the body of Christ to the equally unambiguous reference to the church, by way of the deliberately ambiguous references to the body of Christ *and* the body that is the church.

It is quite clear that both here in 1 Corinthians and in Colossians the main thrust of the body metaphor is to emphasize the essential unity of the body (the church), the diversity of the gifting of its members, and their interdependence. But in the 1 Corinthians passage there is also an important line of teaching contrasting the brokenness of the body of Christ with the dividedness of the Corinthian church. The body of Christ motif identifies the church as a *suffering* church.

Turning to the Colossian epistle we find Paul, in 1:18, identifying Christ as 'the head of the body, the church'; and in 2:19 he explains the relationship between head and body:

> It is the head that adds strength and holds the whole body together, with all its joints and sinews — and this is the only way in which it can reach its full growth in God (JB).

And there is further reference to the body in 3:15. But with the concept of the *suffering* body in mind, 1:24 is of paramount importance:

> Now I rejoice in my sufferings for your sake, and in my flesh I complete what is lacking in Christ's afflictions for the sake of his body, that is, the church.

The subsequent verses make it plain that Paul is not, here, setting himself over against the church, but is speaking of himself as part of the church, a 'minister' according to the divine office which was given to him for the sake of the church. He is a servant *(diakonos)* and as such he suffers.

It is to be regretted that both the Revised Standard Version and the Good News Bible bring together two phrases which are, in fact, separated from each other in the Greek text: 'Christ's afflictions' and 'for the sake of his body, the church'. In fact we might rephrase the verse:

> Now I rejoice in my sufferings for you. For the sake of his body, the church, I will fill up what is still lacking in Christ's afflictions.

All that we have done here is to make it clear that Paul is *not* speaking of 'Christ's afflictions for the sake of the church', but simply of 'Christ's afflictions'. But what *are* these 'afflictions' to which Paul refers? At least seven explanations have been offered, and they are here presented in ascending order of probability.

THE CHURCH

1. That Paul's sufferings in some way completed the vicarious sufferings of Christ in redemption. This interpretation flies in the face of the rest of Paul's teaching on the completeness of Christ's passion.

2. That when Paul said 'I am crucified with Christ', he was expressing the idea that in some way he shared in Christ's passion sufferings and that, similarly in some unexplained way, these sufferings of his benefited the church. But against this is the observation that Galatians 2:20 stands in the context of a doctrine of sanctification and not of salvation.

3. That when the church today suffers, Christ suffers with the church, in the spirit of Isaiah 63:9: 'In all their affliction he was afflicted.' But while, certainly, we may expect that when the church suffers the Head *sympathizes,* it is difficult to see what could be meant by the ascended Lord in glory *suffering,* experiencing *thlipsis,* which is surely more than mental anguish.

4. That the sufferings of Christ which Paul experienced are those sufferings which Christ would have endured had he continued his life on earth. But the nature of such sufferings can only be conjectural.

5. That the sufferings of Christ are to be equated with those sufferings which Christ foretold as preceding the end time, so that to endure *those* sufferings (Mt. 24:21 uses *thlipsis* for the end-time sufferings) is to suffer so that the period of tribulation may end and the eschatological kingdom be ushered in.

6. The sufferings of Christ are sufferings such as Christ endured quite apart from his redemptive sufferings: compassionate sufferings, the sufferings of self-denial, of unremitting labour, and of persecution, for all of which *thlipsis* is a suitable denomination.

7. The sufferings of Christ are not the sufferings which Christ himself endured, but sufferings which Christ announced to be part of the on-going experience of the church. The genitive ('of ')[16] is not a genitive of possession but a genitive of association. The sufferings are not 'his' which he experienced, but 'his' which he foretold for the church.

Paul, then, as part of the body of Christ, the church, is experiencing and so completing the tale of suffering which Christ had foretold as the

---

[16] For an invaluable study of the genitive from the standpoint of the linguist, see E. A. Nida and C. R. Tabor, *The Theory and Practice of Translation* (Brill, Leiden, 1969), p. 43ff., and John Beekman and John Callow, *Translating the Word of God* (Zondervan, Grand Rapids, 1974), chapter 16.

on-going experience of the church. Those sufferings comprise all the sufferings of the church from Calvary to the parousia, the revelation of Christ as King. They are missiological in character; they necessarily accompany the proclamation of Christ; they are the concomitant of being Christ's witnesses (Acts 1:8; 2 Tim. 1:8-12). The parousia comes not through garden parties and cosy chats but through hardship and suffering. Paul comments:

> Five times I have received at the hands of the Jews the forty lashes less one. Three times I have been beaten with rods; once I was stoned. Three times I have been shipwrecked; a night and a day I have been adrift at sea; on frequent journeys, in danger from rivers, danger from robbers, danger from my own people, danger from Gentiles, danger in the city, danger in the wilderness, danger at sea, danger from false brethren; in toil and hardship, through many a sleepless night, in hunger and thirst, often without food, in cold and exposure. And, apart from other things, there is the daily pressure upon me of my anxiety for all the churches (2 Cor. 11:24-28).

These are the sufferings which Paul experienced as the emissary of the church, as a servant of the church — sufferings which were used to increase the church. They are missiological sufferings. They echo the biblical concept of the church as a *broken* body, the continuing and visible representation of the body of Christ.

In this transition there is to be found the source of the discomfort which some have felt over the Pauline metaphor. Where is the continuity, where, indeed, the *congruity,* between the perfect body of Christ and the manifestly imperfect body, the church? The answer lies in that experience of the one church which truly unites, the experience of suffering for Christ.

2.2.4 The church as 'people of the Way'

Early in the history of the church, Christians are designated as people of 'the Way'.[17] The designation appears at most two years after the passion: Saul of Tarsus asks for authority to arrest any he might find who belonged to the Way. It is not entirely clear whether the designation comes from within the church, as Haenchen believes,[18] or whether it was a label given to the church by the Jews. In either case it is evident that the church was remarkable and distinct not only on account of its teaching concerning the Messiah Jesus, but also on account of its man-

---

[17] Acts 9:2; 19:9, 23; 22:4; 24:14, 22. It is difficult to decide whether some other passages should be added to those which RSV identifies as referring to a special movement by capitalizing, 'the Way'. For example, in Acts 18:26 Priscilla and Aquila expound to Apollos the (?)Way of God.

[18] In his commentary on Acts. He disagrees with Michaelis, who restricts the meaning of 'way' (*TDNT*, article *hodos*), to 'teaching' when used in these particular passages.

ner of life. It is worth noting that the designation 'Christians', which was applied to the church by those outside it (Acts 11:26), must have been given in recognition of the fact that the people of the Way lived a distinctive lifestyle clearly related to that of Jesus the Christ.

There is a suggestive parallel here with the theme of the way as it appears in Isaiah. The theme is used as a significant bridge between the two principal parts of the one prophecy, 1 − 35 and 40 − 66. In chapter 35 we have a picture of the revivified desert across which runs the way of holiness. Bridging the historical interlude supplied by chapters 36 − 39, chapter 40 identifies the way as the way of the Lord. And in the remaining twenty-five chapters of Isaiah no fewer than seventeen contain some reference to the way. The theme thus runs parallel with that of the servant of the Lord which itself extends from chapter 41 to the end of chapter 53.

The Way, in the New Testament, depicting the path taken by the church, is also the way taken by her Head; and this Way may be understood in part by reference to the way of the servant of the Lord in Isaiah. That this is reasonable exegesis is suggested by the necessity of multiple interpretation of the servant in Isaiah. The servant is clearly Israel in some passages, Israel the faithful remnant in others, and Israel's Redeemer, the Messiah, in others.[19]

In his commentary on Isaiah, Franz Delitzsch illustrates this multiple understanding of the servant of the Lord by a three-staged pyramid. At the lowest level is all Israel; at the second stage is Israel-after-the-Spirit; and at the top is the individual mediator of salvation, the Messiah.[20] Extending our understanding and application of Isaiah into the New Testament, we may add a second pyramid to Delitzsch's to make it clear that the servant of the Lord has been all Israel, Israel-in-the-Spirit, and, uniquely, the Messiah; and is now the church, the church-obedient-to-the-Spirit, and the Head of the church, Jesus the Christ.

The theme of the servant reaches it climax in Isaiah 52 − 53. Isaiah 52 is first missiological and then soteriological, while chapter 53 is first soteriological and then missiological. We note especially in 52:7 the prophetic anticipation of world mission:

> How beautiful upon the mountains
>   are the feet of him who brings good tidings,
> who publishes peace, who brings good tidings of good,
>   who publishes salvation,
>   who says to Zion, 'Your God reigns'.

[19] Cf. Is. 41:8, 'But you, Israel, my servant, Jacob, whom I have chosen, the offspring of Abraham, my friend', with Is. 49:6, 'It is too light a thing that you should be my servant to raise up the tribes of Jacob and to restore the preserved of Israel; I will give you as a light to the nations, that my salvation may reach to the end of the earth.'

[20] F. Delitzsch, *The Prophecies of Isaiah* 2 (T. & T. Clark, Edinburgh, 1890), p. 165.

Isaiah pictures Israel as God's servant, as a light to the nations, as a people walking a way, the way of holiness, the way trodden by the Lord. This picture of the people of the Way, which reappears in Acts, further illustrates the nature of the church.

2.2.5 The church and the kingdom

The New Testament church is, in some sense, a continuation of the Old Testament congregation, a body of people whose essential function as God's servant cannot ultimately be frustrated by the variety of structures adopted by the church ostensibly to facilitate her ministry. The church is, in some sense, a continuing incarnation, the 'body of Christ', experiencing those sufferings foretold by Christ as inevitable where the missiological imperative is obeyed. The church is a people walking a certain way, the way of holiness, a way which demands holiness of the traveller, a way over which the exemplar-Christ has already passed, a way that ultimately leads on to Zion. Our attention is, therefore, directed beyond the immediate missiological concerns of the church to the eschatological fulfilment of the church in the ushering in of the kingdom of God. As John Macquarrie says, 'the church is much less than the kingdom of God',[21] but the church *is* part of a series that culminates in the kingdom. In a remarkable phrase Macquarrie defines the *kingdom* as 'the entelechy of the church', 'the perfect unfolding of the potentialities which are already manifesting themselves in the church'.[22] The church's present nature is to struggle, to endure, to endure even her present ugliness in the marvellous expectation of her imminent transformation in the kingdom of God.

2.3 THE FUNCTION OF THE CHURCH

We must now consider the *function* of the church which is defined by those didactic elements of Old and New Testaments which throw light on the function of the Old Testament congregation and the New Testament church, and by the illustrations and analogies used to describe them.

A study of these elements of Scripture suggests that the church exists for *worship,* for *community* and for *mission.*

2.3.1 The worship of the church

The church's worship is demanded by the nature of God and is effected through the new relationship between God and man made possible by the death and resurrection of Christ. In the Old Testament the congregation is the servant *('eḇed)* of Yahweh, and so offers worship *(ᵃḇôdâ),* while in the New Testament the Christian is designated the

[21] *Principles of Christian Theology* (SCM, London, 1976), p. 349.
[22] *Ibid.*

servant (*doulos*) of God (Acts 4:23-30; 1 Pet. 2:16), offering worship (*latreia*).

The concept of the people of God as his *slaves* should not lead us into interpreting that concept in terms of modern ideas of slavery. The Old Testament '*ebed* was not a man robbed of all rights as a human being, subject to every whim of his master. That was the Roman concept. The '*ebed*, in fact, surrendered certain rights, receiving in return certain compensating rights, consonant with his new relationship to his master. The master might, in fact, stand in something approaching the relationship of a father to a son. Thus when Ahaz, the '*ebed* of Tiglath Pileser, king of Assyria, was attacked by Syria and Israel he was able to send to his master for help: 'I am your servant *('ebed)* and *your son*. Come up, and rescue me' (2 Ki. 16:7).

The dual designation of servant and son corresponds to a dual designation of master and father. This carries through to the New Testament doctrine of the church, but the process is complicated by the fact that the word *doulos* employed in the Greek New Testament does not have the same meaning as its nearest Hebrew equivalent, '*ebed*; the status of the two referents is different.[23]

There is, in fact, a clear tension in the New Testament between the recognition that we are indeed slaves, and yet not slaves in the normal sense of *douloi*, individuals without rights. Still, we are not allowed to forget that we *are* servants, and unprofitable servants at that (Lk. 17:7-10). But still we are sons, part of the Master's household and as such sharing special privileges and experiencing special indignities:

> A disciple is not above his teacher, nor a servant above his master; it is enough for the disciple to be like his teacher, and the servant like his master. If they have called the master of the house Beelzebul, how much more will they malign those of his household (Mt. 10:24-25).

The church worships because she is the servant, the slave, of the one she rightly calls 'Lord'. As Jesus said to his followers: 'You call me Teacher and Lord; and you are right, for so I am' (Jn. 13:13).

But perhaps it should be emphasized that the demand for worship is unconditionally made by God, not only of the church, but of all people, simply because he *is* God. The church is privileged to respond to the divine imperative because she acknowledges Jesus Christ as Lord.

2.3.2 The church and community

The family of God is not removed from society, but is left in society; thus the church must express *community*, and give expression to its

---

[23]The problem is very evident in the Septuagint, where the translators recognized that they could not regularly translate '*ebed*, with its dual connotation of servant and son, by *doulos* with its central

responsibility for the society within which it is found. The responsibility is *not* limited to the Christian element of society alone. Paul encouraged the church in Galatia:

> As we have opportunity, let us do good to all men, and especially to those who are of the household of faith (Gal. 6:10).

This verse recognizes the special relationship which must inevitably exist between Christians, a relationship which is frequently designated by the Greek word *koinōnia*. The word *koinos*, 'common', is the opposite of *idios*, that which is one's own. Note the condition of the post-Pentecost Jerusalem congregation:

> No one said that any of the things which he possessed was his own (*idios*), but they had everything in common (*koinos*) (Acts 4:32).

The Christian *koinōnia* develops out of a common faith (Tit. 1:4), a common salvation (Jude 3), and even from the sharing of the divine nature (2 Pet. 1:4). The trinitarian formula which closes Paul's second letter to Corinth (13:14) selects precisely the word *koinōnia* to relate to the Spirit: the *fellowship* of the Holy Spirit (which might be set in contrast with the *koinōnia* with demons referred to in 1 Cor. 10:21).

The question of the wider aspect of *koinōnia* is important missiologically because it helps to clarify the nature of Christian evangelism. There is a great deal of confusion between Christian *mission* to the world through evangelism and Christian *service* to the world through acts of philanthropy. Each is incumbent upon the church, but mission is not philanthropy. The spirit of community ought always to drive the church to feed the hungry and to heal the sick, to house the homeless and to relieve distress of whatever nature. But this is not evangelism. It is certainly part of the church's *witness* to Christ, indicating the truth of the statement that God loved the world and gave his only Son for it. But evangelism makes the good news explicit.

But having said that the church must express its spirit of community, and will often do so through acts of philanthropy, we would be wrong in supposing that *missionary* societies ought necessarily to engage in such activities. Their structures are not always appropriate to famine relief, their personnel not always trained for community development. There is quite clearly room for two distinct vehicles for the church's outreach to the world, one for evangelism and one for community. But it is equally vital that these two vehicles should be seen not as competi-

---

concept of slave. The Septuagint, therefore, renders '*ebed* now as *doulos*, servant, now as *pais*, son. It is precisely this problem of rendering the '*ebed* concept that lies behind the Greek of Acts 4:27, '... gathered together against the holy *pais*', translated literally in the AV as 'child', but properly understood as 'servant' in RSV.

tive but as complementary, being sent by the one church and dedicated to the service of the same Lord. Too many mission societies and mission agencies have been hustled into philanthropic work for which they are ill equipped because of a failure to distinguish between these two vehicles and to identify their own proper objectives.

2.3.3 The church and mission
There is a sense in which the liturgical and sociological aspects of the life of the church are to be seen as subsidiary to the missiological task of the church.

The chief end of man is, of course, as the Westminster *Shorter Catechism* puts it, 'to glorify God and to enjoy him for ever'. But the reason the church is left here on earth is not *so that* we might glorify God and enjoy him for ever. The church is left here in order to be a witness to Christ. And since the church is left in the world, she is separated from Christ, denied that immediate presence which will eventually make worship what it ought to be. In the realized kingdom of God worship will be of a very different quality from even the most rapturous experience of worship which, from time to time, and all too briefly, sweeps us into glory now. The church is not left here *so that* she might worship God.

Nor is the church left here *so that* Christians might experience and practice community. Our churches, even the best of them, are far from being perfect examples of Christian *koinōnia*, only too often marked by deep-seated animosities, divisions, quarrels. True fellowship will be our experience only in the realized kingdom.

Of course, being on earth we *shall* worship, and being on earth we *shall* do our utmost to develop the spirit of community. But that is not why we are left on earth. We are left here *so that* we might be Christ's witnesses.

We are unscriptural, however, if we separate the various concerns of the church into watertight compartments. Paul writes to Rome:

> I appeal to you therefore, brethren, by the mercies of God, to present your bodies as a living sacrifice, holy and acceptable to God, which is your spiritual worship *(tēn logikēn latreian)* (Rom. 12:1).

This appeal stands at the head of a lengthy sequence which deals with the Christian in the world and the Christian in the church. It would seem that spiritual worship is at least *linked with* our relationships with other believers in the church (the theme of verses 3-13) and with the unbelieving world outside the church (the theme of verses 14-21). Quite obviously our *latreia* is not *comprehended* by these relationships, but worship is clearly linked with them. So worship, community, and witness are to be seen as interrelated and even as mutually dependent. Worship is not to be seen as separate from mission, as teaching has been separated from preaching. Each activity depends for its validity on our submission to the one Lord. Without that willing submission, liturgical activity is not worship. With it mission is also worship.

There is always the danger that worship will become exclusively liturgical or exclusively praxeological: the enthusiast for God is either for ever in church or so busily engaged in mission or community that he is never in church. This second possibility has too often been allowed to undermine and devalue much of Protestant and especially evangelical mission. The missionary has been formally a member of a church in his home country, but is, of course, only rarely able to be there, even when on his so-called furlough. And while he is overseas, either there is no church for him to join, or he is so heavily engaged in mission that apart from an occasional appearance he does not attend the church that *is* there.

Or even worse, the church that is there has been seen as 'their' church, a church to which the missionary is not required to belong, or 'my' church, of which the missionary is chief executive. The missionary has, as a consequence, been left churchless, his *latreia* unbalanced. In the long term the missionary has often lost altogether the ability to *worship* in any liturgical sense. If he attends a church his concern is primarily with the 'address', the 'sermon', and his basic need to worship *in community* is lost.

The situation has improved in recent years, and most missionaries are now members of local churches in the countries in which they live. But the imbalance in so many missionaries does have important consequences, particularly where the missionary is a church planter. His own attitude to the church as local congregation will inevitably be reflected in the churches that are planted, and thus the whole concept of the church as a teaching, preaching, healing, caring, praying, worshipping, serving, growing community may be lost. Missionaries should have in their training a greater element of ecclesiology.

2.4 THE IDENTITY OF THE CHURCH

It is one thing to talk in the abstract about 'the church', but quite another thing to identify the church, and embarrassing to attempt to identify what is *not* the church even though it might claim to be so. There is a remarkable spectrum of organizations all claiming to be the church of Jesus Christ, most of them having discordant ideas on which of the other organizations can also be accorded recognition. Where do they all fit in — Methodists and Salvationists, Baptists and Anglicans, the Roman Catholic Church, the Church of Christ, Seventh Day

THE CHURCH

Adventists and Quakers, Jehovah's Witnesses and Lutherans?

According to the Chicago-Lambeth Quadrilateral of 1886,[24] the one church is to be identified by its acceptance of four principles: the authority of the Scriptures, the adherence to the Nicene Creed (and the Apostles' Creed?), the observance of the two sacraments of baptism and the Lord's supper, and the possession of the historic episcopate. Unfortunately there is no agreed interpretation of any one of these deceptively simple principles, even were they to command general acceptance.

The 1920 Lambeth Conference went one step further, acknowledging the membership in the one church of all who believe in Christ and have been baptized. Even with so brief an identification it is difficult to see that it allows for the inclusion of all Christians or that it excludes those who might 'believe in Christ' in a very different way from that envisaged at Lambeth.

And yet it is quite clear that there *is* only one church (Eph. 4:4). Granted this fact, it is still difficult to identify those factors which are held in common by all the churches. Even John Macquarrie's tentative suggestion that at least all the churches share the same Bible[25] must be qualified. Roman Catholics and Protestants disagree on the status of the Apocrypha; ultra-conservative groups recognize only the Authorized (King James') Version as having authority as the English-language rendering of the original Scriptures, and fringe groups tend to produce their own translations. And there is no western version of the Bible which corresponds precisely to the Ethiopic Bible, still used by the Ethiopian Orthodox church.

The essential unity of the church is challenged by denominational divisions which usually have their origins in doctrine, but it is challenged also by divisions which are essentially racist. Macquarrie comments:

> We do in fact hear from time to time about churches which exclude from their membership and even from their worship persons of a different race from the members; and often enough, such churches pride themselves on their orthodoxy and their conservative (not to say reactionary) theology. No matter how orthodox these congregations may be, they have cut themselves off from true catholicity by denying the universal character of the Church.[26]

---

[24]The Quadrilateral was approved first at the Chicago convention of the Protestant Episcopal Church in 1886. For details see R. Rouse and S. C. Neill (eds.), *A History of the Ecumenical Movement 1517-1948* (SPCK, London, 1954), pp. 250, 264ff.

[25]*Principles of Christian Theology*, p. 362. See also Sean P. Kealy, 'The Canon, an African Contribution', *Biblical Theology Bulletin*, IX, 1, 1979.

[26]*Principles of Christian Theology*, p. 366. It is surely arguable that the homogeneous unit principle developed by some writers of the Church Growth movement is racist in its exclusivism. See chapter 5, below.

A more general type of exclusivism would appear to demand a similar condemnation. If only Roman Catholics are to enter heaven; or if all Christians except Roman Catholics are to enter heaven; or, to put it more crudely, if only pre-millennialists or only charismatics are 'truly' in the church; where is the one body?

Such exclusivism, whether racial or denominational, brings into question our commitment to the one body, the church. The Bible offers to us no middle ground between the church and that which is not the church. One is either part of the body or else apart from the body. Our arrogant exclusivism unscripturally dismembers the body of Christ.

And yet the biblical position is unambiguous:

> I therefore, a prisoner for the Lord, beg you to lead a life worthy of the calling to which you have been called, with all lowliness and meekness, with patience, forbearing one another in love, eager to maintain the unity of the Spirit in the bond of peace. There is one body and one Spirit, just as you were called to the one hope that belongs to your call, one Lord, one faith, one baptism, one God and Father of us all, who is above all and through all and in all (Eph. 4:1-6).

In writing these words Paul was not unaware of the real differences that existed even then between the local congregations which he knew. But Paul insisted that a measure of diversity need not interfere with the essential unity of the one church. Diverse patterns of gifting emerge in the local congregations, and these make possible the fulfilment of the church's threefold task: worship, community, and witness. The very words that Paul uses at the beginning of the passage make it clear that he saw the difficulty of preserving unity in the context of diversity, and the danger of disharmony and competition. His words speak to us with renewed power today. Like the proliferation of denominations, the proliferation of mission agencies testifies to an unhealthy spirit of competition rather than to a total submission to the teaching of Scripture.

But it must be acknowledged that it is simply not possible to include within the concept of the one body of Christ all that carries the label 'church'. There is a biblical exclusivism that we have no liberty to deny. That exclusivism is based now on doctrine, now on praxis. A church, so-called, may demonstrate its status as a non-church overtly by denying that Jesus Christ is Lord (most of 2 Peter is concerned with this situation), or implicitly by denying the lordship of Christ in behaviour.

The Lordship of Christ and the full implications of that phrase might take volumes to work out, but it clearly ultimately transcends the *notae* of the church (holiness, unity, catholicity, and apostolicity) and all other attempts to define humanly the spiritual reality. Jesus is Lord!

THE CHURCH

As Lord, Jesus Christ commands mission. Both the Protestant Jürgen Moltmann and the Roman Catholic Hans Küng agree here: the truly apostolic church is the church engaged in mission. From Latin America Orlando Costas agrees: the church is, for us, identified praxeologically by what she *does*, and not only, or even chiefly, by what she *says*. Where a church professes Jesus as Lord and yet fails to follow through that profession by the open confession and proclamation of Jesus in mission, it must be doubted whether Jesus is really Lord, there, at all.

The one church is, for us, to be identified by her activity in the world. The apostolic church will be engaged in apostolic mission to the world, a visible activity confirmed by the apostolic preaching of the cross and the activity of God in that preaching. Of course, it is true that to be involved in world mission instead of devoting all the available material and spiritual resources to the well-being of the already existent church is to risk death. To refuse to be involved in world mission is to guarantee it! In so many parts of the world the church only guarantees her own demise when she so loves life that she establishes some kind of *modus vivendi* with the godless world around, and settles for a peaceful, but fossilized, existence.

The one church is the community of God's people, the body of Christ, called out from the world in order to be sent out into the world. She worships the one Lord, liturgically in the gatherings of her people, and praxeologically through the scattering of the members of the one body into the world.

3
The task of the church

The nature of God demands worship from man, and the church is able to offer worship because of the relationship established between God and his redeemed people in Christ. The church is left here on earth not so that she might worship, nor so that she might experience community, but so that she might be Christ's witness on earth.

Three questions arise out of this summary: what is man, what is meant by being Christ's witness, and what means are provided to enable man to become effective in witnessing? This chapter attempts to answer these three questions and to consider some of the alternative answers proposed.

3.1 WHAT IS MAN?

Religion is essentially anthropocentric. All religions are concerned with man's quest for the meaning of life. Indeed, a religion may conveniently be defined as *any coherent system of philosophy which purports to answer man's fundamental questions*. There are three parallel series of fundamental questions. The first series is: who am I, where did I come from, where am I going, and why? The second series recognizes that man lives in community and asks: who are you, where did you come from, where are you going, and why? The third series relates to man's environment and asks: what is this world, where did it come from, where is it going and why?

The ultimate concern of religion, so defined, is the salvation of man. Obviously the term 'salvation' is variously conceived: in Christianity as deliverance from the power of sin; in Hinduism as deliverance from the cycle of existence, *samsara*; in Buddhism as attaining *nirvana*; or in Communism as freedom from capitalist oppression. Religions[1] all

---

[1]The definition given allows us to include atheistic philosophies as religions where those philosophies, as in Communism, seek to answer the fundamental questions. Nihilism, however, is not a religion. In its original form, nihilism was indistinguishable from anarchy, but its later form has been described as 'mood of despair over the emptiness or triviality of human existence' (*The Encyclopedia of Philosophy*, Macmillan, London and New York, 1967, article 'Nihilism'). The nihilist, believing

assume that there are answers to the ultimate questions and that those answers can supply a rationale for a particular way of life. In some sense, of course, religions may also supply some kind of explanation for the existence of other forms of life apart from human life, but this is essentially 'spin-off' and not the central concern of religion, which is always *man*.

3.1.1 Man's place in the universe

Perhaps unconsciously, perhaps necessarily, man places man at the centre of the universe, as the focus of the universe. It does not seem remarkable to man that he should gratuitously assume this, and, as a consequence of the assumption, that he should exploit both the resources of the earth and the potentialities of space for himself. True enough, man is sufficiently aware of the limited extent of the world's resources to be concerned at their over-exploitation, but only exceptionally is this out of any concern for the resources themselves. Rather, his concern is expressed out of his own long-term concern for himself.

If this anthropocentric interpretation of life by man is remarkable, much more remarkable is the anthropocentric interpretation of life revealed in the Bible. It would appear that man is not mistaken in placing himself at the centre of the universe, since that is where, for whatever reason, God has placed him:

> Yet thou hast made him little less than God,
>   and dost crown him with glory and honour.
> Thou hast given him dominion over the works of thy hands;
>   Thou has put all things under his feet (Ps. 8:5-6).

What *is* man? Viewed macroscopically, man appears to be utterly insignificant. As we look out into the universe we can see the individual stars of our own galaxy and the faintly shining blurs which identify other galaxies. It is computed that one galaxy might contain between a billion (a thousand million) and a thousand billion stars, and that there might well be some ten billion galaxies. If the entire population of the world were to be distributed in just one galaxy, each one of us would be the unchallenged ruler of more than three hundred stars! — unchallenged, that is, except by the God who created them and us.

But while we feel ourselves reduced to insignificance by the inconceivable vastness of space, when we look at man *microscopically* the impression changes. Man *does* stand out uniquely from his environment. He is not a passive element in the universe, but an actor, shaping his own environment (for better or for worse), planning his future,

---

that all philosophical systems are absurd and irrelevant, is necessarily an atheist, but the atheist is not necessarily a nihilist, as Nietzsche has shown. Jean-Paul Sartre (*Being and Nothingness,* New York, 1956) is probably the best known of the modern nihilists.

investigating his past, demanding a reason for his being and a purpose behind mere existence. He creates religions and constructs sciences to assist him in his aspirations. He adopts moral codes for society, and judges his own kind in the event of their failing to observe them.

From the specifically Christian point of view, man is unique because he is the recipient of the divine self-revelation, a self-revelation that meets man in his role of thinker, and offers an answer to his questions. God's self-revelation is not in terms of pure philosophy, but in terms of concrete historical events which relate directly to the fundamental enigmas of birth, suffering and death. Man is then expected by God to respond to the divine self-revelation. The response is polarized between two options: either to submit himself humbly to the God who is revealed, in the hope of being conformed to the image of man which was, in the beginning, in the mind of God; or to reject the revelation in favour of a proud self-assertiveness guaranteed only to achieve his own ultimate destruction.

Christianity recognizes that part of the divine self-revelation is to be seen in creation itself:

> Ever since the creation of the world his invisible nature, namely, his eternal power and deity, has been clearly perceived in the things that have been made (Rom. 1:20).

The cosmological argument for the existence of God is not entirely unreasonable, but Paul indicates that man's ability to profit from this aspect of self-revelation is limited. Hence God reveals in other ways what cannot otherwise be discerned by man. Through Abraham and Moses, through David and the prophets of a double-edged holiness made up of righteousness towards God and justice towards man, through the incarnation, and now through the church, God has revealed himself to man. And especially through the incarnation:

> In many and various ways God spoke of old to our fathers by the prophets; but in these last days he has spoken to us by a Son (Heb. 1:1-2).

3.1.2 Man's need of redemption

Man is placed in a perplexing universe, but within that universe he exhibits unique powers, unique abilities. Yet these powers and abilities are limited. Able to control his environment and to invent machinery of incredible complexity, he is nonetheless incapable of controlling himself. Again and again man is driven to nihilism, to the conviction that life is futile. It is God's purpose through his self-revelation to put an end to this futility, to illuminate darkened minds that not only *will* not, but *cannot* see. In a word, God's purpose is the *redemption* of man.

THE TASK OF THE CHURCH

In speaking of the biblical doctrine of redemption we are making reference to a trio of lexically related words: *apolytrōsis*, 'redemption'; *lytron*, 'the price paid for redemption', and the verb *lyō*, meaning 'I loosen', 'I set free'. In the New Testament, redemption is consistently presented as *deliverance from misfortune by the payment of a price*. These three elements are steadily in mind: a misfortune, deliverance from that misfortune, and the payment of a price. The actual nature of the misfortune is left open: in Greek culture the concept of redemption might have been applied to the ransoming of a prisoner of war, to the payment of compensation to the plaintiff in a court action, or to the manumission of a slave; freeing the prisoner from the misfortune of captivity, the accused from the threat of the law, and the slave from his slavery.

It is Jesus himself who introduces to us the concept of man's status as a slave to sin: 'Every one who commits sin is a slave to sin' (Jn. 8:34); and it is again Jesus who introduces the idea of a ransom: 'For the Son of man also came not to be served but to serve, and to give his life as a ransom (*lytron*) for many' (Mk. 10:45).

Paul takes up this concept of slavery in Romans 6:17-18:

> You who were once slaves of sin have become obedient from the heart to the standard of teaching to which you were committed, and, having been set free from sin, have become slaves of righteousness.

The sequence here is quite clear: 'you were once slaves of sin', 'you have been set free', and 'you have become slaves of righteousness'. This last phrase is probably to be understood by metonymy as 'slaves of Christ'.

Romans 6 does not detail the price paid in the transaction, but the price is detailed in three places in the New Testament. First there is the word of Christ: 'to give his *life* as a ransom for many' (Mk. 10:45). Secondly there are Paul's words to Timothy: 'Christ Jesus ... who gave *himself* as a ransom for all' (1 Tim. 2:6).

Thirdly, and in more detail, Peter links the act of redemption with the Old Testament sacrificial representation of redemption:

> You know that you were ransomed[2] from the futile ways inherited from your fathers, not with perishable things such as silver or gold, but with the precious blood of Christ, like that of a lamb without blemish or spot (1 Pet. 1:18-19).

In his discussion of the trio of words under consideration here,

---

[2] RSV, an improvement on AV's 'redeemed'. The change is required by the explicit reference to the price paid.

Büchsel, in *TDNT*, appears determined, against the evidence, to eliminate the crucial concept of *ransom* from the New Testament usage of the words.[3] He is driven to admit an element of ransom-theory present in the usage of the words elsewhere because of the irresistible testimony of the Septuagint and non-biblical sources. But he eliminates the concept from the New Testament by supposing that the New Testament writers themselves created a new meaning for *apolytrōsis* which excluded the idea of ransom. Obviously any writer is at liberty to create a new meaning for any word, but as Leon Morris points out,[4] Büchsel's contention regarding the New Testament writers cannot be established from the New Testament. Of the ten occurrences of the word *apolytrōsis*,[5] the price is explicitly expressed three times and is implicit in two other passages.

The meaning of the *lytron* group of words may be illustrated from the Old Testament where the Septuagint makes use of *lytron* as the equivalent of three important Hebrew words: *kāpar*, *gā'al* and *pāḍâ*.

The root meaning of *kāpar* is 'to cover', and when *lytron* is used as its equivalent it 'always denotes a vicarious gift whose value covers a fault, so that the debt is not just cancelled'.[6] The second word, *gā'al*, is associated with the responsibility of a family to avenge a murder. The vengeance, the death of the guilty person, 'frees' the blood of the murdered man which otherwise goes on demanding the price of murder. The word *gā'al* may also be used in the context of redeeming a member of the family who for some reason has been forced to sell himself into slavery (Lv. 25:48). Thirdly, *lytron*, used in the Septuagint as the equivalent of *pāḍâ*, represents a substitutionary payment (always of something which has *life*), which releases a condemned man from the death sentence.

While it might be argued that a very long period of time intervenes between the rendering of the Septuagint and the writing of the New

---

[3]F. Büchsel, article *luō* in *TDNT*. Bultmann shares Büchsel's opposition to the ransom concept, but takes a more radical axe to the problem, simply denying that Mark 10:45 represents a genuine saying of Jesus at all (*The History of the Synoptic Tradition,* Blackwell, Oxford, 1963, p. 93). I recall my astonishment when I came to the study of theology after studying physics for some years, when I first began to read Bultmann. Perhaps it was unfortunate that I should choose his *New Testament Theology* to commence with. I had scarcely begun when I found such statements as: 'The passages which speak of the "sons of this age" and of the reward in the age to come for having followed him are secondary' (p. 5), and 'At Mark 10:30 the present time as the opposite of the "age to come" is secondary' (p. 5), and 'The introductory formula (the kingdom heaven is like) is due to the editing of the evangelist' (p. 9), and 'The saying about the building of the "Church" is, like the whole of Mt. 16:17-19, a later product of the church' (p. 10). Admittedly it becomes tiresome to repeat endlessly 'In my opinion', but it seemed to me then, and it still seems to me now, that suppositions such as these need to be supported by some kind of evidence or admitted to be the inevitable end-product of certain presuppositions.

[4]*The Apostolic Preaching of the Cross,* chapter 1, where something of a running commentary is given on Büchsel's *TDNT* article.

[5]Lk. 21:28; Rom 3:24; 8:23; 1 Cor. 1:30; Eph. 1:7; 14; 4:30; Col. 1:14; Heb. 9:15; 11:35.

[6]Büchsel, *art. cit.,* p. 329. Nu. 35:31 is an example: no *lytron* can be found to cover the fault of a murderer and there can be no substitution for his death.

Testament, and that the meanings of words may change rather rapidly, the fact remains that there is remarkable agreement between the meaning given to the *lytron* group of words in the Septuagint, in non-biblical sources and in the New Testament. All are consistent with the notion of ransom.

The point at issue here is, of course, the nature of man. Is he a free agent, free to work out his own salvation, free to use his own ideas in a continuing critique of religious insights; or is he a slave, in such a condition that he must be ransomed, so far in debt that only the grace of God can set him free? This issue is crucial for an understanding of the nature of mission.

3.2 WITNESSING AND DISCIPLING

Man is presented in the Bible as being something of a sociological schizophrenic, given a dominant role in his creation by the Creator and yet disqualified from fulfilling that role by his captivity to sin. The missiological task of the church addresses itself to this schizophrenia, bringing to an otherwise helpless mankind an offer of redemption which alone can ultimately fit us for our proper place in creation.

There would seem to be at least two stages in the missiological task — the first stage, which is concerned with confronting enslaved man with the liberating Christ; and the second stage, in which those who accept the offer of liberation are discipled not merely into being docile members of some more-or-less imperfect local community but into being believable members of Christ's body and so, in their turn, his witnesses.

3.2.1 'My witnesses'
In the hiatus between Passover and Pentecost Christ promised his followers:

> You shall receive power when the Holy Spirit has come upon you; and you shall be my witnesses in Jerusalem and in all Judea and Samaria and to the end of the earth (Acts 1:8).

The key phrase here is my witnesses, *mou martyres*. This is not, as the English rendering might lead us to suppose, a genitive of possession, 'witnesses who belong to me', but an objective genitive, 'witnesses who speak *about* me'.[7]

It is instructive to notice how this commission worked out in prac-

---

[7]*C.f.* J. Beekman and J. Callow, *Translating the Word of God* (Zondervan, Grand Rapids, 1974), p. 256, where we are given four examples of this type of genitive:
Mk.1:1, 'the gospel of Jesus Christ', the gospel is *about* Jesus Christ,
Acts 13:44, 'the word of God', the message which is *about* God,

tice: of all that Jesus was, said and did, what was it that the disciples chose to speak about?

The evidence of Acts shows that the focus of the testimony of the disciples to Jesus was his *resurrection*. The events surrounding the crucifixion of Christ were not the focus of their testimony because these events were not in dispute. It was the claim to resurrection, a resurrection that validated all that Christ had claimed for himself, and designated him Son of God in power (Rom. 1:4), that was in dispute. The emphasis on the resurrection in the first witness of the church is unmistakable.

In seeking a replacement for Judas, Peter says: 'One of these men must become with us a witness to his *resurrection*' (Acts 1:22). In his speech at Pentecost, Peter announces the facts of the passion in a single verse, but ten verses are devoted to an *apologia* for the resurrection, concluding: 'This Jesus God *raised up*, and of that we all are witnesses' (Acts 2:32). In chapter 4 it is precisely the proclamation of the resurrection that is singled out for mention in the account of the arrest of Peter and John:

> And as they were speaking to the people, the priests and the captain of the temple and the Sadducees came upon them, annoyed because they were teaching the people and proclaiming in Jesus the *resurrection* from the dead (Acts 4:1-2).

It is, of course, not surprising that the Sadducees should object to the preaching of the resurrection, but it is the Sanhedrin as a whole that deals with the preaching activities of Peter and John.[8] For the entire Sanhedrin the issue is clear: 'By what power or by what name did you do this?' (Acts 4:7). The leaders of the Jews had been united in their condemnation of Jesus. The Roman power had sentenced him to death. He had been crucified and buried. That should have been the end of the matter. But here now are the disciples of Jesus preaching the *resurrection*, the validity of their message being attested by an act of power.

The task of the church, to be witnesses about Jesus, focused on his resurrection as a historical event seen to validate his claims, and an event which was validated further by the evidence of an otherwise inexplicable new quality of life experienced by his followers.

Gal. 3:10, 'the book of the law', the book which is *about* the law,
Gal. 4:3, 'the mystery of Christ', the mystery which is *about* Christ.
On Acts 1:8 B. M. Newman and E. A. Nida suggest: 'The phrase *witnesses of me* must often be shifted to a verbal expression, for example, "tell people what you know about me" (*A Translator's Handbook on the Acts of the Apostles*, United Bible Societies, London, 1972, p. 18).

[8]Although the Sadducees were powerful, particularly since they tended to represent the wealthy patrician element in the nation, they were by no means the most powerful group in the Sanhedrin, able to use the Sanhedrin for their own purposes.

3.2.2 To make disciples

The first Christians walked a certain Way, and behaved in a definable manner readily identified with the walk of Jesus, so that it soon became reasonable to call them *Christianoi*. The new way of life observed by the Sanhedrin in Peter and John could be transmitted, and appeared in those who believed through the witness of the first disciples as they multiplied disciples.

In Matthew 28:19 we have Jesus' commissioning of his followers: they are to 'make disciples', to disciple the nations. The English noun represents the Greek *mathētēs*, from a verb meaning 'to learn'. The root belongs exclusively in Scripture to the gospels and Acts.

Just as the New Testament concept of the *ekklēsia* has its roots in the Old Testament *qāhāl*, so the New Testament *mathētēs* reflects the Hebrew concept of the disciple, the *talmîd*.[9] The Jewish disciple was essentially a companion of his teacher, learning both from what his teacher *said* and from observation of what he *did*.[10] The *talmîd* was not passive absorber of esoteric information, engaged primarily in scribbling notes from lectures, but was concerned with the total praxis of his teacher.

The essential identity which ought to exist between *mathētēs* and teacher is expressed by Jesus:

> A disciple is not above his teacher, nor a servant above his master; it is enough for the disciple to be like his teacher, and the servant like his master (Mt. 10:24-25)

Clearly Jesus has in mind the establishing of a relationship of such a character that his followers would become *like* him, and that the likeness should go beyond mere similarity of thought or even identity of teaching. Discipleship, in this sense, is more than a meeting of minds. A new way of looking at life, a new quality of life which Jesus called the life of eternity, would so identify the *mathētēs* with his teacher that the experience of the teacher would become the experience of the disciple:

> If the world hates you, know that it has hated me before it hated you. If you were of the world, the world would love its own; but because you are not of the world, but I chose you out of the world, therefore the world hates you. Remember the word that I said to you, 'A servant is not greater than his master.' If they persecuted me, they will persecute you; if they kept my word, they will keep yours also (Jn. 15:18-20).

---

[9] *Cf. TDNT*, article *mathētēs* by K. H. Rengstorf.
[10] Birger Gerhardsson in *The Origins of the Gospel Tradition* cites the example of two disciples of a certain rabbi, who hid in his bedroom to observe his conduct in bed!

It is instructive to note the way in which the discipling process made use of structures which have only comparatively recently been identified by students of group dynamics. It is clear from the gospels that from time to time Jesus had many followers. They fall into identifiable groups. There is, first, the amorphous and largely anonymous mass. Secondly, Luke records the existence of a group of seventy[11] 'others', presumably seventy in addition to the group of messengers mentioned in chapter 9 as having been sent to a Samaritan village. The third grouping is the twelve; and finally there is the familiar grouping, Jesus with Peter, James, John and occasionally Andrew. These four groups correspond to the well-known group categories of group dynamics, the *familiar*, family-sized group (two to six persons), the *small group* (seven to sixteen), the *large group* (twenty-five to about eighty), and the *crowd*.[12] Each group has its own characteristic. Within the *familiar* group there is the greatest potential for the development of individuality. For Jesus' familiar group cohesiveness was strengthened by the fact that James and John were brothers, as were Peter and Andrew. In Jesus' small group, the group of twelve, each member would have grown to know each other member very well, to know their weaknesses and strengths; and this became important when in the early church the apostles were given a particular leadership role. The upper limit of the large group marks the maximum number of people who can adequately get to know one another by name, to relate in a measure to one another. Beyond this size some members will inevitably be overlooked. The crowd remains a crowd unless it can somehow be discipled into smaller groups.

It is evident from this brief observation that when Jesus called people to discipleship the level of actual commitment of those who responded varied, so that levels of intimacy with Jesus developed corresponding to the levels of commitment. But these levels of intimacy must be clearly distinguished from vertical tiers in some kind of academic hierarchy.

It must be recognized, however, that the level of intimacy accorded to any individual was not entirely determined by his own response to

---

[11] Lk. 10:1. Or possibly seventy-two were in this group: the text is uncertain here. The number seventy is usually taken as a reflection of Moses' choice of seventy (or seventy-two if Eldad and Medad are added) elders to assist him (Nu. 11; *cf.* Ex. 24:1), or of the seventy nations of Gn.10. Commenting on this last suggestion S. G. Wilson says: 'That the Pentecost narrative (Acts 2) can be read as a reversal of the story of the tower of Babel (Genesis 11) might add a little support to this interpretation of Luke 10:1f.'(*The Gentiles and the Gentile Mission*, CUP, London, 1973, p. 46).

Not surprisingly, attempts have been made to provide details of the composition of the seventy. Eusebius names Barnabas, Sosthenes, Cephas (not the Peter of the Twelve), Matthias, Joseph Barsabbas and Thaddaeus *(Historia ecclesiastica* I, 11). Origen adds Mark to the number. See Bruce M. Metzger, 'Seventy or Seventy-two Disciples?' *NTS,* 5 (1958-59), and A. Plummer's *St Luke* in the *International Critical Commentary* (T. & T. Clark, Edinburgh, 1896, [5]1922).

[12] See, for example, W. R. Bion, *Experience in Groups* (Tavistock Publications, London, 1961), G. S. Gibbard, J. J. Hartman, and R. D. Mann (eds.), *Analysis of Groups* (Jossey-Bass Publishers, Washington, 1974) and L. Kreeger (ed.), *The Large Group* (Constable, London, 1975).

THE TASK OF THE CHURCH

Jesus' preaching. As we shall see, below, the discipleship pattern developed by Jesus rested on the unique feature that it was Jesus who chose his disciples, not the disciples who chose Jesus. He selected them with a particular purpose in mind: 'I chose you and appointed you that you should go and bear fruit' (Jn. 15:16).

The figure of speech, 'bearing fruit', refers back to the image of the vine at the beginning of the chapter, and the 'going' is a reference to 'the mission of the apostles to the world'.[13] Thus the apostles are chosen *by* Jesus (the *egō*, 'I', in Jn. 15:16 is emphatic), and he has a specific task for them: to engage in world mission, in their turn to make disciples.

It is, in fact, vital to observe that there were fundamental differences between the concept of discipleship evidenced in the *talmîd* of the Jewish rabbi and the discipleship initiated by Jesus. First of all, although the disciple was to become like Jesus in many ways, Jesus was, and knew himself to be, more than rabbi, more than *didaskalos*, 'teacher'. He was Lord (Jn. 13:13). Moreover, Jesus was instituting a new order of discipleship in which the disciple would not have the privilege of walking with his master, of seeing for himself the master's way of life. It was to be a discipleship *in absentia*. Thirdly, the Christlikeness would not be due to a mere external affectation of the way of the master, but to an inner transformation effected by the real presence within the disciple of the Holy Spirit. Fourthly, the relationship between disciple and master would come not through an interested student attaching himself to an interesting teacher, but through radical conversion, through rebirth.[14] And, as we have already seen, the disciple did not choose his master but was chosen by him.

It was to this concept of discipleship that Jesus called first his apostles and then, through them, his church. There was a discipline to be observed and there was teaching to be learned,[15] but the relationship between Jesus and his disciples would always be conditioned by the fact that Jesus is *Lord*.

---

[13]C. K. Barrett, *The Gospel according to Saint John* (SPCK, London, ²1978). John Marsh in SCM'S *Pelican Commentary* on *St John* (Penguin, Harmondsworth, 1963; SCM, London, 1977) is prepared to go further: 'This saying reflects the imagery of the vine, which in turn reflects the symbolism of the wine at the Eucharist. All the more reason, therefore, to see in the use of "go" *(hupagēte)* a reflection of the fact that the Son is about to "go" to the Father. The going of the disciples into the world will demand sacrifice too.' Barnabas Lindars (*The Gospel of John, New Century Bible,* Oliphants, London, 1972, p. 492), however, objects to this interpretation: the phraseology here is 'too weak to bear the sense of "go the way of the cross" '.

[14]Rengstorf's summing up of his article *mathētēs* in *TDNT* is important: 'Notwithstanding the formal kinship between the *talmîd* of late Rabbinic Judaism and the *mathētēs* of Jesus, there is between the two no inner relation. The reason is that both in origin and nature the disciples of Jesus are moulded by the self-awareness of Jesus. He is for them, not the rabbi-*didaskalos*, but their Lord. The fact that they are *mathētai* does not affect this. The relation in which the disciples are set by Jesus to Himself implies already that witness to Him is the task to which they are called as His disciples.'

[15]*Cf.* Harald Riesenfeld's suggestion in *The Gospel Tradition and its Beginnings* (Mowbray, London, 1957), that Jesus not only expected his disciples to learn, but, like all rabbis of the time, expected them to learn by heart.

3.3 POWER FOR MISSION

The reason why the church is left on earth is missiological: to be Christ's witness, to express through her life the reality of the resurrection of Christ. The church was to offer to all an entirely new quality of freedom-life, the life of eternity through the redemptive act of Christ in the passion, and to disciple those who respond to the proclamation of Christ into the pattern of life demonstrated in Jesus.

But *how* is this new quality of radical discipleship to be lived out? Certainly not by a simple decision to follow Christ and to do one's best to imitate him in the sense that the Muslim is expected to imitate the lifestyle of Muhammad. The church's proclamation of Christ and the hearer's response to Christ are alike conditioned by the need for an external and enabling power: the power of Pentecost.

The general failure of theologians to relate the origin of the missiological task of the church to Pentecost, and the consequent missiological malaise of the church in the area of witness, have been powerfully demonstrated by Harry Boer in *Pentecost and Mission*.[16] He summarizes:

> Pentecost has not played a determinative role in missionary theological thinking. Suggestive, even penetrating, thoughts have been presented but, except by Roland Allen, a missionary theology centring around Pentecost and its continuing meaning for the church has not been developed.

The recognition that it is Pentecost which alone makes available *power* (*dynamis*, Acts 1:8) to complement its *authority* (*exousia*, Mt. 28:18) for mission should lead every Christian to an awareness that witness is inescapably *conflict*, conflict with intangible spiritual forces which, apart from our appropriation of Pentecost power, are invincible.

3.3.1 The insufflation

The period intervening between the Passion and Pentecost is a unique period in the church's history. Christ was risen but for forty days not ascended. And then Christ was ascended but the Spirit's power had not yet been given. The fifty days, no less than the forty days following the resurrection of Christ, do require some explanation.

If we are prepared to take the biblical evidence seriously we must explain the interval in terms of the origins of the two determinative feasts, Passover and Weeks. Primarily Passover celebrated the crucial

---

[16] Harry R. Boer, *Pentecost and Mission* (Lutterworth, London, 1961), p. 63. Dr Boer's book says in greater detail and with greater clarity all that I am here attempting to express of the origin of mission and the task of the church. *Pentecost and Mission* ought to rank with Roland Allen's *Missionary Methods* in the study of mission.

events of the Hebrew exodus from Egypt, events which took place in the month Abib (later known as Nisan), the month in which harvesting began. The offering of a sheaf of barley at the beginning of Passover (Lv. 23:15-16) is sufficient to show that in theology the connection of Passover with the beginning of harvest is not to be treated as a mere chronological coincidence. At the other end of the fifty days, Pentecost marks the completion of the harvest. The two central events of soteriology, the passion and Pentecost, are deliberately related to these two Jewish festivals.

The reason for this would seem to me to be part of a comprehensive system of explanation of profound spiritual truths through a multitude of individually simple illustrations taken from the life of the common people. It is just not possible to expound the total significance of the life, death, resurrection, ascension and saving life of Christ in terms of theological propositions; and so through the Old Testament sacrificial system and through the system of feasts and fasts we are encouraged to throw light on what might otherwise be only a dimly perceived mystery.

Thus the fuller significance of Christ's death is to be understood through an examination of all that relates to the Passover story, and other legitimate Old Testament sacrificial pericopes. Similarly, the fuller significance of Pentecost will come through an understanding of the Old Testament regulations concerning it.

I have no intention here of developing such a detailed interpretation of the passion and Pentecost, but reference is made to this aspect of New Testament chronology to explain the apparent hiatus between the resurrection of Christ and the empowering of the church for mission, a hiatus which has tended to produce a certain vagueness in the understanding of the status of the post-resurrection pre-Pentecost church.

The fifty days do represent a unique period in the church's history, but it is not a period in which the apostles are Spirit-less. They are granted the Spirit through the insufflation of John 20:22, but they must await the specific missiological *empowering* of the Spirit at Pentecost. It would be as disastrous to think of the early church in the fifty days as being without the Spirit as to think of Christ as being without the Spirit before his baptism. A visible descent of the Spirit and an evident empowering of the Spirit must not be taken to imply the Spirit's total absence prior to the visible descent. Pentecost marks not so much the birth of the church as the birth of mission. But while mission cannot commence until Pentecost, it is inaugurated immediately after the resurrection.

Matthew records the words which have become known as the Great Commission, Matthew 28:18-20. But John's record of the insufflation is of comparable importance, missiologically. Mission is given a Christological component: 'As the Father has sent me, even so I send you'

(Jn. 20:21; *cf.* 17:18). His words are then supplemented by action: 'And when he had said this, he breathed on them, and said to them, "Receive the Holy Spirit." '

Jesus here introduces a decisive intervention in human history: as in the first act of creation in Genesis, so here the creation of life is dependent on the breath of God, and only subsequently is man able to fulfil the role for which he is created. As C.K. Barrett comments:

> That John intended to depict an event of significance parallel to that of the first creation of man cannot be doubted; this was the beginning of the new creation.[17]

In fact, Jesus is inaugurating mission by giving birth to his church, which cannot be left *orphanous*, 'desolate' (Jn. 14:18), Spirit-less, unsure of its task. Sir Edwyn Hoskyns expresses it clearly:

> The Resurrection scenes in the Fourth Gospel are all preparatory scenes, preparatory for the mission. What the Lord will do invisibly from heaven he does here visibly on earth. The mission is inaugurated, but not actually begun.[18]

The insufflation, therefore, is a vital stage in the commissioning of the church in which the apostles are 're-created' by the breath of their Lord, given the Holy Spirit as the guarantor of incorporation into Christ (Rom. 8:9; Eph. 1:14), and are told of their task. The actual empowering for mission, however, awaits the dawning of Pentecost.

Of course we are not to suppose that at Pentecost the disciples received 'more of' the Spirit as though he were somehow divisible. But the *gifts* of the Spirit are diverse, and it is the descent of missiological enabling that they must await, as Jesus awaited the descent of the Spirit on him before opening *his* mission.

3.3.2 Understanding Pentecost

There are three primary links between the events of Pentecost and the Old Testament: the phenomenon of glossolalia, linked to the Babel confusion; the Joel prophecy, alluded to by Peter; and the calendrical association with Weeks.

---

[17] *The Gospel according to Saint John*, p. 570. Barrett, however, sees the insufflation not as additional to the Acts 2 descent of the Spirit in power, but as a doublet of it. Leon Morris, in his commentary on John (*The Gospel of John*, New International Commentary, Eerdmans, Grand Rapids, 1971), notes that the best Greek texts do not include the words 'on them' to define the breathing out although Barrett comments that those versions which do supply *autois* rightly interpret the act: it is a breathing on them as God originally breathed on Adam. Among German scholars, J. Koehler sees the insufflation account as evidence of Johannine polemic against Luke's Acts (see Bultmann's commentary on St John's gospel, *ad loc.*) In an acute observation Bultmann interprets: 'Easter and Pentecost therefore fall together' (*The Gospel of John*, English translation by G. R. Beasley-Murray, Blackwell, Oxford, 1971, p. 692).

[18] *The Fourth Gospel* (Faber and Faber, London, ²1956), p. 547.

THE TASK OF THE CHURCH

Babel, with its tower-ziggurat, is our introduction to Babylon, which stands, throughout the Bible, as a symbol of human rebellion. The Babel rebellion appears to be directed against the proto-missiological commission of Genesis 1:28: 'Be fruitful and multiply, and fill the earth and subdue it.' The commission is repeated to post-diluvian man, together with an assurance of safety in carrying it out: 'Be fruitful and multiply, and fill the earth. The fear of you and the dread of you shall be upon every beast of the earth, and upon every bird of the air' (Gn. 9:1-2).

Chronologically the commissioning may be traced through Abraham, Moses and the prophets. Abraham is called out not merely to occupy Canaan, but to be a blessing to the whole earth: 'By you all the families of the earth shall be blessed' (Gn. 12:3 mg.)

Moses is chosen to lead the exodus from Egypt in a renewed evidence of the uniqueness and even exclusiveness of the people of God:

> For how shall it be known that I have found favour in thy sight, I and thy people? Is it not in *thy going with us*, so that we are distinct, I and thy people, from all other people that are upon the face of the earth? (Ex. 33:16).

Isaiah finds Israel a sedentary people, engaged like the surrounding nations in amassing property, unfit for mission:

> Woe to those who join house to house,
>   who add field to field,
> until there is no more room...
> Woe to those who rise early in the morning,
>   that they may run after strong drink...
> Therefore my people go into exile (Is. 5:8, 11, 13).

Israel was constituted a nation with a particular mission to the world, but rejected that mission in favour of the preservation of Israel as a nation, a preservation which they hoped to guarantee (as had the proto-Babylonians of Gn. 11) by 'settling down'. The commission must, therefore, be given to another:

> It is too light a thing that you should be my servant
>   to raise up the tribes of Jacob
>   and to restore the preserved of Israel;
> I will give you as a light to the nations,
>   that my salvation may reach to the end of the earth (Is. 49:6).

Malachi in his condemnation of Israel deliberately describes the debased way of life of Israel in the context of her missionary relationship to the surrounding nations:

> From the rising of the sun to its setting my name is great among the nations, and in every place incense is offered to my name, and a pure offering; for my name is great among the nations, says the Lord of hosts. But you profane it (Mal. 1:11; *cf.* 2:10; 3:12).

And so we reach the New Testament across the silent years, to find the commission that should send the people of God into the world to be a light, a blessing, to the nations, repeated to the church:

> Go into all the world and preach the gospel to the whole creation (Mk. 16:15).

In this sequence the Babel event and the Pentecost experience are the two missiological poles. The confusion of tongues *at* Babel[19] and the scattering of the people *from* Babel must be related to the 'tongues' of Pentecost and the power for mission granted at Pentecost.

Babel, of course, is a missiological denial: ordered to fill the earth, the people simply settled down. Pentecost is a positive restatement of the missiological imperative. At Babel we have a rebellious people, refusing to fill the earth and engaged in an attempt to coerce God into coming down through their *bâbel*, 'gate of God'. At Pentecost, by contrast, we have an obedient people gathered together to await the right time for the Spirit to be 'poured out'. At Babel the people were scattered and divided; at Pentecost they were united and empowered.

Surprisingly, the commentators have been reluctant to recognize the relationship between Pentecost and Babel, concentrating attention, rather, on parallels with the giving of the law at Sinai and the Pentecost experience.[20] J.G. Davies, however, has made out a compelling case for viewing Acts 2 as being deliberately based on the Septuagint of Genesis 11. Speaking of the upper room in Jerusalem where the disciples were obediently gathered and waiting, he says:

> From this centre of unity the good news of redemption and atonement can now go forth: from Babel God scattered abroad

---

[19] Hebrew *šam*, 'there', God confused their language. The attempt to make the confusion of language depend on the natural consequences of the scattering *from* Babel does violence to the text. See pp. 128-138 of my *Language and the Christian* (Bagster, London, 1978) for a rather fuller consideration of the significance of Babel.

[20] Rabbinic tradition suggests that the decalogue, promulgated by a single voice, was heard in each of the seventy languages corresponding to the seventy nations of Gn. 10, thus providing a plausible connection between Pentecost and Sinai. For example, Jubilees 1:1 and 6:21, taken together, show that tradition interpreted Pentecost as a feast with two points of reference, Weeks and Firstfruits, and associated it with two events, the covenant with Noah and the law-giving at Sinai. But of course this is *tradition* and not Scripture. There is no plausible evidence in Scripture for associating Pentecost with Sinai. Unfortunately a preoccupation with rabbinic tradition and so with the Sinai link to Pentecost has led to the neglect of the more significant link between *Babel* and Pentecost.

(diespeiren) the people to live at variance with one another; from Jerusalem the members of the church were scattered abroad *(diesparēsan)* and 'went about preaching the word' that the people of the earth might live in concord one with another.[21]

And this is the significance of Pentecost. The creation purpose of God is restated in the Great Commission and in the words of Jesus which preceded the insufflation, but the church awaits that power which alone can enable it to fulfil the commission. Pentecost is an example of what Irenaeus spoke of as 'recapitulation'. It is human weakness redeemed by an act of grace. And in particular it is to be seen as Babel redeemed. In the gift of tongues we have a *symbolic, partial* and *temporary* healing of the linguistic divisions of Babel: symbolic, partial and temporary since the apostles do not appear to have continued to exercise a preaching ministry in tongues and since the gift of tongues has demonstrably not been given to all Christians. Since the Pentecost experience, which involved the speaking of specific, identifiable languages to native speakers of those languages by individuals who had never learnt them, missionaries have had to spend years of hard work in language study to enable them to communicate across the Babel-barrier.

The second strand that links Pentecost to the Old Testament is the prophecy of Joel. The Joel prophecy is a reminder that Pentecost is both missiological and eschatological.

Mission and eschatology are, of course, conjoined by Jesus:

> And this gospel of the kingdom will be preached throughout the whole world, as a testimony to all nations; and then the end will come (Mt. 24:14).

Peter affirms that the events of Pentecost are the fulfilment of a particular prophecy by Joel:

> It shall come to pass afterward,
> that I will pour out my spirit on all flesh (Joel 2:28; Acts 2:17).

The prophecy itself is set in the context of famine, a literal grain famine parallel to and indicative of spiritual disaster of the first magnitude:

> What the cutting locust left,
>   the swarming locust has eaten.
> What the swarming locust left,

---

[21] J. G. Davies, 'Pentecost and Glossolalia', *JTS* 3, 1952, p. 229.

> the hopping locust has eaten,
> and what the hopping locust left,
> > the destroying locust has eaten (Joel 1:4).
>
> The seed shrivels under the clods,
> > the storehouses are desolate;
> > the granaries are ruined
> > > because the grain has failed (Joel 1:17).

But as the prophecy proceeds it becomes apparent that the famine is related to national apostasy:

> Put in the sickle,
> > for the harvest is ripe.
> Go in, tread,
> > for the winepress is full.
> The vats overflow,
> > for their wickedness is great (Joel 3:13).

This is no simplistic vision of a temporary agricultural disaster, followed by a miraculous harvest-home. Joel joins Isaiah in the latter's vision of the glorious figure marching from Edom, the garments of the warrior-servant stained red not with his own blood, shed redemptively, but with the blood of nations brought to judgment. The prophecy is a reminder that the proclamation of salvation is both a missiological and an eschatological event, that alongside the offer of redemption there is also both a proclamation of *present* rebellion against God and of a coming judgment by God.

Indeed, the power given by Pentecost might proleptically usher in eschatological judgment. Ananias and Sapphira die at the words of Peter; Elymas is struck blind by the word of Paul. Great fear comes upon the church.

More briefly, we note the connection between Pentecost and the Feast of Weeks, the *ḥaḡ šāḇû'ôṯ*, suggestively also designated *ḥaḡ bikûrîm* (Ex. 23:16), a designation which again directs attention to the exodus and the redemption of the *bᵉḵōr*, the firstborn.

So then, Pentecost is to be seen as that event which gave to the church the power it needed to carry out its missiological task, a task which can be traced back through the life of Israel and to creation itself. Pentecost represents a unique enabling of the church to obey the creation commission to man to go into all the world, to fill it with a worshipping community. And Pentecost reminds us that the church is commissioned for mission which is always carried on in the context of eschatology, in the sense of urgency necessarily created by the realization that the Day is at hand.

3.4 PROCLAMATION AND PERSUASION

The Christian is designated a witness about Jesus and is charged with the task of making disciples. To enable him to fulfil this task he is empowered by the Holy Spirit. In recent years there has developed a measure of controversy concerning the character of our witnessing — its character as *proclamation* and its character as *persuasion*.

3.4.1 Evangelism and persuasion
In 1919 the Archbishops' committee of enquiry into the evangelistic work of the church defined evangelism in the following terms:

> To evangelise is so to present Christ Jesus in the power of the Holy Spirit that men shall come to put their trust in God through Him.

Objection to the monosyllable 'so' ('so to present'), was raised by John Stott at the Lausanne Congress in 1974: 'This is to define evangelism in terms of success. But to evangelise is not *so* to preach that something happens.'[22] The dilemma is, however, apparent in the immediately following statement by Stott: 'Of course the objective is that something will happen, namely that people will respond and believe.'

In saying this much, Stott goes a long way towards accepting the element of persuasion present in biblical evangelism. The fact is that we must maintain a biblical balance. On the one hand, we must recognize that in the New Testament the verb *euangelizomai* does simply mean the proclamation of good news, whether that news is believed or not. On the other hand, surely those who emphasize the element of passion in preaching are right in insisting that our preaching cannot be passionless? Surely there must be in the evangelist and in the witness something of the evident longing of Jesus, of his passion and his compassion, as we, like him, see the crowds like sheep without a shepherd? Certainly we would not consider evangelism to be so to preach that people did *not* believe!

Is the element of passion demonstrable from Acts? Consider, as an example, the conclusion to Peter's address at Pentecost: he 'testified with many other words and exhorted them, saying, "Save yourselves from this crooked generation" ' (Acts 2:40). Again, following the healing of the cripple outside the Jerusalem temple, Peter concludes his witness with a lengthy appeal which begins: 'Repent therefore, and

---
[22]'The Biblical Basis of Evangelism' in J. D. Douglas (ed.), *Let the Earth Hear his Voice*, the record of the 1974 International Congress on Evangelization, Lausanne (World Wide Publications, Minneapolis, 1975), p. 69. Interestingly enough, Stott appears to have moved away from the position indicated by his 1961 Payton lectures, when he quoted the Archbishops' committee definition with approval, and then commented: 'True evangelism seeks a response. It expects results. It is preaching for a verdict'. *The Preacher's Portrait* (Tyndale Press, London, 1967), p. 37.

turn again, that your sins may be blotted out, that times of refreshing may come from the presence of the Lord' (Acts 3:19).

Even more conclusively we find Paul arguing, explaining and proving the necessity of the passion, so that as a result 'some of them were persuaded (*peithō*), and joined Paul and Silas' (Acts 17:4). The same concept of persuasion is present in Acts 18:4, again of Paul: 'And he argued in the synagogue every sabbath, and persuaded Jews and Greeks.' And again, writing to the church at Corinth in the context of the eschatological judgment seat of Christ, aware of the fact that each Christian must one day account for his life's work, Paul comments: 'Therefore, knowing the fear of the Lord, we *persuade* men' (2 Cor. 5:11).

In the expectation of judgment, in the light of Christ's own command ('compel people to come in', Lk. 14:23), out of our concern for people, evangelism will always be more than 'just' proclamation.

3.4.2 Evangelism and proclamation

But the New Testament maintains a close connection between evangelism and proclamation, between *euangelizomai* and *kēryssō*. On twelve occasions we have the phrase which brings the two concepts of evangelism and proclamation into the closest possible relationship. Michael Green says flatly:

> It remains true that for a great many of its occurrences in the New Testament, *kērussō* means precisely the same as *euaggelizomai*.[23]

But the Acts accounts of evangelism do not end with the proclamation of the good news about Jesus. Evangelism is that form of proclamation which initiates a dialogue, not mere debate and point-scoring, but a dialogue which engages mind and will in those who hear, the goal of which is decision.

For example, in Acts 8, following the persecution of the believers in Jerusalem, we find those who were scattered going about preaching (*euangelizomai*) the word. In particular Philip proclaims (*kēryssō*) Christ:

> And the multitudes with one accord gave heed to what was said ... unclean spirits came out of many ... and many who were para-

---

[23] *Evangelism in the Early Church* (Hodder and Stoughton, London, 1970), p. 59. The Greek verb *euangelizomai* occurs fifty-five times in the New Testament, with twenty-five of these ocurrences in Luke-Acts. In the fifteen occurrences in Acts the subject of the preaching is described simply as 'the gospel' ten times. In 8:12 it is 'good news about the kingdom of God and the name of Jesus Christ'. In 8:35 it is 'the good news of Jesus'. In 10:36 it is 'good news of peace by Jesus Christ'; and, more fully, in 13:32 the good news is the fact that 'what God promised to the fathers, this he has fulfilled to us their children by raising Jesus'. In three other places the emphasis is slightly different: in 5:42 it is 'Jesus as the Christ' who is preached; in 11:20 they preach 'the Lord Jesus'; and in 17:18 Paul preaches 'Jesus and the resurrection'.

lysed or lame were healed. So there was much joy in that city ... When they believed Philip as he preached good news *(euangelizomai)* about the kingdom of God and the name of Jesus Christ, they were baptized, both men and women (Acts 8:6-12).

Proclamation-evangelism is thus more than delivering theological lectures, more than making speeches about God. It is preaching for decision, it is preaching with passion. But even where such preaching is not followed by the response of faith on the part of anyone who heard it, in the New Testament sense of the word those people who listened have been *evangelized*. Ultimately Stott is right in his objection to the Archbishops' committee's definition of evangelism: to evangelize is *not* so to preach that something happens, for no such methodology is available to us. There is no technique that the preacher can follow which will guarantee that his listeners *will* respond in faith. But New Testament evangelism will always mean proclamation in the earnest *hope* that faith will be the outcome in the listeners.

3.5 LIBERATION THEOLOGY

Liberation theology has arisen from a culpable misinterpretation of Scripture, but also from a genuine concern for the oppressed and exploited masses of the world. The theologians of liberation criticize traditional theologies, and specifically those of what they term the North Atlantic churches, for ignoring important strands of biblical teaching and so developing defective systems of theology which are then allowed to determine church praxis. In particular, traditional theologies are accused of neglecting the biblical teaching on social justice. Mission, it is said, has consequently been concerned with the salvation of the individual, a salvation which is largely to be experienced in the future; while for the present, man is expected to continue to live, uncomplainingly, in an oppressive and unjust society.

Thus liberation theology adds to the traditional concept of mission a revolutionary element explicitly absent from traditional mission practice.

That the Bible *is* concerned for social justice is indisputable. Isaiah castigated the oppressor of his day:

> 'What do you mean by crushing my people,
>   by grinding the face of the poor?'
>   says the Lord God of Hosts (Is. 3:15);

and Amos joins him:

> For three transgressions of Israel,

> and for four, I will not revoke the punishment;
> because they sell the righteous for silver,
> and the needy for a pair of shoes —
> they that trample the head of the poor into the dust of the earth,
> and turn aside the way of the afflicted (Am. 2:6-7).

Elijah confronted Ahab on his acquisition of Naboth's vineyard (1 Ki. 21:1-24). Nathan dealt with David's cynically legalized murder of Uriah (2 Sa. 11:1 – 12:14). It is quite clear that justice *(mišpāṭ)* is demanded of Israel, and especially of her rulers, and it must be admitted that there has been a tendency amongst missionaries to overlook this genuine biblical teaching and its implications. On the other hand, those of us who were weaned theologically on Snaith's *Distinctive Ideas of the Old Testament*, and were lectured exhaustively on the moral teaching of the eighth-century prophets, and were glad to follow in the very practical footsteps of General Booth of the Salvation Army, might be pardoned for wishing to qualify the accusations of the liberation theologians.

3.5.1 The propositions of liberation theology

Liberation theology is in essence a Latin American phenomenon: 'all its spokesmen are Latin Americans',[24] and is primarily concerned with replacing the traditional concept of *salvation* with that of *liberation*, which then becomes *political* liberation: 'Sin demands a radical liberation which in turn necessarily implies a political liberation.'[25]

It is not basically the case that liberation theology ignores the concept of sin; on the contrary the domain of sin, the *hamartiosphere*, is enlarged to include some areas which have been overlooked in more conventional theologies. Sin becomes 'a social, historical fact, the absence of brotherhood and love in relationships among men, the breach of friendship with God and with other men, and, therefore, an interior, personal fracture.'[26]

It is this 'personal fracture' which then leads to oppression, exploitation and alienation. Liberation from oppression and exploitation results from class conflict:

> Liberation expresses the aspirations of oppressed peoples and

---

[24] Orlando Costas, *The Church and its Mission* (Tyndale House, Wheaton, 1974), p. 221. In an extended footnote Costas provides a useful guide to the foremost exponents of liberation theology. In particular Rubem Alves is labelled the *prophet,* Hugo Assman the *apologist* and Gustavo Gutiérrez the *systematic theologian* of the movement. Costas recognizes that the movement developed largely as a reaction against Roman Catholic rationalization of the oppressive political systems of Latin America (and a study of Gutiérrez confirms this), but the movement also reacts violently and immoderately against North Atlantic pietism.

[25] Gustavo Gutiérrez, *A Theology of Liberation* (SCM, London, 1976), p. 176.

[26] *Ibid.*, p. 175.

social classes, emphasizing the conflictual aspect of the economic, social and political process which puts them at odds with wealthy nations and oppressive classes.[27]

Having identified the oppressor as the sinner it is surprising and surely illogical to find salvation conceived for the oppressed. We are then left with the paradox of the unsaved sinner, the capitalist, and the saved saint, the prole!

The soteriology of liberation theology is augmented by the Marxist interpretation of history in terms of the class struggle; this, in its turn, is augmented by Marxist economic theory. The world is divided into the capitalist oppressors and the proletarian oppressed.[28]

But the Marxist analysis of society will not do, because it is contradicted by the facts — the facts of history now being made and the facts of history already recorded. Costas would insist that Jesus is decisively on the side of the poor:

> Jesus not only challenged the universal claims of the Empire and underlined its corrupt moral nature. His political option involved also an identification with those who were the victims of the powerful and the mighty. He took sides with the weak and destitute. He emptied himself, Paul says, and he took the form of a servant. He did not stand alongside the haughty and rich (cf. Luke 6:24-26). Rather he stood on the side of the hungry, thirsty and naked, strangers and prisoners, harlots and publicans.[29]

But this is shamelessly selective exegesis. Reading Costas one would never suppose that Jesus called Nicodemus to discipleship, that Joseph of Arimathea was one of his followers, that Zacchaeus was one of the saved, or that wealthy women, including the wife of Herod's steward, were allowed to supply Jesus' material needs.

As a consequence of adopting Marxist ideas of class conflict, something new has appeared in the Latin American church: a new schism, a potentially disastrous division. The International Ecumenical Congress of Theology held in Sâo Paulo in 1980 proved, in fact, to be a

---

[27] *Ibid.*, p. 36.

[28] Andrew Kirk's *Liberation Theology* (Marshall, Morgan and Scott, London, 1979) provides in chapter 3 a useful and understandable summary of 'Some Basic Themes'. Note especially p. 30 on the adoption of 'the classical Marxist categories of oppressors and oppressed'. In chapter 16 Kirk considers more closely the reasons for and the consequences of the adoption in liberation theology of Marxist socio-political theory. Lesslie Newbigin, in *The Open Secret* (SPCK, London, 1978) has devoted one closely reasoned chapter to a sympathetic but highly critical consideration of liberation theology, and specially of the importation into Christianity of the Marxist idea of class struggle.

[29] *The Church and its Mission*, p. 243. The literature on liberation theology is enormous, and much of it ephemeral. Marcuse's work, *An Essay on Liberation* (Penguin, Harmondsworth, 1969), built on Jürgen Moltmann's *Theology of Hope* (SCM, London 1967). For a cogent summary see Bonino's *Revolutionary Theology Comes of Age* (SPCK, London, 1975), and Andrew Kirk's two works, *Liberation Theology*, and *Theology Encounters Revolution* (IVP, Leicester, 1980).

gathering only of so-called 'popular' churches. The Spanish term is explained as referring to the churches of the working class, peasants, and the poor.[30]

The fundamental text of liberation theology is the Old Testament account of the exodus, which is interpreted primarily, if not exclusively, in terms of political liberation. Of course it *was* political liberation, but the text itself precludes any attempt to make it exclusively or even primarily political liberation. In the exodus account the Hebrews do not mount a revolt against their Egyptian masters; and Yahweh makes clear the symbolic element of the event by the centrality of the act of sacrifice, a sacrifice which becomes for the Jew the central feature of the annual Passover remembrance and which in due course is transformed into the New Testament eucharist.

The interpretation of the exodus in terms of the passion is not a fancy of modern North Atlantic theologians, but goes back to Paul and to Jesus himself. But it is important to notice that attempts to appropriate the connection between exodus and passion for liberation theology by turning Jesus into a political revolutionary fail. While the title-accusation on his cross satisfied the judicial system of Rome, its thesis cannot be supported from the evidence of Jesus' life and teaching. Politically, at least, Jesus left the Jews as enslaved to Rome and as exploited by Rome as he found them.

Properly understood, the exodus must be seen as one pole of the ellipse of Bible history, reflecting light on the cross, which is the second pole. The exodus indicated a spiritual liberation which is partial *and* a political liberation which is partial, and this is then reflected in the cross where a spiritual liberation is effected for individuals *of all classes*, and the acceptance of that spiritual liberation represents the only way in which society can be saved. Violence is the weapon of the oppressor, precisely *not* of the oppressed. Jesus does not strike, but is stricken.

3.5.2 The role of praxis
A further strand of liberation theology is that which raises praxis (action) above principle, behaviour above belief:

> Very concretely, we cannot receive the theological interpretation coming from the rich world without suspecting it and therefore asking what kind of praxis it supports, reflects or legitimizes.[31]

The accusation is clear: the theology of the North Atlantic churches is fabricated so as to validate a particular praxis, in fact capitalism, and

---
[30]*Occasional Bulletin of Missionary Research* 4.3 (1980), p. 127.
[31]*Revolutionary Theology Comes of Age*, p. 91.

does not arise out of any sincere engaging with the biblical text. The validity of any system, then, is to be determined not by reference to an authoritative biblical revelation, but by reference to experience, to action: 'Action is itself the truth.'[32]

Now this is not the same thing as saying that one's true beliefs are revealed by one's praxis. Jesus said as much, though more intelligibly: 'You will know them by their fruits' (Mt. 7:16, 20).

What is being suggested by liberation theology is that action stands above revelation, that theological propositions follow from human action instead of the traditional (western?) view that human action ought to follow from divine revelation. Our witness to Christ is not in terms of the proclamation of what Christ has done for us, but in terms of what I now do for the oppressed. Bonino says:

> God can only be named through the reference to a concrete community of historical existence, in relation to which words define their meanings.[33]

This remarkable piece of prose demands a great deal of interpretation. It could mean that the activity of God is known only through an identifiable body of historical events, and these events then define the theological language which has been developed to explicate them. Or it could mean that I can witness to God only by my behaviour, which then gives meaning to the vocabulary I choose to use in talking about God. If the first is intended, then the statement is merely tautologous. If the second, it is untrue. In view of the subject matter of the relevant section of Bonino's book it would appear that the second is intended.

It simply will not do to suggest that action is itself *the truth* unless a new meaning is given to 'truth'. But what Bonino and the rest seem most of all reluctant to do is to define their terms. In the normally understood sense of the word 'truth', action can be as much a lie as a lie itself can be. Praxis may be a liar.

Obviously the *consistency* between my belief and my conduct provides a good indication of the genuineness of my belief, but it says nothing at all about the truth of the content of that belief. Galileo must be allowed to deny praxeologically what he knew intellectually to be

---

[32] Quoted by Lesslie Newbigin in *The Open Secret*, p. 110, from *Revolutionary Theology Comes of Age*, p. 72. Newbigin's criticism of liberation theology is given added significance by his long association with the ecumenical movement in general and the World Council of Churches in particular, where liberation theology has from its beginning been looked upon with favour.

[33] Bonino, *Revolutionary Theology Comes of Age*, p. 81. One of the irritating features of liberation theology is its extraordinary jargon which often defies all attempts to extract meaning. I could not disagree more with McAfee Brown's commendatory blurb on Bonino's book, 'he writes from the "inside" in such a way as to communicate clearly with those on the "outside" '. I am tempted to invert Sir Winston Churchill's epigram concerning a parliamentary colleague, 'His clarity of speech is a positive disadvantage when he has nothing to say,' and comment of Bonino's liberation theology, 'His impenetrable speech is a positive advantage when he has something illogical to say.'

true. But his denial made no difference to the correctness of what he believed. What his denial did was to show that Galileo did not believe that the establishment of scientific truth was more important than the preservation of his own life.

Similarly, the North Atlantic theologian may demonstrate by his limited involvement that he does not feel that questions of oppression and exploitation should concern him to the extent that they interfere with his creature comforts. But that is not the same as saying that matters of oppression and exploitation do not concern him. The question is, rather, how deeply do they concern him?

Indeed, the identification of praxis as the test of belief is very much a sharp-handled weapon. How much action, what kind of action, will satisfy the liberation theologians that western theologians are concerned about oppression and exploitation? And conversely, what level of praxis is the westerner to demand of the liberation theologian to authenticate *his* theology? It sometimes appears to the missionary that the theologians of both persuasions spend a great deal of time in conferences, on committees and in congresses, writing and publishing books and pamphlets and articles about praxis, while he, the missionary, is left to heal the sick, give recovery of sight to the blind, care for the orphan, preach good news to the poor, and be castigated by both groups of theologians for doing so.

Praxis is *not* truth. Truth *is* absolute. It is independent both of my intellectual assent and of my praxeological commitment to it. As Edward Norman succinctly expressed it: 'Truth does not cease because people give up believing it.'[34]

Although it may still be possible in Latin America to think in terms of Marxist revolution as an answer to political oppression, in the rest of the world it simply is not possible. Demonstrably, Marxist revolution more often leads to deeper oppression than to any genuine liberation of the masses.

Stephen Neill has commented on Bonino's distress at finding Jürgen Moltmann 'already in 1973 retreating from his earlier advocacy of liberation through revolution'.[35] Bonino finds this volte-face extraordinary, but Czechoslovakia provides the explanation. No historian of integrity, no discerning theologian, could watch the cynical destruction of the short-lived Dubček regime and ever seriously advocate Marxism again. Berlin, Hungary, Poland and Czechoslovakia, Cambodia, Angola, Ethiopia and Afghanistan all cry aloud against the folly of expecting society to save itself by Marx-inspired violence.

The theology of liberation and the related politicization of the church has been criticized in depth by Edward Norman in his 1978

---

[34]*Christianity and the World Order* (OUP, London, 1979), p. 14.
[35]*Salvation Tomorrow* (Lutterworth, London, 1976), p. 85. *Cf.* Moltmann's *Theology of Hope*

THE TASK OF THE CHURCH

Reith Lectures and the subsequent book, *Christianity and the World Order*. Significantly, Dr Norman is both a theologian and a professional historian with a special interest in South America.

To the theological and sociological objections raised against liberation theology, Norman has added a third objection, namely to its educational programme. The liberation theologians have adopted the pedagogical principles of Paulos Freire, the key to which is the unlovely word *conscientization*. Freire objected to traditional methods of education as being impositional, the content imposed on the students by the teacher. The student learns what the teacher feels that he should learn, and the content of the curriculum will necessarily depend on the presuppositions of the teacher.

This, according to Freire, should be replaced by a system in which the student determines his own curriculum through being brought to a state of *awareness* of his need. But what is carefully concealed, here, is the inescapable fact that conscientization is itself education. The student is *taught* to demand a certain curriculum. As Norman comments: 'Despite the heavy use of technical language to describe conscientization, it is ordinary political indoctrination.'[36]

When liberation theology espouses conscientization as its educational base, it falls into the perennial trap of marriage to the spirit of the age. And as Dean Inge commented, such a person soon finds himself a widower. Fashions change. Systems pass away. To quote Norman again:

> The vocabulary used is not merely a contemporary rendition of biblical meaning, as those who employ it like to suppose; in reality, this sort of rhetoric indicates those social ideals as originating pretty firmly in contemporary political ideology. The creditability of the ideals is also short-lived, as the orthodoxies of thought within western liberalism now rise and decline with remarkable rapidity, dragging the perpetual re-interpretation of the content of Christianity along with them. Today's solemn declaration of the true purpose of Christ's teachings is tomorrow's reviled illustration of false 'prophecy'.[37]

It has been a saddening experience to observe so many of the scholars of the North Atlantic churches hastening into sackcloth and ashes and vying with one another to confess the truth of every accusation levelled against them by liberation theology. It is an aberrant theology, false in its hermeneutic, wrong in its fomentation of class struggle and mistaken in its epistemology.

(1967), which is overtly Marxist, with his *The Crucified God* (SCM, London, 1973).
[36] *Christianity and the World Order*, p. 55.
[37] *Ibid.*, p. 74.

3.5.3 A confession of failure
And yet. And yet there is a whole area of Christian concern which has been highlighted by liberation theology but often neglected (not 'invariably ignored'!) by the traditional missionary community. There has been too much political opportunism, too many colleges and hospitals and schools named after kings, emperors and presidents because of the value of the expected patronage. Too often the masses have been alienated.

Cone, leading apostle of the Black Theologians, asks:

> What power is keeping you out there? Is it not true that the so-called oppression of which you speak is freely accepted because you are unwilling to pay the price for real freedom?[38]

The missions have often been 'out there', isolated from the masses, because it has not seemed possible to risk the ill will even of regimes quite obviously oppressive. The need to conform has been rationalized:

> 'We cannot operate without the goodwill of government.'
> 'To speak out would mean being sent out.'
> 'We may have to compromise in order to maintain any kind of continuing ministry.'
> 'If we are to contribute to the needs of the under-privileged we must be *here*.'

Perhaps the greatest blot on the history of missions has been the often scandalous treatment of their employees. Wage differentials between missionaries and their 'servants' were often of the order of ten to one. But the price to be paid for ending this obvious exploitation was often too high, and the alternative was to attempt to justify it: 'If we pay any more it will upset the entire economic balance.' (So much the worse for the economic balance.) It has been interesting to observe how what would not be agreed to on such grounds was implemented subsequently when minimum wages were introduced by law.

Actually we continued to be slaves of a system of economic oppression because the price to be paid for freedom was too high: the loss of income, the surrender of an unreal standard of living. Here, at least, our critics are right. We have refused to die, and the cost to mission has been incalculable.

It must be possible to produce a biblical synthesis which will preserve the true nature of mission as a spiritual salvation, a salvation needed equally by everyone, everywhere, in every class of society, while incorporating also the wholly biblical burning indignation against every form of oppression and exploitation.

[38] *A Black Theology of Liberation* (Lippincott, Philadelphia, 1970), pp. 184f.

3.6 CATEGORIES OF MISSION

The task given to the church is to witness to Jesus Christ. This ought necessarily to involve the Christian in a distinctive lifestyle in which he is identified with all who are oppressed, no matter what the nature of the oppression. The commission to be Christ's witness reaches out from where the Christian is to the ends of the earth.

3.6.1 The priority of the Jew
And yet, precisely because the Christian faith is historically rooted in specific events, the Christian does find himself with a unique relationship to one nation: the Jews. It is arguable that this is the only biblically valid category of mission. Paul certainly recognizes a missiological priority for the Jew:

> For I am not ashamed of the gospel: it is the power of God for salvation to every one who has faith, to the Jew first and also to the Greek (Rom.1:16),

and again:

> There will be tribulation and distress for every human being who does evil, the Jew first and also the Greek, but glory and honour and peace for every one who does good, the Jew first and also the Greek (Rom. 2:9-10).

It is, of course, true that for those who are in Christ all ethnic categories are abolished: there is neither Jew nor Greek (Gal. 3:28). But we can no more ignore the evident fact that there *are* Jews and Greeks than we can ignore the fact that there *are* men and women, Paul's 'there is neither male nor female' notwithstanding. Admittedly Paul's phrase 'to the Jew first' might be taken merely as an indication of chronological priority: the gospel *did* come to the Jew first. John Murray, however, comments:

> It does not seem sufficient to regard this priority as that merely of time. The implication appears to be rather that the power of God unto salvation through faith has primary relevance to the Jew, and the analogy of scripture would indicate that this peculiar relevance to the Jew arises from the fact that the Jew had been chosen by God to be the recipient of the promise of the gospel, and that to him were committed the oracles of God.[39]

---

[39] The *Epistle to the Romans* 1 (Marshall, Morgan and Scott, London, 1960), p. 28. On the basis of

The phrase 'to the Jew first' must be allowed to be more than a reference to a mere chronological fact. The Jew continues to stand today in a unique relationship to the covenant and to God's covenant love. Not that there is some alternative route by which the Jew, although not the Gentile, may be saved: the one gospel has the same efficacy, the same power for both. But there is a missiological priority inherent in the phrase 'to the Jew first'.

There are those who would deny any priority for the Jew at all. They would ask: 'Then what advantage has the Jew'? (Rom. 3:1), to which Paul responds: 'Much in every way'; and points in illustration of his assertion to the special advantage the Jew has in that the Scriptures are given to him, and can best be understood by him. This very observation highlights the peculiar position of the Jew, on the one hand the custodian of Scripture in the sense that culturally he is best able to explain it, but on the other hand perhaps more than any other people (not excluding the Muslims) blinded to the meaning of Scripture.

Caught in this unenviable position of special privilege and special responsibility, the Jew ought to be accorded priority in the missionary task. But this is easier to state than it is to implement. The long and painful history of the relationship between Christian and Jew is not one that can give the Christian much satisfaction. That peculiarly Jewish *genre* of literature, the *Memorbuch*, witnesses to the multitudes of Jewish martyrs killed by zealous 'Christians' from the eleventh century and onwards. The Reformation and the Second World War, each in its own way, bear witness to an apparently intractable antisemitism that is easier to chronicle than it is to explain.

3.6.2 Geographical categories of mission

Some see an indication of geographical categories of mission in the phrasing of the Acts commissioning: '... in Jerusalem and in all Judea and Samaria and to the end of the earth' (Acts 1:8). This is certainly a neat encapsulation of the way in which, in fact, mission was effected,

---

Galatians 3:28 and Ephesians 2:14, Anders Nygren says flatly 'The priority of the Jew is abolished' (*Commentary on Romans*, SCM, London, 1952), p. 73. C. E. B. Cranfield, in a more careful consideration of the Greek construction of Romans 1:16, decisively rejects Nygren's judgment: 'The word *te* (though its presence is simply ignored by RV, RSV, NEB, and JB) is suggestive of the fundamental equality of Jew and Gentile in the face of the gospel (the gospel is the power of God unto salvation for believing Jew and believing Gentile alike), while the word *prōton* indicates that within the framework of this basic equality there is a certain undeniable priority of the Jew. The paradoxical insistence both on the fact that there is no *diastolē* (no distinction) (3:22, 10:12) and also at the same time on the continuing validity of the *Ioudaio ... prōton ...* belongs to the substance of the epistle' (*International Critical Commentary* on *Romans*, T. & T. Clark, Edinburgh, 1975, *ad loc.*). It is to be noted that *prōton* is omitted from some manuscripts, notably from Vaticanus. It is possible that '*prōton* here is due to assimilation from 2:9-10, but it is more likely that its omission should be traced to a later, anti-Jewish (Cranfield suggests Marcionite) revision.

beginning in Jerusalem in Acts 2 and finishing in Rome in chapter 28. But is there a suggestion that the preaching in Rome must be conditional upon a prior exhaustive preaching in Jerusalem?

Writing to Rome before his visit Paul commented:

> But now, since I no longer have any room for work in these regions, and since I have longed for many years to come to you, I hope to see you in passing as I go to Spain (Rom. 15:23-24).

His meaning is clarified by his statement,'From Jerusalem and as far round as Illyricum I have fully preached the gospel of Christ' (Rom. 15:19). The word Paul uses, *pleroō*, 'fully' preached, could mean a total, complete preaching, but it could also mean a pervasive preaching which, while not actually exhaustive, was potentially so. For example, Paul did preach in Thessalonica, and then from there 'the word of the Lord sounded forth' and the faith of the Thessalonians had 'gone forth everywhere' so that Paul could comment, almost ruefully, 'we need not say anything' (1 Thes. 1:8).

A study of Acts makes it clear that in fact Paul in no sense evangelized (proclaimed the good news to) *all* the peoples of Asia Minor. A handful of churches was established, but there were plenty of places still left to hear the gospel for the first time when Paul projected his visit to Rome and then Spain. Thus Paul began his witnessing *where he was,* but he did not feel compelled to remain where he was when others had been found to continue the work he had begun:

> I have fully preached the gospel of Christ, thus making it my ambition to preach the gospel, not where Christ has already been named, lest I build on another man's foundation (Rom. 15:19-20).

In fact it is quite obvious that Paul did not stay long enough in any one place to 'preach fully' if we are to assume by that a preaching to every person. But *pleroō* could be used in a third way as a preaching *in depth.* In Colossians 1:25 Paul speaks of his task as being 'to make the word of God fully known', and he uses the same verb. Paul's 'fully preaching' might then mean not 'reaching everyone' but 'preaching everything'. And having passed on the whole gospel he felt free to move on (Acts 20:27).

If this understanding of Paul is correct, it raises a question mark over those missions which have assumed that having first effectively preached Christ so that people turned to God in faith through him, they were then required to spend years in imparting a whole *system* of theology to the converts. It would appear that the essence of the gospel — the whole gospel and not merely a part of it — can be communicated in a short time. And in turn this might suggest that much of what we have been concerned to communicate as the gospel has been, in fact, cultural additions to the gospel.

3.6.3 The category 'missionary'

There is a certain inescapable difficulty in defining the term 'missionary', since the Bible does not present us with any clearly defined category of person or office which corresponds to it. There is a clearly defined *mission*, but no special category of *missionary*. Max Warren solves the problem neatly by equating the New Testament 'apostle' with English 'missionary'. Of the word 'apostle' he says: 'Its true English equivalent, the *only* one, is the word "missionary", that is, "one sent on a Mission with a message".'[40]

But of course it is not. It is true that in their respective languages the two words *apostle* and *missionary* have similar etymological roots ('I send'), but the meaning of a word must be determined by its usage and not by its etymology. There is no particular reason to identify the Twelve as missionaries, in the sense in which that word is used in English today. The word 'apostle' is used in the New Testament of the Twelve, of other prominent church leaders and of Jesus himself (Heb. 3:1), but never in defining an individual because he is engaged on recognizable missionary work.

George Peters devotes seventeen pages of his book on missions to a consideration of the term 'missionary', differentiating between the 'technical, biblical missionary function' and the 'general missionary involvement of all believers'.[41] Peters rejects Max Warren's solution and eventually identifies the missionary as the New Testament *evangelist*, with the cautious qualification that he 'operates mainly in non-church territory'.

The methodology here, however, is open to criticism, since it begins with the assumption that there is a specific category of missionary and that this category can be found in the New Testament. What is missing is any convincing proof that such a category really exists.

If we begin with the announcement of mission to the apostles by Christ it must be apparent that the call to be 'my witnesses' in Acts 1:8, or to 'make disciples' in Matthew 28:19, was given either to the Eleven only or to the whole church. And since Paul, Barnabas, Silas, Timothy, John Mark and Philip all demonstrably engaged in mission but were not of the Eleven, the first rigorist interpretation must be abandoned in favour of a more general application. The whole church is called to mission.

As to the requirement that the missionary is one who is sent on a specific task, the New Testament makes it clear that there is one task,

---

[40] *I Believe in the Great Commission* (Hodder and Stoughton, London, 1976), p. 172.
[41] *A Biblical Theology of Missions* (Moody Press, Chicago, 1972), p. 248.

to be Christ's witnesses. Mission is biblically still mission whether it involves being Christ's witness in my home or being Christ's witness five thousand miles away from my home. There is no geographical category which turns a *martys* (witness) into an *apostolos* (missionary) in Max Warren's terms. A *martys* is a missionary. A *kēryx* is a missionary.

The term 'missionary' today has come to mean for the North Atlantic churches 'a member of a recognized missionary society'. A member of a missionary society, based in London and typing letters or editing a magazine, would claim to be a missionary. A member of a missionary society teaching missionaries' children in Malaysia would claim to be a missionary. A member of a missionary society teaching English as a foreign language in Zambia would claim to be a missionary. But all of these jobs might be done by individuals who do not belong to a missionary society. And if they are done by people who do not belong to a missionary society, then the people who do them are not usually accorded the label 'missionary'.

But membership of a missionary society does not necessarily constitute a person a witness of Christ. Living in Bangladesh does not necessarily turn an expatriate into a witness. Any Christian becomes a missionary when he finds himself sent by God, however near or far, to be his witness.

The task of the church is, then, the proclamation of Christ in the power of the Holy Spirit, in the hope and expectation that those who hear will turn to God in faith. Our message centres on Christ, and particularly on the passion, and here particularly on the resurrection. Our proclamation is validated by acts of power and by the quality of life which we exhibit. The good news presents Christ as one who ransoms man from his otherwise helpless state as a slave of sin. Man's redemption is to be expected to affect his entire lifestyle radically, and thus to undermine the oppressive structures that serve to exploit man's impotence.

The church will expect to find her primary task challenged from time to time, both from within and from outside. She will be protected from the attractions of ephemeral reinterpretations of her task by adherence to Scripture. Salvation is to be seen not in terms of violent political revolution, but in terms of the freedom offered by Christ to all who are oppressed, from whatever class of society they may come.

In her task of proclamation the church recognizes a certain priority to the Jew, but accepts that reaching out to the untouched corners of the earth must not be allowed to await the total completion of the task of witnessing near at hand. And finally the task is not one that is restricted to a particular category of Christian, but one that is incumbent on all. As today the Christian finds himself more a global traveller than could possibly have imagined fifty years ago, so he must be aware that he carries with him, whoever he is, whatever his gifts, the responsibility of being 'my witness'.

4
The end of an era

In the second half of the twentieth century the Christian church closed one era of mission strategy and entered into a new era. It was precisely at the mid-point of the century that World Vision International was formed in North America, to be followed in 1967 by the British equivalent, Tear Fund, The Evangelical Alliance Relief Fund.[1] The creation of these societies marked a fresh recognition of the biblical imperative of a holistic approach to man's need, and coincided with powerful new developments in Third World mission. In April of 1969 the oldest ecumenical journal in existence lost the final 's' from its title to become the *International Review of Mission*,[2] likewise marking the changing nature of mission from a uniflow pattern from the west and north to the south and east, to the pattern of mission in six continents.

Third World missions are not, of course, a unique product of the twentieth century. A fully structured mission organization, the Melanesian Brotherhood, goes back to the 1920s and by the 1930s teams of Melanesian Christians were at work throughout the Pacific islands. But *a hundred years* earlier, Jamaican Christians had gone to West Africa and had initiated Bible translation work there.[3] If not unique to the twentieth century, however, they have certainly proliferated in the twentieth century; and by the early 1970s more than 200 Third World mission organizations had been identified.

[1]Tear Fund has had an interesting history, beginning in 1967 as an integral part of the work of the Evangelical Alliance, but rapidly outgrowing its parent and becoming an independent body. Its earlier ministry was effected through the traditional missionary societies, but this pattern changed under the stress of the operating conflicts with mission structures. New patterns of mission emerged in the ACROSS programme for Southern Sudan and HEED for Bangladesh.

Tear Fund income grew rapidly and topped £1 million in 1977, but the work was limited in that constitutionally it could deal only with social vectors, such as famine relief and community development, unlike its American counterpart, World Vision. Tear Fund could provide bread but not Bibles, build dams but not churches, establish orphanages but not seminaries. This anomalous situation was remedied in 1979 when Tear Fund set up the Evangelism and Christian Education Department of its work.

[2]See comment on the transition in *IRM,* LVIII, 230, April 1969, 'Dropping the S'.

[3]On the Melanesian Brotherhood see A. R. Tippett, *Solomon Islands Christianity* (William Carey Library, Pasadena, 1967), and on the Jamaican mission outreach to West Africa P. Larson, E. Pentecost and J. Wong, *Missions from the Third World* (Church Growth Study Centre, Singapore, 1973).

But while these changes were taking place in mission, many missionary societies failed to take note of them. By nature tempted to be reactionary, some societies lost touch with the supporting constituencies. The churches showed a growing disenchantment with the mission societies.[4] Still determined to accept their commitment to mission, Christians gave more generously to the newer societies such as World Vision and Tear Fund, while the more traditional societies experienced a serious financial decline. In *Crusade*, December 1980, Derek Williams reported Tear Fund income up 37% over the previous year, to a record £3.27 million; but a shortfall of £154,000 in thirteen societies responding to his questionnaire. To understand the bewilderment of the evangelical community of the fifties and sixties we must examine, however briefly, the history of the modern missionary movement.

4.1 THE HISTORY OF CHRISTIAN MISSION

The history of Christian *mission* is not the same as the history of Christian *missions*. The missionary society in the form familiar to the churches of the nineteenth and twentieth centuries has no pedigree to give it permanent validity. George Peters refers to missionary societies as 'accidents of history', and recognizes that they do not have a Bible origin.[5]

In his seven-volume *A History of the Expansion of Christianity*, Kenneth Scott Latourette divides the Christian era into four periods. The first of these, which he labels 'The First Five Centuries', presents the extraordinary spectacle of the apparently insignificant and powerless church reaching out with its good news into the Roman Empire and beyond.

By the end of the second century, Christianity had reached Britain to the west, and the third century *Acts of Thomas* makes it clear that somehow the church had also reached India in the east. By the middle of the fourth century there was a Christian church established in the Axumite kingdom of Ethiopia.

The church then moved into Latourette's second period, 'The Thousand Years of Uncertainty'. These were painful years, in some ways illustrative of the church in Britain in the twentieth century, when the church exhausted itself in playing two disastrous games, politics and philosophy. Politically, the church occupied itself in developing a hierarchical structure modelled on that of the Empire. The philosophical game was baptized and re-labelled theology, but it was philosophy for all that. And out of these two concerns, politics and

---

[4]*Cf.* George Peters, *A Biblical Theology of Missions* (Moody Press, Chicago, 1972), pp. 231f.: "A serious dichotomy between church and mission societies has developed ... we have today many churchless mission societies.'

[5]*Ibid.*, p. 229.

THE END OF AN ERA

philosophy, new links were developed between church and state—links which had begun to be forged in the days of Constantine. The Roman Empire was, of course, preoccupied with the problem of assuring the military security of the state, thus effectively leaving to the church the whole field of social action. So well did the church rise to its new responsibilities that early on in the second millennium the earlier dependence of church on state was reversed, and the church was able to impose its will on the state: or at least it could attempt to do so. In the Gregorian *Dictatus papae*[6] we find not only the ultimate expression of papal authority over the church, but also the clearest possible claim to ultimate sovereignty over the state.

Philosophically the Fourth Lateran Council of 1215 formalized Christology, pneumatology, ecclesiology and soteriology within the confines of a hierarchically structured and authoritarian church. But the thousand years of preoccupation with politics and philosophy left the essential church neglected. Right at the beginning of the thousand years we have the rise of Islam[7] and the shattering collapse of the historic North African churches. By the end of the period the situation was critical:

> The faith seemed threatened with internal disintegration. In Italy the Renaissance had brought a dry rot of scepticism. Even the Popes appeared in morals and aspirations more pagan than Christian. Criticism of the Church and of the clergy was rife. Most of the thirteenth and fourteenth-century movements which had given such evidence of vitality had lost their first enthusiasm, had died out, or had been crushed by persecution.[8]

Yet even the thousand years of uncertainty, the Middle Ages of the church which might have led to a permanent Dark Age, were not without their mission highlights. Pope Innocent sanctioned the formation of the Franciscan Order of Friars, and St Francis, better known as the gentle figure throwing breadcrumbs to the birds, made at least three missionary journeys to the Muslim world. Ramon Lull of Majorca also was closely associated with the Franciscans and, like Francis, was deeply concerned for the Muslim world. An intellectual, he produced a rationale for the church's mission to the Muslim world which has probably not been equalled since.[9] To his concern for the Muslim

---

[6] See Geoffrey Barraclough, *The Medieval Papacy* (Thames and Hudson, London, 1968), pp. 85-89, for a facsimile of the original twenty- seven notes of the *Dictatus*; and, in more detail, W. Ullmann, *The Growth of Papal Government in the Middle Ages* (Methuen, London, 1965). Chapter 9 is devoted to a consideration of Gregory's contribution to papal government.

[7] Which may conveniently be dated from the *hijra* in AD 622.

[8] K. S. Latourette, *A History of the Expansion of Christianity* 2 (Paternoster, Exeter, 1971), p. 448.

[9] *Cf.* E. A. Peers' biography of Ramon Lull, *Fool of Love* (SCM, London, 1946) and the same author's longer biography, *Ramon Lull* (SPCK, London, 1929).

world Lull added a concern for the reform of the church, rightly recognizing that the good news of Jesus Christ was being brought into disrepute by the gross luxury and sensuality of the church. Lull was more than eighty years old when he was stoned to death in Algeria.

The third period, the 'Three Centuries of Advance', takes Latourette to 1800. The period is neatly signposted at each end, at the beginning by the *Turmerlebnis,* Luther's tower experience in which he recovered the principle of justification by faith, and at the end by Carey's *Enquiry.* The one experience may be dated 1513,[10] and the other 1792. Luther recovered the doctrine of justification by faith, and Carey liberated it from the hyper-Calvinism[11] which had immobilized it.

Latourette's final period he calls 'The Great Century' and to it he devotes three volumes, in itself a fair indication of the primacy of this century (which he takes through to 1914) for the theme of his work. The great century is marked by the creation of a sequence of missionary societies and an apparently inexhaustible stream of missionaries who were undeterred by the knowledge that the expectation of life of the newly arrived missionary in some parts of Africa could be measured in weeks. It was a century of great contrasts in mission. It was a time when missionaries laboured for hours each day learning new languages and reducing them to writing, translating the Bible, establishing schools, building clinics and hospitals, fighting malaria and a dozen other diseases then scarcely known to western medicine. Of such missionaries the world was scarcely worthy. But on the other hand it was a time when missionaries sat and stagnated, waited on by their 'boys', functioning as political agents (with gunboats to back them up if needed).[12]

In fulfilment of Jesus' words the seed died. All over the mission world the graveyards were planted. There can scarcely be a mission

---

[10]James Atkinson places the experience in the summer of 1513 (*The Great Light,* Paternoster, Exeter, 1968, p. 19) but the *Oxford Dictionary of the Christian Church* (edited by F. L. Cross and E. A. Livingston, OUP, London, ²1974) places it between 1512 and 1515.

[11]It is interesting to note that at the end of some three centuries it is Calvinism which has come to dominate ecumenical theology through the period, through its *soteriological* emphases, rather than Lutheranism which, in its earlier stages, seemed to be moving towards an important and distinctive *sociological* emphasis. Soteriology is a much safer topic for public debate than sociology.

[12]*Cf.* Geoffrey Moorhouse, *The Missionaries* (Eyre-Methuen, London, 1973), a disturbing but highly readable book which provides a balanced corrective to the mission hagiographies to which we have become accustomed. In chapter 5 Moorhouse traces the development of missions in West Africa, where mission activity explicitly assumed British Government protection. He chronicles the destruction of Calibar Old Town by a British gunboat in response to the demands of Samuel Adgerley, other missionaries of the United Presbyterian Mission and the rest of the expatriate community.

See also Roland Oliver, *The Missionary Factor in East Africa* (Longmans, London, ²1965). In chapter 2 a graphic account is given of the 'Republic' established and administered by missionaries of the Church of Scotland at Blantyre in Nyasaland, and of the judicial floggings ordered (and executed with such severity that one man died). The battle of Mengo, near Kampala, in 1892, fought between Catholics and Protestants, is not a creditable aspect of missionary endeavour. These things need to be said, and today's missionaries need to know about them.

The publisher's blurb to Moorhouse's book states: 'If there had been no missionaries, there would have been no Battle of Mengo between Catholics and Protestants in Uganda in 1892, but there might not have been a modern Africa, either.'

station anywhere in the world more than twenty-five years old that does not have its quiet corner where husbands, wives, and children were laid to rest from the relentless struggle. And out of it all came the miracle: the seed died and the church sprang to life. To Latourette's Great Century, Ralph D. Winter could add *The 25 Unbelievable Years,* spanning the years from 1945 to 1969. On every continent the church was born, and proved to be no sickly child. Between 1956 and 1968 the world-wide Protestant community almost doubled in size, from 162 million to 316 million.

4.2 THE MODERN MISSIONARY MOVEMENT

We may conveniently take Carey as the prototype of a century of missionary thinking. He expounded missionary work in terms of five factors:[13]

1. The preaching of the good news.
2. The study of language and culture as a necessary preliminary to the translation of the Bible.
3. The more general study of anthropology to act as some kind of guide to the formation of the church.
4. The establishment of self-supporting churches which should transcend the traditional Indian caste limitations.
5. The opening of educational establishments, particularly with the thought of training church leaders.

To these five principles was quickly added a sixth, the establishment of medical services, peripatetic at first, but developing in scope until fully equipped hospitals and even teaching institutions became a common feature of mission outreach.

4.2.1 A self-destruct programme

What went generally unnoticed was the fact that such a programme, if successful, was inevitably self-destructive. For if the good news was preached and accepted, and if the church was formed and then adequately trained and became self-supporting, then the church leaders would inevitably displace the expatriate missionaries. The process would be almost irresistible, since, because of his understanding of culture and his command of language, the national is almost always a better Bible teacher and evangelist than the expatriate. Thus the second generation of *evangelists* was largely composed of nationals, while the expatriate missionaries turned their attention to their educa-

---

[13] On Carey's missionary principles see the doctoral thesis by A. H. Oussoron, published as *William Carey, Especially his Missionary Principles* (Suthoff, Leiden, 1945).

tional and medical programmes. The evangelistic vector in missionary work tended to be replaced rather rapidly by other concerns, while the churches shouldered the responsibility for church growth. It is very significant that precisely when the traditional missionary societies find the majority of their missionaries involved in institutional work, the younger Third World missions report that 89% of their mission activity falls into the two categories of evangelism and church planting.[14]

The next stage in the developing pattern of western mission was predictable; the educational programmes were popular and successful, and increasing numbers of children passed through the schools and on into higher education, embarrassing government which could not absorb the young graduates into the existing labour market. The missions employed some of their graduates as teachers, nurses and doctors, and once again the missionary found himself displaced. The change was accelerated by growing nationalism and by the very real dangers posed to governments which failed to provide employment for their intelligentsia. Schools were nationalized. Hospitals were taken over. It was something of a relief to some missionary societies to be able to lay down the rapidly increasing financial burden of the educational and medical work, but once again the scope of missionary work had been curtailed. New patterns of medical work developed. The South American Missionary Society reported in 1976:

> During the last few years the missionary medical contribution in South America has undergone a gradual change. The stress today is no longer on an independent medical service based on mission hospitals: rather it is to work within the context of national health services. Where that cover is comprehensive, as in Chile, missionaries work in governmental hospitals and clinics, and alongside Chileans in the rural health programme. In northern Argentine the government health service does not yet have the resources and personnel to cover the Indian area, so the missionary doctors and nurses are in a pioneer situation, serving in an intermediate capacity, implementing government policy until such time as the government is in a position to assume more direct responsibility.[15]

The situation was sometimes complicated by the growth of mission medical projects which were developed by ambitious doctors without any particular reference to their missions or to the local church — projects which the missions were not capable of administering. The Sudan Interior Mission faced this problem in its work in West Africa:

---

[14]*Readings in Third World Missions* (William Carey Library, Pasadena, 1976), p. 104.
[15]Eddie Gibbs in the SAMS medical newsletter, *Share*, March/April 1976.

And let's face it, in some cases SIM may have over-extended its medical outreach. Maybe we've let some projects grow beyond what we can adequately handle. If that's the case, and we really can't recruit enough staff, we're prepared to re-define our limits.[16]

With church planting and evangelism taken over by the church, and with government taking responsibility for education and medical care, missionaries moved into other work. There was still Bible translation. This had almost invariably been given high priority by the missionaries, although the results of the translation programmes were uneven. Stephen Neill comments:

> Many of the early translations were rough-hewn and imperfect, in some cases laughably so; a great deal had to be re-done, and perhaps Henry Martyn's Urdu version of 1810 is unique is being still the basis of the version current more than a century after the translator's death.[17]

The Wycliffe Bible Translators was founded by W. Cameron Townsend and L. L. Legters in 1934, and it was this society which, when most other mission societies were contracting, demonstrated a remarkable expansion. From 1960 to 1970 the total Wycliffe personnel leaped from 550 to 2,150 and by 1977 to 3,400. The mission set a target of 8,000 missionaries by 1985. But here again the tide of events was running contrary to mission thinking. A reaction set in against the pre-empting of Bible translation programmes by expatriate missionary societies. Although other missionary societies began to develop their own linguistic programmes, partly to take up missionaries made redundant by the loss of other activities, it became increasingly evident that translation was essentially a task for the national church rather than for the expatriate. The national Bible Societies began to develop their own translation programmes and to train nationals in the principles of translation, often assisted by Wycliffe missionaries. And so, once again, the expatriate missionary found a closing door.

4.2.2 Traditional missions and social action

One more door of opportunity was open to the missionaries: development. A series of socio-economic disasters in the 1970s demanded rapid response. The Sahel region of Africa was one such disaster zone, while India, Pakistan and Bangladesh presented a long series of crises. Tens of thousands of people in the disaster zones had to be fed, housed

[16] *Africa Now*, 4th quarter, 1976.
[17] *A History of Christian Missions*, p. 254. Not even the genius of Carey could overcome the inevitable shortcomings of the expatriate's translation. His finest translation, the Bengali, has long been superseded.

and rehabilitated. The missionaries were often well suited to meet the immediate needs: they knew the local languages and customs, often they had the confidence of the people. Sometimes suitable church structures already existed to facilitate area projects. But once the immediate emergency was past, the missionaries were often unable to cope with the more sophisticated aspects of long-term relief and rehabilitation.

This is scarcely surprising: they were not recruited for relief work. The evangelical missions had often preached a rather limited gospel which was concerned with souls. Missionaries were recruited either for that or for the institutional side of mission. Certainly in the early years the prime requisite in the potential missionary was spirituality, as it was then conceived.

The recruiting of missionaries is almost caricatured in Spurgeon's *Lectures to my Students*. A certain Matthew Wilks had been asked to interview an applicant for missionary work with the London Missionary Society in India. Wilks gave the young man an appointment for 6 a.m.

> The brother lived many miles off, but he was at the house at six o'clock punctually. Mr Wilks did not, however, enter the room till hours after. The brother, wonderingly, but patiently, waited. At last Mr Wilks arrived and addressed the candidate in his usual nasal tones, 'Well, young man, so you want to be a missionary.' 'Yes, Sir.' 'Do you love the Lord Jesus Christ?' 'Yes, Sir, I hope I do.' 'And have you had any education?' 'Yes, Sir, a little.' 'Well now, we'll try you; can you spell "cat"?' The young man looked confused and hardly knew how to answer so preposterous a question. His mind evidently halted between indignation and submission, but in a moment he replied steadily, 'c, a, t, cat.' 'Very good', said Mr Wilks; 'now can you spell "dog"?' Our young martyr hesitated, but Mr Wilks said in his coolest manner, 'Oh, never mind: don't be bashful; you spelt the other word so well that I should think you will be able to spell this: high as the attainment is, it is not so elevated but that you might do it without blushing.' The youthful Job replied, 'D, o, g, dog.' 'Well, that is right; I see that you will do in your spelling, and now for your arithmetic; how many are twice two?' It is a wonder that Mr Wilks did not receive 'twice two' after the fashion of muscular Christianity, but the patient youth gave the right reply and was dismissed. Matthew Wilks at the committee meeting said, 'I cordially recommend that young man; his testimonials and character I have duly examined, and besides that, I have given him a rare personal trial such as few could bear. I tried his self-denial, he was up in the morning early; I tried his temper and I tried his humility: he can

spell "cat" and "dog" an can tell that "twice two make four" and he will do for a missionary exceedingly well.'[18]

An incident such as this is indicative of a certain attitude to missionary work and a certain concept of the missionary. In my own student days (but not, I hasten to add, in my own college) it was not unknown for a certain training college principal to kick over the bucket of water being used by some unfortunate missionary candidate (as part of his quota of household chores) in order to test his sanctification.

Such missionaries had character, and some of them, especially in the earlier days, were well educated. But a perceptible change came over the situation as missionary training colleges began to proliferate, especially in the United States of America, but also in Britain. A stereotyped career missionary emerged, impeccably orthodox in his adherence to a clearly defined body of doctrine, but not always quite clear on the distinction between the essence of the gospel and the cultural wrappings within which he found it. The missionary could cope with the routine of teaching in a Bible School a limited curriculum that was simply a watered-down version of the courses he had himself taken. Indeed, to offer anything else probably never even occurred to the majority of the missionaries. There was a minimum of administration and a minimum of planning involved. As Stephen Neill said of the situation in India: 'Protestant missions have never been distinguished by having any plan at all.'[19]

This was not entirely surprising, since, in the main, missions did not attract planners. But as the traditional tasks of missions were lost, first to the church and then to the state, new and more demanding programmes began to open up. But the move into the area of social service sometimes proved disastrous. The missionaries simply were not trained to cope with the administrative structures which were now necessary. As we have seen, the early stages of emergency work suited the abilities of the missionaries admirably. But when the consolidation stage was reached, then the missionaries were, inevitably, out of their depth.

---

[18] C. H. Spurgeon, *Lectures to my Students* (Marshall, Morgan and Scott, London, 1954), pp. 39f. By the 1950s, apart from the medical missionaries, graduates were the exception amongst UK missionaries in the evangelical societies. The situation tended to be self-perpetuating. Since the missionaries were non-graduates and the home deputation workers tended to be appointed from amongst the missionaries they tended to fish the same pools from which they had themselves been fished. Some missions, of course, did better than others.

[19] *Salvation tomorrow* (Lutterworth, London, 1976), p. 129. With his customary fairness, Neill adds that missions in India did tend to follow the principles of the Jesuit de Nobili. The Abyssinian Frontiers Mission also provides an example of a mission with a careful plan of operation: to establish a base in Addis Ababa from which a thrust towards the southern border of Ethiopia might be supplied. This would then meet a north-directed thrust into the same area being planned from Kenya. See my *Born at Midnight*, chapter 1.

Still there was great pressure on the missions to be involved in relief work. Theologically they were reminded that they must minister to every part of man: *holistic* became the key phrase. Politically they soon discovered that visas were forthcoming for missionaries involved in relief work. Economic pressures appeared and comparatively enormous sums of money were made available to those missionary societies that would involve themselves in social work.

The financial pressure was a very real one. Missions had been accustomed to working on almost nothing, but now money began to pour in. It was evident to the Christian public at home that money sent to a mission for relief work was not siphoned off for other purposes. All over the world other agencies were being discredited by stories, some of them substantiated, of funds being misapplied. And so even the government agencies of the developed world began to offer money to the missions. US-AID; the Canadian International Development Agency, CIDA; the corresponding agency in Sweden; the Dutch government's programme financed through the church tax; all added to the money available for this new aspect of mission work. In some cases the social side of the work became paramount: there were missions where the budget for the relief programmes exceeded the budget for all other mission activities combined.

With some reluctance senior missionaries moved into the relief programmes. Mistakes were made. Administration either proliferated until the work was strangled by its own structures, or else was minimal so that the work done was unrelated to any plan. Disillusionment set in. Many missionaries returned home. Short-term workers returning to their sending countries were often less than complimentary about what they had seen.

4.2.3 Missions and the sending constituency

During this period deputation meetings lost their snap. Most missionary societies had long ago developed a furlough system,[20] and missionaries on furlough were expected to interest the home churches in their work. The missionaries for the most part owned cameras and they were able to photograph the people and the churches of the lands to which they had gone. But no-one showed them how to take photographs, still less how to present their slides to their audiences. In earlier years it didn't much matter. They had a story to tell and they spoke of countries which were totally unknown to the home churches. The fact that the slides were poorly exposed, projected haphazardly and did not show very much mattered little. But after World War II it be-

---

[20] Usually a term of five or six years, followed by a one-year 'furlough'. The system had the disadvantage that the missionary was effectively isolated from his supporting church. The length of the term of service was gradually reduced, along with the length of the furlough. Air travel made the new arrangement feasible, and the collapse of the traditional sea transportation made it inescapable.

gan to matter very much. The audiences had *seen* the rest of the world. Nightly the television brought fresh insights into events in the world.

A revolution was taking place in the whole process of communication. But of course many missionaries were unaware of what was happening at home. *They* didn't have time to sit in front of the television when they came home. Some of the larger societies were able to provide films and sound strips for their missionaries, but often the missionaries themselves preferred the old and tried methods and ignored the new techniques. Attendances at missionary meetings dropped. In some cases 'deputation meetings' turned out to be counter-productive. Missionary giving dropped and so did recruitment.

There was a third problem: that of the increasing complexity of mission work. With the involvement in social action, reports were needed. The sending agencies wanted reports, the host governments wanted reports, the mission wanted reports. There were enquiries from newspapers. Because of the increasing amounts of money being channelled to the missions, careful financial controls had to be provided. Committees and sub-committees multiplied. In an odd reversal, the number of missionaries decreased steadily, but the number of missionaries involved in the various areas of administration increased. In the five years ending in 1976 the total UK missionary force decreased in numbers by some 20%, but in the same period there was an average increase of 50% in the number of missionaries involved in administration.[21]

A fourth problem emerged: the inevitable problem of ageing personnel. In the Overseas Missionary Fellowship in 1977, 13% of the total mission force was on the retired list, compared with only 5% a decade earlier and only 1% in 1947. In 1977 the Overseas Division of the Methodist Church listed 196 retired missionaries and only 207 actually overseas, with 45 on furlough.[22] So there was added the further complication of the financial support of large numbers of retired workers at a time of falling income.

4.3 THE NEW WORLD FOR WORLD MISSION

The financial problems of the missionary societies were aggravated by the world economic climate of the seventies and eighties. Inflation reduced the real value of apparently increasing missionary giving. In Britain the unemployment situation worsened and so people found it hard to maintain their level of giving. The prestige of the church declined, and with that went the prestige both of minister and of missionary.

---

[21]Figures taken from P. W. Brierley's detailed and informative *UK Protestant Missions Handbook*, published in London in 1977 by the Evangelical Missionary Alliance. The statistics ought to have produced a storm in mission circles: in fact they caused scarcely a ripple.

[22]*Ibid.* Those missionaries listed as retired are only those for whom the mission has some direct financial responsibility.

Recruitment to the theological colleges faltered, and in the Anglican and Baptist churches this was reflected by the closure of some colleges and the amalgamation of others.

Such mergers indicated a realistic approach to the growing pressures for some measure of evangelical co-operation. The pressures being brought to bear were not only financial, although they were crucial since they could not be ignored. The ecumenical movement, with its early campaign for organic unity but its more visible expressions of unity in local ecumenical services, added to the pressure. The lay evangelical community, in general, approved of Christian co-operation, although their approval invariably stopped far short of what the professional ecumenists wanted. These pressures reached the missionary societies, and they, too, began to consider seriously the possibility of closer co-operation, urged on by the urgent financial difficulties.[23]

MECO emerged, the Middle East Christian Outreach, a merger of the Middle East General Mission, the Arabic Literature Mission and the Lebanon Evangelical Mission. In the same year, 1976, Christian Witness to Israel appeared from the marriage of the Barbican Mission to the Jews and the venerable (1842) Society for the Evangelization of the Jews. Even the larger societies began to consider suitable mergers: in 1978 the Sudan Interior Mission, with over 1,200 missionaries, opened negotiations with the tiny North Africa Mission.

The logic was obvious: missions simply could not afford the duplication of administration, the plurality of mission magazines, and the welter of ineffective, disheartening, competitive missionary meetings. An era was drawing to a close. A new era was beginning.

4.3.1 Third World missions
One further strand which influenced the changing pattern of mission must be referred to: the rise of the world church and the development of Third World missions.

The church in the world was not structured for mission. The rise of missionary societies in the western world reflected the church's inability to engage in mission, an inability which was imposed on it by its own institutional structures. But these structures were, in general, imposed in turn on the churches which grew out of the work of the missionaries, and were as impotent in mission as were the churches from which the missionaries had come. The situation was analysed with respect to the Asian church by Chua Wee Hian,[24] who specifically identified the new church structures as on the one hand enabling the missionary to retain a measure of control and on the other hand inhibiting mission. But the

---

[23] Of course, missions must not merely have an increasing income: it must increase at least in proportion with inflation. SAMS in 1978 was reporting an increase in income of 7% to be set off against inflation estimated at 300% in parts of Chile and Argentina.

[24] 'Encouraging Missionary Movement in Asian Churches', *Christianity Today* XIII, 19, June 1969.

call to mission could not be resisted. The churches accepted their own responsibility for mission. And an additional pressure on the churches came from Third World governments which indicated their willingness to accept Third World missionaries and their reluctance to accept western missionaries.

In 1977 the first Nigerian missionaries of the Evangelical Missionary Society, the missions arm of the Evangelical Churches of West Africa, arrived in the Sudan, and the Society reported 127 full-time missionary families deployed. The Far East was moving, too. In August 1977 some 1,600 Chinese Christians met in Hong Kong for the Chinese Congress on World Evangelization. And yet the church has remained largely unpersuaded of its responsibility for mission. The people of Hong Kong did not even need a passport to cross into the neighbouring Kwangtung province of China. There are 500 churches in Hong Kong and 50 missionaries registered with the Hong Kong Association of Christian Mission in 1980. But of these 50, 45 work amongst Chinese communities in the USA, the UK or Australia. Only five are actually involved in the kind of cross-cultural situation which is, in fact, immediately to hand.

Third World missions and churches began to absorb their parent expatriate missions. From the Latin America Mission CLAME emerged, the Community of Latin American Evangelical Ministries. LAM missionaries were expected to submit themselves to the CLAME personnel co-ordinator, who then circulated details of applicants to the partner agencies in Colombia and Costa Rica. Deployment depended on acceptance by one of the partner agencies.

The Quito Consultations of December 1976 and October 1978 uncovered deep-seated hostility on the part of some South American evangelicals towards the North Atlantic missions. These missions had imposed upon them a dependency which demonstrated four aspects:

> ... systems of theological education which are not relevant to our reality;
>
> ... proliferation of literature and educational materials which are mainly translated and are not relevant because they have come from a different cultural situation;
>
> ... the formation of structures and institutions which are imposed with neither consultation nor respect for Latin American reality and which will never be financed without foreign help;
>
> ... the propagation of a theology which makes no distinction between the biblical context of eternal value and the temporal cultural trappings of the missionary.[25]

[25] The Quito Consultations were called by an *ad hoc* committee, and brought together evangelical representatives of the Latin American churches and mission societies working in Latin America.

Everywhere the emphasis in mission began to move away from the uniflow mission concept of the North Atlantic churches to the multiflow biblical pattern of mission, mission *to* all the world and *from* all the world.

To many in the West, Third World missions are a new concept. But when *Missions from the Third World*[26] was published in 1973, there were already 200 Third World mission agencies with 3,000 missionaries. The Third World churches had often been critical of missionary societies which acted as a filter between them and the sending churches. The new world mobility and the new missionary societies of the Third World began to bypass the filter, so that through the seventies there was a gathering momentum in the movement for direct cooperation between the traditionally sending churches and the traditionally receiving churches. The traditional labels were rapidly being discarded.

4.3.2 New mission structures

The situation at the end of the 1970s was radically different from that obtaining at the end of the Second World War, when missions had taken up their task again. The missionaries had done their job well, and the world church was planted. True, there were still countries with minute Christian populations, and Islam remained essentially unreached, but there was no continent without a powerful Christian community.

Independence for the nations had come in like a flood, and the positions of special privilege enjoyed by expatriate missionaries were swept away. In Britain in the 1970s, missions seemed irrelevant and missionary meetings often failed either to inform or to enthuse. The mission malaise was, in fact, only a part of the general malaise affecting the entire church in Britain. Tom Houston, Executive Director of the British and Foreign Bible Society and a former Minister of the Nairobi Baptist Church, commented in 1978:

> The picture in the larger denominations is one of unabated decline of a very serious nature. There are variations but the same theme is recognizable ... It is interesting to see that the rate of decline in the members is much faster than in the paid staff or the buildings. This means that more money will be needed from fewer people to support the structures.[27]

Despite some very plain speaking at the first Consultation, the final communiqué was agreed unanimously. Quito II assembled in October 1978, but subsequent reports on the Consultations do not encourage the belief that any substantial progress had been made towards solving the tensions. See particularly *Partnership* 13, February 1979, for a report on Quito II.

[26]P. Larson, E. Pentecost and J. Wong, *Missions from the Third World* (Church Growth Study Centre, Singapore, 1973).

[27]*UK Protestant Missions Handbook* 2 (Evangelical Alliance, London, 1978), p. 7.

But Houston went on to question the accepted response to the situation: retreat. He commented:

> Looked at with management eyes, the churches still represent a tremendous pool of resources in personnel, plant and money. The business man would look for ways to re-deploy these for growth. They would sack or retire many leaders and rationalise both plant and finance and they would have done it a long time ago.[28]

No such large-scale reconstruction has taken place either in the churches or in the missions, possibly because both church and mission hierarchies tend to be self-perpetuating. Certainly in the majority of evangelical missionary societies the constituents who provide the finances have virtually no say in the membership of the mission councils. There appears to be no way in which mission societies can be called to account for their effectiveness or ineffectiveness except through the sanction of withdrawal of finance. Mission structures resist reform.

The Quito Consultations, already referred to, commented on these structures:

> We have become conscious of the complexity of missionary structures based in North America ... neither the validity nor the authenticity of the missionary impulse which has created these structures can be denied, but there is consensus that these structures need to be reformed.

The development of mission structures has proceeded spontaneously, arising out of an original situation in which an individual went where there was no church, and progressing to the new situation where there is both an overseas church and an overseas-church mission society. Diagrammatically the development is striking.

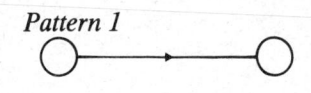

Let ◯ represent the individual missionary;
▫ represent the church; and
△ represent a mission organization.

Pattern 1

◯⟶◯

The first and simplest pattern of mission represents a missionary without direct mission or church structures in support, going to a situation where there is no church. This might parallel the situation Gladys Aylward faced in China.

[28]*Ibid.*

Pattern 2

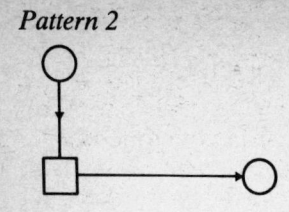

At the second stage of complexity the missionary is sent out by his home church; here we might consider Paul sent out by the church at Antioch.

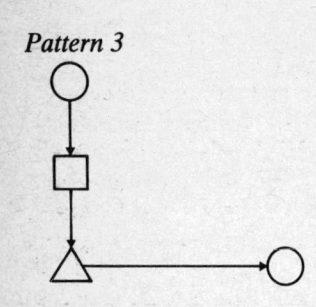

Pattern 3

Next in complexity (but not necessarily the next step chronologically) we have the formation of a mission society to which the church recommends the missionary and through which the church channels its financial support. The church has not yet developed in the host country.

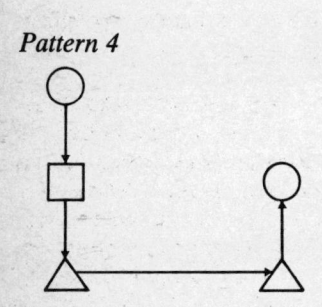

Pattern 4

As the number of missionaries deployed overseas increases, so does the mission structure overseas; some kind of 'field' council is established.

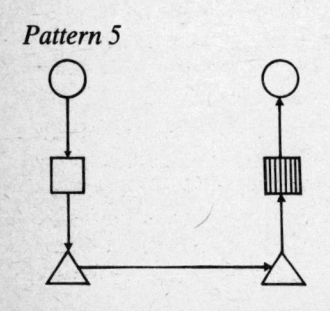

Pattern 5

The work advances and churches begin to be established. They in their turn begin to develop some kind of structure, even a church headquarters, through which the missionary is now appointed to his work.

Pattern 6

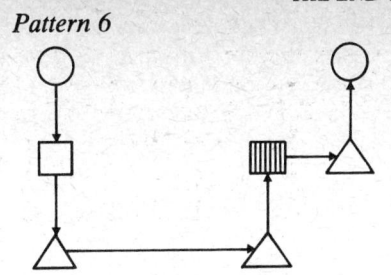

Finally the overseas church establishes its own missionary society as a separate entity from the church, and it is to that society that the missionary must now relate.

Two things may at once be said about these simplified relational diagrams: first, that they are all uniflow diagrams, the action is all in one direction; and secondly, that the final diagram emphasizes the increasing isolation of the missionary society from the decision-making. At the home end missionary-sending churches are beginning to demand some say in what happens to the money they raise and the people they recommend. Thus in North America the Association of Church Missions Committee, ACMC, was formed in 1975 with a group who believed that the success of missionary enterprise depends on the local church but found that the local church had almost no influence on the mission strategies of its denomination. What is very possible here is the complete isolation of the two mission triangles from the lower part of structure 6, as the home and overseas churches join together in multi-flow partnership in mission.

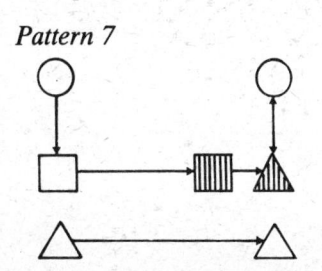

Pattern 7

Pattern 7 indicates what has already effectively happened to those missions which persisted in acting as monitoring agencies for communication between the home and overseas churches. So great has the pressure for such direct links become that they are now irresistible. Bodies such as International Needs and Christian Nationals Evangelism Commission promote direct church-to-church links and the channelling of funds and personnel directly to the overseas situations where they are needed.

Of course these fundamental changes have not come about smoothly, nor are they all entirely for the good of world evangelism. Very often missionary societies had very good reasons for filtering out certain applications being made for scholarships or for funds for buildings. A system of nepotism existed and continues to exist in many of the Third World churches. But in the light of the state of the church in

Britain it was patently absurd to look upon Britain any more as the centre for world evangelism. With the church in South America mushrooming, with revival in Korea, with the flourishing revival churches of Africa, it was evident to everyone else, if not to the British, that it was time for Britain to become a receiving country. And so ended an era.

But the chapter cannot end there. It would be totally wrong to forget that there are no territorial categories in mission. Where there is a church, where there is even one Christian, there is the missionary mandate. The church in Britain cannot be allowed simply to turn all its attention on itself. The commission is not suspended while we put our house in order. An old and well-tried vehicle of uniflow mission has been used and has been wonderfully successful. A new vehicle must be found for the same commission. But it would be utterly wrong for the church in Britain to abandon world mission. Missionaries will always be needed and must always be trained and sent, because the Bible will always challenge and commission.

A new awareness of the Church Growth movement is appearing in Britain. This movement challenges the traditional way of conducting mission, the traditional way of building the church. Here we could well find a new, radical approach to the holistic concept of church and mission that will revolutionize the life of the church and its world mission. We consider the Church Growth movement in the next chapter.

5
The Church Growth movement

5.1 INTRODUCTION

The twentieth century, missiologically speaking, has been the century of assemblies, congresses, conferences and consultations.[1] The World Missionary Conference held at Edinburgh in 1910 and the Lausanne International Congress on World Evangelization of 1974 must be recognized as having vitally affected world mission at the grass-roots level; most other congresses have done little more than provide material for research reports, books, and historical research for the academic missiologists.

Of course this is a sweeping generalization, but it is generally true that conferences descend to mere dispute amongst the theorists without necessarily any practical relevance. And again, the great names of

---

[1] Starting, perhaps, just outside the twentieth century with the 1892 Edinburgh meeting of the Student Volunteer Missionary Union and including the following:

1910	The World Missionary Conference, Edinburgh, which paved the way for the establishment of the International Missionary Council, delayed by the World War but finally implemented in 1921.
1928	The first IMC Conference, the second World Missionary Conference, at Jerusalem.
1938-9	The Tambaram (Madras) IMC Conference on World Mission.
1947	The first post-war IMC Assembly at Whitby, Canada.
1952	The Willingen, Germany, Assembly.
1958	The last World Conference to be sponsored by the IMC before its integration with the World Council of Churches, held at Legon, Ghana. In the same year there was the first All-Africa Christian Conference, held at Ibadan, Nigeria.
1961	The Third Assembly of the World Council of Churches, at which the IMC was integrated into the WCC and became the Commission on World Mission and Evangelism, CWME.
1963	The CWME organized its first Assembly at Mexico City.
1966	The Evangelicals' Congress on the Church's Worldwide Mission, Wheaton, Illinois. In the same year there was the World Congress on Evangelism in Berlin.
1968	The 4th General Assembly of the WCC, Uppsala.
1972-3	The 8th Conference on World Mission, with the theme 'Salvation Today', at Bangkok.
1974	The International Congress on World Evangelization, Lausanne.
1975	The 5th Assembly of the World Council of Churches, Nairobi.

Stephen Neill, in his *A History of Christian Missions*, comments on the phenomenon of the Edinburgh Conference, 1910: 'This brought into being a new era, which may be called the era of Councils' (p. 542). If there remains any doubt about this we have only to note that Dr John Mott was in the East from 11 November 1912 to 11 April 1913 — a period of five *months* — and convened and presided over twenty-one conferences!

mission, J. H. Oldham, John Mott, and, in more recent years, Visser 't Hooft, Hans Hoekendijk and Max Warren, have tended to be associated with the organization of conferences and the circulation of reports rather than with the actual practice of mission. That is not the case with Donald McGavran, Dean Emeritus of the School of World Mission, Pasadena, California, and creator of the Church Growth movement. The basic concepts of the Church Growth movement[2] have transformed the outreach of mission societies, of individual missionaries and of the churches of the United States of America, wherever those missions, individuals and churches have been prepared to think through what McGavran is saying to them.

It is usual to trace the origins of Church Growth thinking to the publication in 1955 of McGavran's *The Bridges of God*.[3] Since then there has been a constant flow of books and articles on the subject. The movement was accorded a special number of the *International Review of Mission*,[4] although the majority of the articles (and all of those contributed by WCC staff and the academic missiologists) were negative towards the movement.

Although a great deal has been written on the subject of Church Growth, it is possible to summarize McGavran's contribution to mission strategy simply and briefly. He insists that *the primary concern of mission is the numerical increase of the visible church*. All else that has been written on Church Growth is commentary on this premise. It is as a consequence of this allegedly simplistic approach to the task of world mission that McGavran has been accused of an unbiblical position, of being concerned, for example, with ecclesiology rather than with missiology,[5] and with numerology rather than with pneumatology. Even so, while there have been some changes in terminology (especially in the understanding of the 'people movement'), and while there has been a growing concern for a more thorough biblical basis[6] to Church Growth thinking, the basic thrust has remained unchanged. Mission means planting churches and it means growing churches. The primary concern of the missionary should be with assessing his own church-planting and church-growing activities, and with improving his methodology in order to maximize these activities.

---

[2] The best introduction is probably still D. A. McGavran, *Understanding Church Growth* (Eerdmans, Grand Rapids, 1970), but see the bibliography for other works.
[3] D. A. McGavran, *The Bridges of God* (World Dominion Press, London, 1955).
[4] *IRM* LVII, 227, July 1968. The articles are largely a disappointment. While much of what is said is critical, the criticism lacks the factor of involvement. Quite obviously most of the criticism comes from people who do not understand the concepts of Church Growth, had not followed the developing debate in America and had not used Church Growth principles in action. Frankly much missiological writing suffers from the failure of the writers to engage in mission.
[5] Orlando Costas, *The Church and its Mission* (Tyndale House, Wheaton, 1974), pp. 134f.
[6] *Cf.* Alan Tippett's *Church Growth and the Word of God* (Eerdmans, Grand Rapids, 1970). Tippett is an excellent anthropologist, but is not at home in biblical exegesis.

5.2 SOME AXIOMS OF THE CHURCH GROWTH MOVEMENT

Of the many concepts that could be taken as axiomatic for the Church Growth movement, just five are presented here. These five raise in the most precise way the concerns of Church Growth and the criticisms made of Church Growth. But these five axioms should not be taken as having some legitimization from the Pasadena School. Rather they are to be understood as interpretative, axioms drawn from debate with Dr McGavran and his associates, from lectures given at the Seminary and in London Bible College, from my experience of the application of Church Growth principles in Africa, and from my study of the writings of the many specialists in the field as compared and contrasted with Scripture.

5.2.1 Numerical church growth[7] is a proper and prime concern of mission

If mission is essentially witnessing about Jesus in the expectation that people will come to believe in God through him, then mission ought always to be concerned to see if this is, in fact, taking place. In the study of group dynamics[8] we have become aware of the necessity for any group to have a prime goal if that group is to continue to function as a group. In conflict with this concern is the tendency to develop some secondary or surrogate goal which enables the group to continue to function comfortably, without stress, apparently productively, but not in the manner originally intended, nor with the results initially expected. In the context of the local church, the primary goal of the church council or diaconate would be to encourage, to facilitate and to monitor the ministry of the church in its three aspects of worship, community, and mission. The secondary surrogate may become the furthering of the ambition of the minister, the building of a larger sanctuary, or the preservation of a pattern of worship. In the same way a mission may begin with the determination to witness to Christ but might finish as an inward-looking, self-perpetuating reactionary community. McGavran would require the mission to measure itself not by its monthly income, nor by the size of its missionary staff, but by the results of its ministry measured in terms of numerical church growth.

The criticisms of the academics could be anticipated. J. G. Davies, who is Edward Cadbury Professor of Theology at Birmingham University, complains:

> To think in terms of church growth is to plan for survival, and this is the antithesis of the pattern of life laid down for us by Christ ...

---

[7] See chapter 5 of *Understanding Church Growth*.
[8] *Cf*. P. M. Turquet, *Leadership: the Individual and the Group* (Tavistock Publications, London, 1967). He distinguishes between the 'sophisticated work group', which is concerned with the primary task of the association, and the 'basic assumption group' whose goals arise from within itself. Such

The strategy of deliberately planned Church Growth is a limitation of the free activity of the Holy Spirit.[9]

It should be at once apparent that neither of these assertions is true. It is the church that does *not* engage in mission, that fails to move out into the world, and that refuses to examine its ministry, that is planning for survival, a survival that must lead to death. It is precisely the church that assesses its work and prepares to dismember itself, to send out labourers (to use a good New Testament phrase), in the expectation, but never the certainty, of planting new congregations, that dies, and can therefore expect to live. And to suggest that the active criticism of mission methods is a limitation of the Spirit is patently absurd. A concern that something should be done cannot be equated with the assumption that it can be done alone.

In fact the Church Growth movement is totally misunderstood if it is conceived as an infallible method for growing churches. Rather it is an expression of concern that the missiological task of the church should be clearly defined and that its effectiveness should be maximized. The missionary is so to conduct himself that he does not unnecessarily hinder mission. He is so to live that the work of the Spirit through him is maximized. The Spirit cannot be limited to using the Christian as a mere machine to be manipulated. The doctrine of redemption is a holistic doctrine; man's *mind* is redeemed, his thought processes transformed:

> Do not be conformed to this world but be transformed by the renewal of your mind, that you may prove what is the will of God, what is good and acceptable and perfect (Rom. 12:2).

Or, as the Jerusalem Bible so clearly expresses it:

> Do not model yourselves on the behaviour of the world around you, but let your behaviour change, modelled by your new mind. This is the only way to discover the will of God and know what is good, what it is that God wants, what is the perfect thing to do.

Church Growth thinking asserts that the human intellect is redeemed in Christ, and that it is a legitimate sphere of operation for the Holy Spirit. Thus the human intellect, redeemed in Christ and subject to the authority of Christ, of his Spirit and of the Word, and so made aware of the nature of mission, ought to be used to monitor the processes involved in mission.

The monitoring of mission work is inevitably a comparative exer-

---

concepts apply aptly to church hierarchies.
[9] 'Church Growth, a Critique', *IRM* LVII, 227, July 1968.

cise, and it is usually illegitimate to interpret statistics absolutely as Alan Tippett does in his survey *Peoples of Southwest Ethiopia*. Of one church community he writes:

> The fact remains that 15,000 constituents with 4,000 of them full communicants, in a population of half a million, is not great growth for forty years among a people showing a disposition towards religious change.[10]

An observation such as this makes sense only where it can be demonstrated that *comparatively* a similar constituency under similar socio-economic conditions has experienced significantly greater growth. And even then the observation should not be pejorative, as Tippett's tends to be, since the redeemed human intellect will always bear in mind the total sovereignty of the Spirit. The observation of numerical church growth is concerned with the reverent application of the redeemed intellect to establish *facts*. No value judgment is necessarily implied in the determination of a statistical fact. But the observed fact may then be used to ask relevant questions bearing on the fact: is literacy higher in this growing group; are the evangelists more acculturated; is the Bible known and understood; is growth expected?

So then, the first axiom of Church Growth thinking involves a concern with numbers, a concern that people should be *churched*. To that extent it represents an ecclesiology and not a missiology only. But this identifies and corrects a weakness in much pseudo-evangelism: conversions are recorded but the churches do not grow. The situation is not helped by the pious hope that the invisible church has grown even though the converts have not been discipled into the visible church. The church is commissioned to make disciples, not converts, and to be discipled must involve discipling into the local *ekklēsia*.

But is the concern with numbers a re-emergence of David's sin in numbering Israel (2 Sa. 24)? Those who have pressed this point choose to ignore the numerous head-counts recorded without adverse comment in Scripture. Thus in Genesis 46:8-27 we have a careful enumeration of Jacob's family (seventy persons), and in Exodus 12:37 we have the exodus people numbered at some 600,000 men, plus women and children. In the context of warfare we find the Benjaminites of Judges 20:15 numbered at 26,000, while Israel mustered 400,000 (verse 17). On a different occasion David was not criticized for numbering his people: he totalled the Levites at 38,000 and used his computation for a meaningful division of labour (1 Chr. 23:3-6).

The events of 2 Samuel 24 are obviously of a different nature from those of other passages which deal with numbers. David was con-

[10]*Op. cit.*, p. 247.

cerned to number the people in order to convince himself of his status. His action might be taken as akin to the practice of some denominations which publish annual membership figures that are *not* used for the development of mission strategy!

The use of numbers in mission work is simply a recognition that as we cannot keep honest accounts without writing down numbers, so we cannot account for our ministry without recourse to arithmetic. It is, perhaps, trite to point out that the Scriptures do no less: numbers *are* recorded in Acts and presumably someone took the trouble to count a few heads.

But the counting of heads is not an end itself. It is not done with a view to the setting up of a league table of mission. It simply provides a comparative tool for use in assessing the effectiveness of our ministry.

5.2.2 The church should concentrate its mission activity on the responsive elements of society[11]

There is in this second axiom a recognition of the group principle. There *are* resistant groups and there *are* responsive groups. Once again it would be wrong to accuse the Church Growth movement of perverting the commission to go into *all* the world and to make disciples of *all* the nations. What is being said is that it is criminal for there to be groups of people who are responsive to the gospel and yet to fail to give to those people the labourers who will be adequate to the task of gathering in the harvest.

In Ethiopia the story of the town of Sókota well illustrates the point. A Muslim sheikh, by the name of Zacharias, somehow became a Christian and acquired an Arabic New Testament. Through his teaching a considerable number of Muslims became Christians, but Zacharias refused to identify himself with the Ethiopian Orthodox Church which he considered to be unbiblical. He was eventually tried before Emperor Menelik (Emperor from 1889 to 1913) but acquitted of acting against the Ethiopian Church and given a Writ of Toleration, allowing him freedom to preach. Dr Lambie[12] estimated that as many as 5,000 Muslims were converted through his preaching. Zacharias was succeeded by Yusuf who, in his turn, was opposed by the Orthodox Church. Yusuf came south, to Addis Ababa, where he met Dr Lambie, then of the United Presbyterian Mission. Lambie introduced him to Haile Selassie (or, since this was in 1924-5, more correctly Ras Tafari Makonnen), who inspected Menelik's Writ of Toleration which Yusuf still had and confirmed the former order allowing Yusuf to

---

[11]See chapter 12 of *Understanding Church Growth*.

[12]Dr T. A. Lambie was a medical missionary in Ethiopia with the American United Presbyterian Mission, then with the Abyssinian Frontiers Mission and finally as Director of the Sudan Interior Mission, 1919 to 1936. He wrote a number of popular books on his experiences as a missionary, including *A Doctor without a Country,* a book which traced his difficulties following his decision to abandon his American citizenship and become an Ethiopian. He died in Jerusalem in 1954. 'Dr T. A. Lambie: Some Biographical Notes', *Journal of Ethiopian Studies* X, 1, January 1972.

preach. Yusuf asked Lambie for help. They needed teachers, Bibles. Lambie gave him Arabic Christian literature and promised to send help when it was available. Ten years later Lambie at last reached Sokota. The movement had dwindled to almost nothing. Yusuf had been murdered. The Governor, a blind man, offered to give the mission land if they would only send missionaries. But on 3 October 1935 the Italians crossed the Mareb river and invaded Ethiopia. The missionaries were expelled and the movement came to nothing. Church Growth would say that where such situations arise the church *must* concentrate its resources so as to be consonant with the response.

Of course, the formulation of the principle assumes that responsive elements of society can be identified, and recognizes that society is non-homogeneous. It may, of course, be categorized in many ways: by age, separating young from old; by income, separating rich from poor; by colour, separating black from white; by sex, separating men from women; by employment, separating manual workers from white-collar workers; by politics, separating Conservative from socialist; by locus, separating the urban dweller from the rural dweller; or by religion, separating Muslim from animist. And there are, of course, many other possible categories. The assumption is, then, that people tend to move not as individuals, but as groups, and that they tend to respond as groups to new patterns of buying, new concepts in clothing, new styles of living and to some fresh presentation of religion.

Here again, it is easy to be shocked at so matter-of-fact a way of looking on mission, but it is well illustrated by Paul's decision to turn away from the resistant Jewish audience and concentrate his attention on the responsive Gentile audience at Antioch (Acts 13:46). What we are looking for in the search for responsive elements in society are the *relevant* groupings or 'homogeneous units'[13] of that society. For Paul the relevant units were Jews and Gentiles, but for his purposes a *geographical* categorization, though valid as identifying a unit (the 'homogeneous unit of the residents of Antioch'), would have proved irrelevant.

Once it is accepted that there *are* identifiable groupings in society, and once it is recognized that movements take place within such groupings, the question arises: how can we identify a spiritually responsive unit? The first answer is obvious: because the people within an identifiable 'homogeneous unit' are responding, while people in other units are not. To refer again to Ethiopia, it was observable that the formerly animistic Wallamo and Sidamo peoples of the south were responsive, while the Muslim Arussi Galla, also of the south, were not. This observation is readily made from the work of the various Lutheran

---

[13]For the concept of homogeneous units see *Understanding Church Growth*, pp. 85-87, and the *Pasadena Report on the Homogeneous Unit Principle of Church Growth*. This is a product of the Lausanne Continuation Committee's discussions, published in *Explaining the Gospel in Today's World* (Ark Publishing, London, 1980).

missions in Ethiopia or from the work of the interdenominational Sudan Interior Mission. Both missions concentrated their resources on the responsive unit, resulting in a combined church of almost half a million people by the end of the 1970s.

5.2.3 Conversion takes place in many ways: individually and through multi-individual decisions[14]

One-by-one discipling, which has tended to characterize evangelism in the western world, is not the only pattern presented in Scripture. Missionaries who came across the phenomenon of group conversions were often perplexed by what appeared to be a novel approach to conversion. The experience varied from the determination of a patient exposed to the good news in hospital to return home, bring back his family and then make a joint commitment to Christ, to cases where an entire village would hear the good news, discuss the implications of changing religion, and then together commit themselves to Christianity. In Acts 9:35 we observe that 'all the residents of Lydda and Sharon' saw Aeneas healed of his paralysis, 'and they turned to the Lord'.

The concept of a people movement is important since on the whole Britain has lost its sense of cohesion. We do not relate, generally, to other people. At the turn of the century the situation was very different. As examples of the transformation we may take the effect of television, which ended the social aspect of cinema going, and the wider distribution of the car, which tended to complete our isolation from one another. This breakdown of society presents a very severe sociological problem, but it is not evident in the Third World. In most Third World societies any change of behaviour is a matter of concern for the entire community. Any individual who considers change must also consider his changed relationship to the community. If he feels that the change demanded by the gospel is worth while, then he will consider it to be good for his community. The preaching of the gospel does involve an inevitable call for decision for change. The listener acquires a certain body of information, regarding the meaning of life and the significance of death, regarding the present life and its mores and the life to come. All this he will weigh up against the body of knowledge he already has. But only rarely will he decide unilaterally on change.

The concept of a people movement is recognized in the Bible, and we may note that the principle was not even rediscovered by McGavran. McGavran relevantly quotes Latourette's *Missions Tomorrow*; writing in 1936 Latourette said:

> More and more we must dream in terms of winning groups, not merely individuals. Too often, with our Protestant, nineteenth

[14]On people movements see chapter 16 of *Understanding Church Growth*.

century individualism, we have torn men and women, one by one, out of the family, village or clan, with the result that they have been permanently de-racinated and maladjusted. To be sure, in its last analysis, conversion must result in a new relationship between the individual and his Maker, in radiant, transformed lives. Experience, however, shows that it is much better if an entire natural group — a family, village, caste or tribe — can come rapidly over into the faith. That gives reinforcement to the individual Christian and makes easier the Christianization of the entire life of the community.[15]

It is to be noted that both Latourette and McGavran avoid the concept of a 'mass' movement, and each recognizes that ultimately the group movement is consummated by the establishing of new relationships between God and the individuals of the group. A mass movement would be a mindless movement, an unthinking movement.[16] People movements are not mindless. On the contrary, McGavran separates two stages in the movement, a discipling stage and a perfecting stage — a stage at which people commit themselves to following Christ and a continuing stage in which the people learn what is involved in following Christ. Quite properly we recognize that before the act of commitment it is possible to transmit only a very limited knowledge of the content of Christian living. Only when man's spirit is revitalized can the perfecting stage go forward.

The strategic significance of the people movement is that it provides an environment within which Christians can develop socially. Too often in the past, converts were gathered out of their own society and employed by the missionaries as catechists, teachers, gardeners, dressers and so on. This meant that they were removed from their own society, and their new manner of life was not available for inspection or testing. The unconverted were unconvinced. The 'conversion' was too often seen as a prudent insurance policy against dismissal. The alternative appeared to be the lonely isolate.

What McGavran saw was the long-term instruction in the Christian faith of groups, who could then move together into their new faith, and form a new sociological unit. Peter Berger has pointed out in his *A Rumour of Angels*[17] that the *possession of cognitive deviation* (the possession of knowledge or ideas not shared by the majority) demands a specific response from the deviant. He may conceal his knowledge; he

[15] *Op. cit.*, p. 159, quoted in D. A. McGavran, *Understanding Church Growth*, p. 298.

[16] D.A. McGavran, *The Bridges of God*, p. 13: 'We do not use the term "mass movement". This unfortunate term implies unthinking acceptance of Christ by great masses. While it does fairly represent one aspect of a People Movement — that the group usually numbers many persons — it totally obscures the facts *a.* that any one group is usually small in numbers, *b.* that each member of the group has usually received much instruction in the Christian faith, and *c.* that large numbers are achieved only by the conversion of a series of small groups over a period of years'.

[17] P. Berger, *A Rumour of Angels* (Penguin, Harmondsworth, 1970), chapter 1, especially pp. 31ff.

may reinterpret his knowledge to make it conform, generally to the knowledge of other people; he may protect his deviance by total withdrawal from the rest of society; or he may set about converting society to his own way of thinking. This last option is the missiological option, and leads eventually to what *was* the norm becoming itself deviant. But this cannot happen without the propagation of the deviant knowledge. So the group is instructed *together* and becomes together the deviant group, but from within its own homogeneity can reach out to offer a sociological shelter to new converts.

5.2.4 People prefer to make their commitment to Christ without crossing unnecessary cultural barriers[18]

It is generally recognized that missionaries have failed to distinguish between the essence of the gospel (which crosses all cultural barriers) and the vehicle of the gospel (which is culture-specific). Thus while the good news always remains the same it may be presented, explained and expressed in ways appropriate to different cultures. But what is meant by culture? It can be readily defined. A person's culture is *the totality of his normal behaviour in his own society*. We refer to *normal* behaviour since that behaviour can be disturbed by abnormal circumstances. The presence of a stranger, the appearance of a tape recorder, the offer of money, can all produce atypical conduct. Culture is exhaustively defined in terms of a person's *total* behaviour, since culture includes his language, his religion, his music or literature (oral or written), his dress, his eating customs, his sexual mores and so on. In this sense of the term there can be no such thing as an 'uncultured' person, a pejorative term which usually signifies simply a person who behaves differently from the way in which *I* behave.

All culture is equally judged by Scripture. There is no such thing as Christian culture, although there are un-Christian elements in all cultures. Christianity judges all cultures, recognizing the various elements of those cultures as being in one of three categories; those elements which are consonant with Christianity and required by it, those which are inimical to Christianity and are condemned by it, and those which are neutral. For example, in America it is culturally normal for a person to drink a glass of milk. Such an element of culture is neutral, so far as the gospel is concerned. It is not required by the gospel; it is not inimical to the gospel. But in the Atete fertility cult of the Chabo people of south-west Ethiopia, the cow is taken as a symbol of the cult, and all that attaches to the cow is sacred to Atete: horns, hide, hair, dung,

[18]*Understanding Church Growth*, chapter 11. It will be noted that McGavran begins his chapter: 'Men like to become Christians without crossing racial, linguistic, or class barriers.' In my submission this is asking for the impossible. In mission we very commonly find that the evangelist (as in Philip and the Ethiopian) is of a different race or social class from that of the hearer, and the Holy Spirit will continue to use evangelists *across* cultural barriers until the Commission is rescinded; while that lasts we shall have to go into all the world, and people will come to Christ across cultural barriers. As missiologists we are concerned to eliminate *unnecessary* cultural barriers.

and, of course, the milk. To drink milk from the Atete cow is to identify oneself with the Atete cult. It would not be possible in Chabo thinking to drink a glass of milk *and* to be a Christian. What is neutral in the American culture is not neutral in the Chabo culture. Very real difficulty arises when what is inimical to Christian conduct in one culture is unthinkingly defined as inimical to Christian conduct in all cultures, or what is neutral in one culture is taken to be neutral in all cultures.

The Christian has a specific quality of life which is called the life of eternity ('eternal life').[19] The definition of 'Christian' may then be adduced by a consideration of those elements which are considered to be of the essence of the life of eternity. The process of identifying these essential elements is frustrating, since many elements assumed to be of the essence turn out on inspection to be culture-specific.

A Christian may be conceived as a person who attends church and there worships God through Christ, in the Spirit. But in Muslim countries there may well be no recognizable church *building* and indeed there may be no 'two or three' to gather together to form an *ekklēsia*. In the same general context we might distinguish Christian from Jew by recognizing that the former worships on Sunday and not on Saturday, or from the Muslim by recognizing that he does not worship on Friday. But Seventh Day Adventists recognize Saturday as their sabbath, and in Muslim countries the Sunday may well be established as a normal working day (and in any event Paul indicates that the day is irrelevant).[20] Frequently the new life is related to a pattern of tabus: the Christian does not smoke, drink, dance, gamble or go to cinemas and theatres. But some of these tabus are shared with Islam,[21] while there is no general agreement on the others. In North America evangelicalism in the southern states allows chewing tobacco but forbids mixed bathing, while in the northern states it forbids chewing tobacco but permits mixed bathing.

In a more theological vein the Christian might be defined as one with certain doctrinal beliefs; but James shows the inadequacy of a definition which omits practice when he reminds us that our theological beliefs are shared by demons.

These superficial observations, which uncover a very real problem of identification, suggest a different approach to the problem of iden-

---

[19] Eternal life is a quality of life which we receive now ('he who believes in the Son *has* eternal life', Jn. 3:36; 'he who hears my word and believes him who sent me *has* eternal life;... *has* passed from death to life' Jn. 5:24), not something we shall receive at death. It is a quality of life which transcends physical death, which takes a man from this world on into the next. And in biblical terms, if we have not *got* it then we are not going to *get* it.

[20] 'One man esteems one day as better than another, while another man esteems all days alike. Let every one be fully convinced in his own mind' (Rom. 14:5). 'Let no one pass judgment on you ... with regard to a festival or a new moon or a sabbath' (Col. 2:16). 'You observe days, and months, and seasons, and years! I am afraid I have laboured over you in vain' (Gal. 4:10-11).

[21] *Sura* 5; 'The table' forbids alcohol, gambling and sorcery.

tifying the Christian. What activity in an individual would serve as a clear indication that he is *not* a Christian? The question leads to the concept of the *crux decision*.[22] When an individual is exposed to the gospel he is being led inevitably to a choice between a new commitment and fidelity to the existing way of life. It is an either/or confrontation. The confrontation is not necessarily immediate, although, as in the case of Candace's treasurer, it may be so. But in time the decision must be made, whether overtly or by default. The decision is marked by a crux. The term is chosen deliberately:

> Then Jesus told his disciples, 'If any man would come after me, let him deny himself and take up his cross and follow me' (Mt. 16:24).

The cross of which Jesus spoke was obviously a visible symbol. The man carrying his cross was a man unmistakably defined to anyone who had eyes to see him. More than that, the cross, so far as the carrier was concerned, was an intolerable burden; it literally weighed him down, but it provided a poignant comment on his future: he was in principle already dead to the world that surrounded him.

The crux decision is similarly *a decision which irrevocably separates a person from the society of those who are not Christians and commits him to a new loyalty to Christ and his people.* The crux decision is culture-specific, and may in some cases be recognized only by those who belong to the culture concerned. Traditionally the crux decision has often been taken to be the act of baptism, and it has been assumed that this crux is cross-cultural.

A biblical example of the crux decision comes from Judges 6. Gideon is chosen to deliver Israel from the Midianite oppression, but this involves a prior confrontation with the apostate society of which he was a part. Gideon is to be marked out as God's man by an act which would irrevocably separate him from apostasy:

> That night the Lord said to him, 'Take your father's bull ... and pull down the altar of Baal which your father has, and cut down the Asherah that is beside it; and build an altar to the Lord your God ... then take the second bull, and offer it as a burnt offering with the wood of the Asherah which you shall cut down' (Jdg. 6:25-26).

The crucial nature of the act is confirmed by the response of the people, who demanded Gideon's death.

The crux decision frequently involves a direct challenge to former tabus. Alan Tippett refers to such a situation in his paper *Religious*

---

[22] F. P. Cotterell, 'The Conversion Crux', *Missiology* II, 2 (1974).

Group Conversion in Non-western Society.[23] A woman named Kapiolani turns to Christ from the religion of Pele, and shows the change first by trespassing on the volcanic crater sacred to Pele and then eating berries prohibited to women:

> 'Jehovah is my God. He kindled these fires. I fear not Pele.' She cast some stones defiantly into the fiery gulf. Then she ate some of the sacred Ohelo berries, sacred to the goddess herself and forbidden to all women.

A number of possible crux decisions can be suggested: prayer facing Mecca is exchanged for prayer facing Jerusalem, the convert eats pork, the wearing of the turban is abandoned, the hair is cut or is allowed to grow, customary gifts to ancestors are not offered, a hitherto forbidden object is touched, or traditional death customs are abandoned. Alternatively the crux decision may mean participation in some distinctively Christian function such as baptism or the eucharist.

Failure to identify a true crux may result in the establishing of a substitute crux, a crux which is not, in fact, crucial. Such a substitution is a serious matter, since it results in a temporary transition, a tentative and negotiable, reversible, retractable adherence to the church. Where the government of a church has been in the hands of expatriates for many years and the crux decisions of the expatriates have become unquestioningly the crux decisions of the new church it is common to find that in times of stress the 'converts' revert to former practices, consulting the *shaman* or sacrificing to an ancestor.

So then, the church is confronted with the reality of the transition demanded by our preaching, a commitment to turn to God from idols and to serve a living and true God (1 Thes. 1:9). But the reality of the transition is not made apparent by cross-cultural patterns of behaviour, by adopting *a* common culture, but by the appearance of a crux decision, culturally determined.

This might suggest a relativity about Christianity which is quite unscriptural, but we must distinguish between the culturally determined response to the preaching of the Word and the cross-cultural essential content of that preaching. Here the normative role of Scripture is paramount. Paul defined the gospel as being that gospel which we received, in which we stand and by which we are saved *if we hold it fast,* if the transition to Christ is irrevocable. He then indicated the specifics of the preaching of the gospel:

> Christ died for our sins (and didn't merely die)
> He was buried (and did not revive in the tomb, burial was con-

[23] A. R. Tippett, *Religious Group Conversion in Non-western Society* (No. 11 in the Pasadena School of World Mission 'Research in progress' pamphlets, published in August 1967). p. 8.

firmation of death)
He rose on the third day (as confirmation of his deity, Rom. 1:4)
He appeared to various witnesses

These are taken to be historical events, not early-church mythology. There was a cross on which Christ died, there was a tomb in which he was buried and there was a stone that was rolled away from the mouth of the tomb. There were grave-clothes to be seen inside the tomb and there was no body in the tomb on the morning of the resurrection. Positively, there was a risen Christ whose living, physical body could be seen.

It is recognized that precisely under the pressure of unbelieving culture the clear record of historical events may be misinterpreted. Paul urges Timothy:

> Do your best to present yourself to God as one approved, a workman who has no need to be ashamed, rightly handling the word of truth (2 Tim. 2:15).

Paul assumes, here, that it is possible to handle the word of truth *wrongly*. The word that he employs, *orthotomeō (temnō*, I cut), means 'to cut straight'. But where the Word of truth wishes to cut straight there may be a culturally determined wish to cut in a different direction. The word itself is a ploughing word, and the unashamed ploughman would be the one who cut a straight furrow.

The Word of truth (a genitive construction signifying that what God says is true) may be deflected from its straight-cutting path by one of two types of interference, *proactive* or *retroactive* interference. Proactive interference with the Word of truth occurs when philosophical or theological presuppositions are held prior to the study of the Word, presuppositions by which the Word is interpreted or even judged. Retroactive interference occurs when the Word is read and understood, but is found to be incompatible with the quality of life already determined upon, so that future goals are allowed to dictate the interpretation of the Word.

While it is recognizably difficult to claim that freedom from such modes of interference has been gained, we are not, in fact, thrown back upon such a subjective claim. The Word *is* true, and its truth is mediated to us *not* through human intelligence, nor through human experience, but through the eternal Spirit: *he* leads us into all the truth, *he* brings to our attention all that Jesus has said, *he* enables us to submit ourselves to the Word of truth, even when that Word stands in condemnation of *our* culture.

We therefore recognize that all culture stands under the judgment of God, that there is no one Christian culture, and that we cannot construct such a culture. At the same time we recognize that there are culture-specific crux decisions which mark the essential transition from the non-Christian world to the kingdom, and that a person is brought to this transition through the straight-cutting exposition of the Word of truth, the meaning of which is mediated to us by the Holy Spirit.

In mission we recognize that in making the transition to Christ some cultural boundaries *must* be crossed. We recognize also that we have often in the past required people to cross *unnecessary* cultural barriers. It is in the recognition of the true nature of culture and in the identification of those elements of culture which are truly inimical to the essence of the gospel that the way to Christ is properly opened up.

It is painfully possible to become Pharisaic in our acquisition of the gospel, neither understanding it ourselves nor truly offering it to others:

> But woe to you, scribes and Pharisees, hypocrites! because you shut the kingdom of heaven against men; for you neither enter yourselves, nor allow those who would enter to go in. Woe to you, scribes and Pharisees, hypocrites! for you traverse sea and land to make a single proselyte, and when he becomes a proselyte, you make him twice as much a child of hell as yourselves (Mt. 23: 13-15).

A mission is not enough. Earnest endeavour is not enough. An apparent orthodoxy is not enough. We may have all this and yet neither enter heaven ourselves nor lead others to Christ. Unnecessary Pharisaic barriers to the kingdom, culturally determined, may exclude both us and them.

5.2.5 The study of anthropology, linguistics, history and geography, is legitimate in developing a scientific and responsible exercise of mission

There is no call for us to be intimidated by the concept of a *scientific* exercise of mission, as though this necessarily excludes the determinative role of Scripture and the leading of the Spirit. We are concerned, rather, with avoiding unnecessary hindrances to the work of the Spirit.

The role of language-learning in mission needs no explanation. Without an understanding of *language* the good news cannot be communicated. But language is more than words, a communication is far more than what is said. Language involves gesture,[24] and also dress. Amongst the Amhara people of Ethiopia an important part of the dress for men and women is the *shamma*, a shawl, usually with some kind of border to it, the border being patterned and coloured in the case of women, often plain for men. The shamma is draped differently for different occasions. There is a proper draping for a wedding,

[24]See my *Language and the Christian*, chapter 1.

another for a funeral and yet another for an appearance in court. The *shamma* itself is a form of communication. In Amhara society, then, communication includes a study of culture, which would itself include some observation of the mode of dress.

But even where the various factors involved in *communication* are properly balanced, there may still be interference through *history*. In Ethiopia, north of Lake Abbaya, is the crescent of territory inhabited by the Wallamo (Wolayta) peoples. Since 1936 the church there has grown at the rate of 10% a year. Missionaries have been sent out into other areas. And everywhere new churches have been formed. There was one exception to this pattern of success: the lowland area inhabited by the Arussi Galla. There, although fine Wallamo evangelists laboured and churches were established, they were almost always churches for immigrants from other areas — never the Galla.

At the impulse of Church Growth thinking an investigation of the area *geographically,* and of the relationships between the peoples *linguistically* and *historically,* was undertaken. Geographically an extraordinary structure was discovered, a vast ditch and mound system which stretched almost the whole way from the Bilate river in the east to the Omo river in the west, a distance of some 40 miles. In most places the system was in ruins, but its course could readily be discerned. Historically it was discovered that the ditch system was built following war between Wallamo and Galla peoples at the end of the nineteenth century. The ditch marked the demarcation line established by the victorious Wallamo after the war.

The line itself extended along the highland region, but significantly the border between the two peoples was, in the 1960s, far beyond that line. The Wallamo had steadily advanced beyond the line into Galla territory, forcing the Galla off the fertile highland and down into the Arussi desert.

Not surprisingly the Wallamo did not make acceptable evangelists to the Galla.

But when the Wallamo evangelists were replaced by evangelists from nearby Kambatta, the picture changed. By 1976 there were thirty churches in the area.

Of course it is true that in the past God has planted his church without there being elaborate studies of history or geography. But as God makes us aware of the significance of these studies we are surely expected to react to them responsibly. It is possible for study to produce radical change in church planting.

In Kaffa province of Ethiopia a mission work was established in 1931. Apart from the period of the Italian occupation, from December 1936 to 1946 the missionaries had a centre at Qochi. A church was established in the town of Jimma, and at Qochi a Bible college serving the entire work of the mission was developed. But the church did not develop. Under the stimulus of Church Growth thinking a survey was undertaken by a graduate of the Pasadena School of World Mission, Paul Baliskey. He found that the area could be pictured as a series of concentric circles. In the centre were the Amhara administrators, nominally Orthodox Christians. In the next ring were the Muslim Kaffa traders, resistant to the church. But in the outer ring, a ring which had never been reached by the missionaries, he found a different people, unrelated to either Kaffa or Amhara. Linguistic study showed that they spoke a dialect of Wolayta, the language used in the area to the east of them, where there was a thriving church. A new strategy was developed. The Missionary Aviation Fellowship was used to overfly the resistant areas. Airstrips were built. A mobile clinic ministry developed. Evangelists from Wallamo went in. And within three years there were some eighteen churches in the area.

It must be said at once that there is no guarantee of any kind that such results will follow the introduction of a more scientific approach to mission. The examples merely come from my own involvement in Church Growth methods, reflecting the experiences of many others, that a scientific approach to mission is at the same time a responsible approach to mission, and that it may, and frequently does, result in our doing what we are sent to do: to make disciples.

5.3 EFFECTIVE CHURCH GROWTH INVESTIGATION

Church Growth investigation envisages a careful survey of the ethnology of the area concerned, an ecclesiological survey and then a missiological appraisal of the situation out of which strategy should emerge. This principle applies equally to the situation in Britain and to the traditional mission situation. The problem is essentially the same and cannot be geographically fragmented.

5.3.1 The ethnological survey

What is needed here is a total understanding of the community to be served. Every aspect of its life may be investigated since there can be no prior certainty of where the ultimately relevant factors so far as mission is concerned will be located. The survey defines the people sociologically, indicating the existence of the various sub-groups and the relationships which exist between them. Do they speak the same language, different languages or various dialects of the one language? Are the sub-groups separated geographically — do miners tend to live in one street and managers in another? What standard of education prevails? Is the literacy rate high, and what types of literature are available? How do the people meet, and where, and when? What do they do when they meet? What games do they play? What tabus exist?

A historical survey is important. Where do the people come from?

What account do they give of their own origins? How do they account for linguistic and cultural diversity? Have they recently migrated or are their roots very deep down?

A study of religion is vital. What concept have they of God? What answers are given to the ultimate questions: Who am I, where have I come from, where am I going to, why am I here? Is there a religious language, a sacred book? Is there a religious calendar with propitious and unpropitious days? What are the moral requirements of the religion? How do the people cope with death?

A study of group behaviour may be necessary. Does this people operate from the base of the extended family, or the immediate family? What rules govern marriage? How are children viewed? How is work divided between husband and wife? What is the status of parents? Of great significance is the discovery and elucidation of the social hierarchy. What determines the place of the individual within the hierarchy: is it sex, age, education, wealth? How is the society ruled? Are rulers elected or appointed, or are they hereditary? What is the proportion of men to women, of children to adults?

A health survey is valuable. What is the expectation of life? What are the principal diseases? Where do these diseases come from? How do the people treat disease and accident? How do they explain illness?

5.3.2 The ecclesiological survey

The survey of the church is essentially parallel to that made of the population as a whole. The concern is to determine first of all whether the church population is a microcosm of the population at large, or whether it differs significantly from it; and secondly to determine the state of the church and its fitness for mission.

Commencing with the church membership itself, we need to know precisely where church members live. Are they scattered throughout the local community, or are there Christian enclaves, aggregates? Here it is vital to take into account the *total* resources of the church (not merely the limited resources of one sector of the church), the membership of all the local congregations.

Where are the churches and the church halls? Are some churches located at particularly strategic positions? Are there significant areas which are devoid of suitable buildings? Are there alternative buildings such as schools and community centres which might be used for Christian work? How well attended are the churches? Although major emphasis is usually placed on attendance at the principal Sunday services, it is, in fact, more significant to note the attendance at other services since such attendance usually signifies a greater commitment to the work of the church. Is there provision for small-group gatherings which can ensure adequate personal relationships within the church? Who are the leaders of the churches and how do they relate to one another? Who are the official leaders? Are there unofficial leaders? What pattern of pastoral care has developed?

There is a need to investigate the numerical growth of the church. Has there been any significant change in the numbers attending the church? Has the financial status of the church changed? Has there been any building programme? How is giving determined: by continuing past patterns, according to needs, or in step with inflation? Has the church's giving increased in real terms?

What is the scale of church outreach? What is understood by the term? Are regular missions held? Is there any programme of visiting the homes of transient contacts? Do the house groups contribute to outreach? Is there a system of training for outreach? Are there special family services, youth services, guest services, open days? Is there any outreach into the local schools? Is there any overt involvement in social action?

And very important are the investigations into the leadership of the church. Is the minister concerned to see his people growing up into Christ? Is he concerned to see the local people being discipled into the church? Or is his concern merely to keep the church filled and the mechanism in working order? Are the church elders spiritually mature or only business-effective? Do they do everything, or do they do nothing? How many people in the church actually have defined responsibilities? What gifts are discernable in the membership? Are the gifts being used? Is there a proper understanding of the biblical teaching on the Spirit's gifting?

Are there divisions in the church? Is there, indeed, a history of divisions? And if so, why? What can be done to end them? Is the church divided socially? Is there a proper understanding of Christian *koinōnia*, fellowship, and is hospitality practised? What happens when visitors attend the church? Is there any system for welcoming them and for following up the visit as may be appropriate? Are the young people integrated into the church, or do they form a 'second world' of their own? What is the situation musically? Can the Christians sing? Is there someone who can lead the congregation into true worship in music?

All these questions need to be asked of any church which is seriously concerned with developing its effectiveness. The facts which are uncovered in church surveys are only *facts*. But they *are* facts, and will not go away simply because they are ignored, nor, on the other hand, will they be dissolved merely by being identified. A survey is a necessary prelude to church action.

5.3.3 Missiological planning
The intention of missiological planning is to take all the information that has been gathered and to interpret it in terms of the purpose of the church: worship, community and witness. But if the preliminary work

has been adequately done, there will be a heterogeneous mixture of information to be processed into which some measure of order must be introduced. This is usually done through the careful use of visual display using maps, pie-charts, graphs, comparative tables and histograms.

Some care is needed in the use and the interpretation of graphs. Where the zero point is concealed it is sometimes possible so to stretch or to compress the vertical scale that growth can be grossly exaggerated or minimized. Where organic growth is being considered, it is necessary to make use of a logarithmic scale on the vertical axis. The point is worth demonstrating.

Let us consider a church of twenty members. If in the first year twen-

CHURCH GROWTH USING A LINEAR VERTICAL SCALE

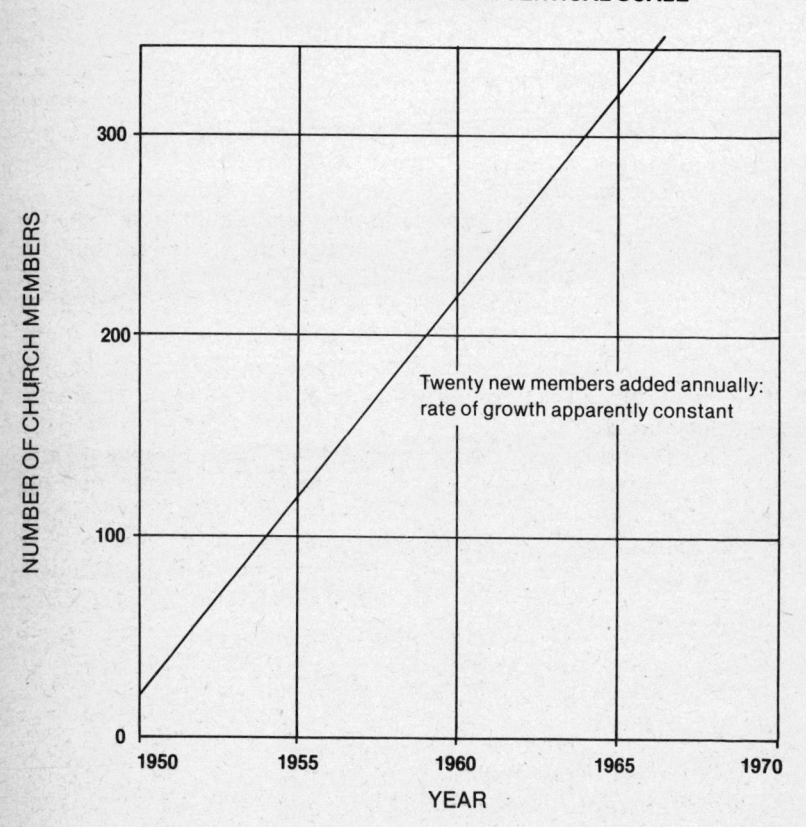

Twenty new members added annually: rate of growth apparently constant

ty new members are added to the church we have 100% per annum growth. If a further twenty are added in the next year this now represents only 50% per annum. The growth rate will steadily decline even though the church continues to add twenty new members each year. A linear scale would present the growth picture as reassuringly constant, concealing the fact that in the first year each member brought in one new member while in, say, the tenth year only one member in ten was bringing in a new member.

Organic growth, therefore, ought to be graphed on a logarithmic scale, and on such graph paper a steady rate of growth will be represented by a straight line. The two types of graph are illustrated and should be compared.

CHURCH GROWTH USING A LOGARITHMIC VERTICAL SCALE

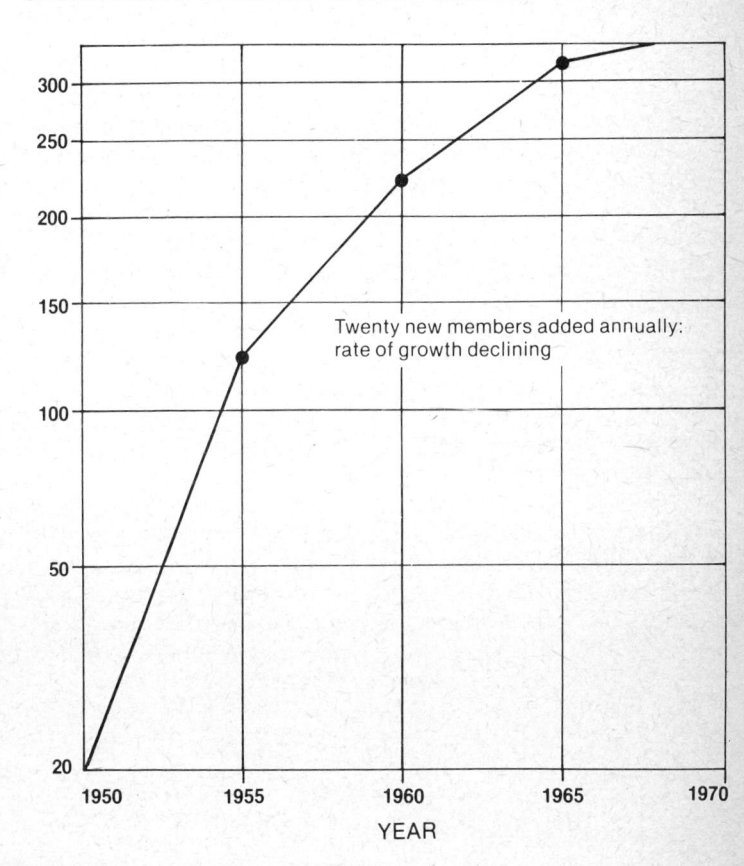

Twenty new members added annually: rate of growth declining

Some of the most interesting and revealing statistical work in British church growth came from David Wasdell's Urban Church Project, reported in the *International Review of Missions*[25] and the periodical publications of the Project. Among other phenomena, Wasdell charted (and christened) the 'hiccup' effect associated with church missions. When church membership has steadied, or when a new minister arrives, a mission might be planned. In the weeks preceding the mission, attendance at the church begins to rise, reaching a maximum during the weeks of the actual mission. But then reaction sets in. Many of the regular members of the church find themselves exhaused by the mission and take a break. Attendance falls, but gradually rises again until it reaches approximately the pre-mission level.

A second phenomenon observed by Wasdell is the self-limiting church. Using Wasdell's own example we may recognize that a business may limit its output in one of two basic ways: by deciding that it will produce only a certain number of items and concentrate on selling them, no matter how large the potential market may be. On the other hand the business might decide to limit production according to demand, allowing for expansion just so long as a market for the product exists. The first business is self-limiting, and the church in Britain tends to fall into that category. For the Anglican communion this is readily demonstrated; there is no direct statistical relationship between the size of the parish and the number of people attending church. In a very general way it would be expected that if 10% of the people in a parish attend church and the size of parish is doubled then the congregation also would double. But this does not happen. There may well be some increase in church attendance, but there is no correlation with parish size. The church is self-limiting in the sense in which Wasdell and Miskin[26] have demonstrated that the size of the congregation depends on the number of clergy, which *in turn* is linked to parish size. That is to say, if the parish becomes large enough and manpower is available, additional clergy may be appointed. In that event the congregation will probably increase; Miskin states that it will increase by an average of ninety Christmas communicants with the first addition, and a further eighty-one Christmas communicants if a second assistant clergyman is appointed. On the other hand, if the parish increases in size but no additional clergy can be found, the increase in attendance is marginal. The results can be presented graphically.

It is noticeable that even where additional clergy are appointed to a

---

[25] David Wasdell, 'The Evolution of Missionary Congregations', *IRM* LXVI, 264 (October 1977). See also the various project reports and workpapers that have come out of the Urban Church Project (available from St Matthias' Vicarage, Poplar, London E14 OAE).

[26] David Wasdell, Urban Church Project Workpaper No. 1, *Let My People Grow*, p. 5, and see the original study by Dr Leslie Paul, 'The Deployment and Payment of the Clergy' (published by the Church Information Office, London, 1964).

THE HICCUP EFFECT

[Chart: Church attendance over time 1975–1976, showing a bump at "Date of mission"]

THE SELF-LIMITING CHURCH

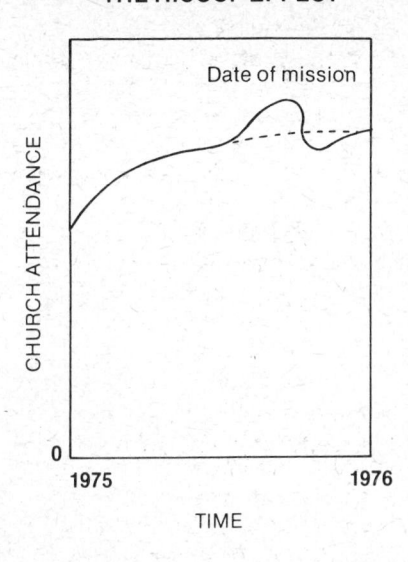

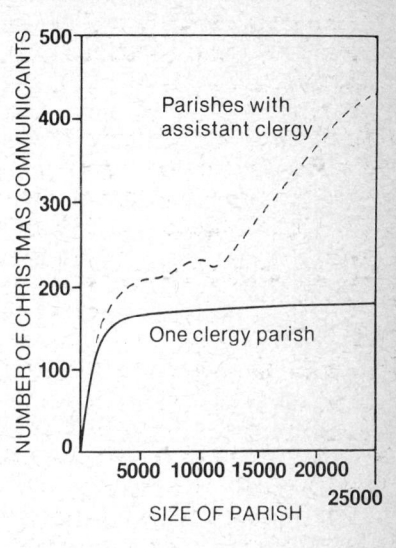

[Chart: Number of Christmas communicants vs. size of parish (0–25000), showing "Parishes with assistant clergy" rising to ~400+ and "One clergy parish" plateauing around 180]

parish, still there is no constant relationship between the size of the parish and the size of the congregation. It would seem that the church's failure to interpret the concept of the ministry correctly, and the establishment of 'clergy' and 'laity', produce a self-limiting church, a positive hindrance to mission.

This study of the Anglican church in the United Kingdom highlights the necessity of a careful definition of terms used. For example, the concept of *membership* needs definition. Statistics for 1979 show that some 26.8 million were baptized in the Anglican church and 8.7 million were confirmed members of the Anglican church. These figures, however, were not reflected in the actual figures of church attendance. The maximum attendance by practising Anglicans was at Christmas when 1.9 million attended the services. It is likely that although they rarely attend church, many of those who have been baptized into the Anglican church would still, in a survey, record themselves as being Anglican. Somehow, out of a confusing range of statistics like these, a meaningful definition of Anglican church membership must be adduced.

**DEGREES OF COMMITMENT:
THE ANGLICAN CHURCH IN ENGLAND 1979**

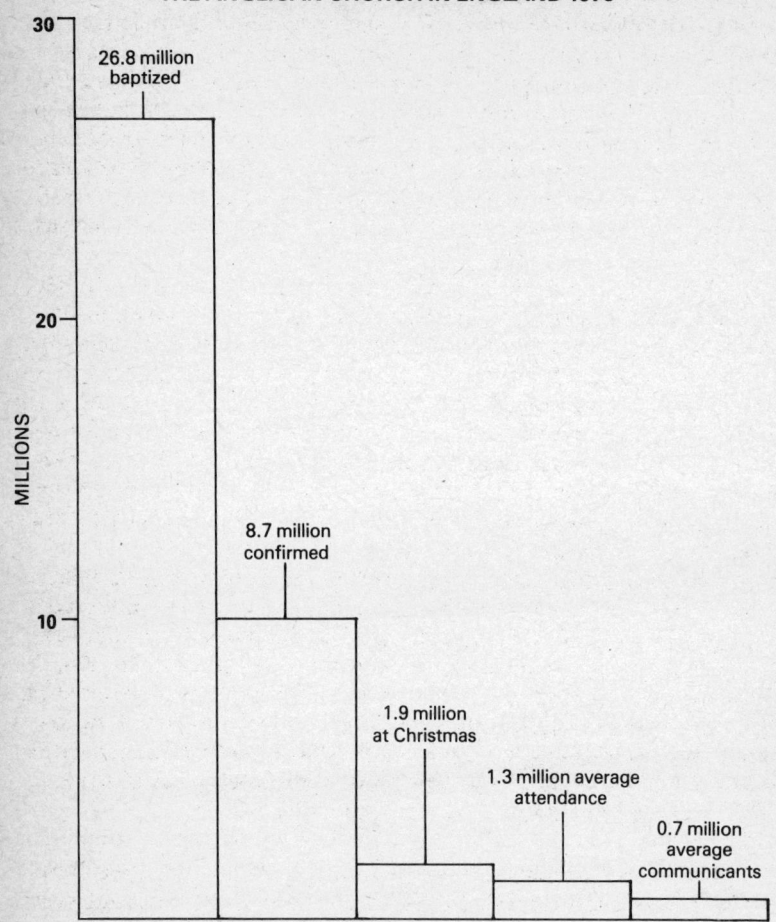

- 26.8 million baptized
- 8.7 million confirmed
- 1.9 million at Christmas
- 1.3 million average attendance
- 0.7 million average communicants

(MILLIONS)

5.4 TYPES OF GROWTH

The recognition of the importance of *definition* in any serious statistical study directs attention to the various types of growth which may occur in a church. Three particular areas of growth are identifiable: the *numerical* growth of a particular church, the *discipleship* growth of church members, and *geographical* growth as the area within which mission takes place is increased.

5.4.1 Numerical church growth

Numerical church growth is measurable with some degree of precision, through physically counting the number of people attending the various church gatherings over an extended period of time, or through examining the church records. The phenomenon of increasing or decreasing numbers at a church, however, is a complex one, related to the movement of the Spirit within the church, the sociological conditions in the 'catchment area', the activities of other churches in the same catchment area, and the relationship of the church to the community, amongst other factors. Three types of growth may be identified here: *biological* growth, *transfer* growth and *conversion* growth. Each type of growth is perfectly valid, but each has its own implications.

By *biological* growth we understand the increase of numbers through the conversion of members of the families which already attend the church. Such relatives stand in a special relationship to the gospel. So far as the *children* of a Christian parent are concerned, Paul strikingly designates them as 'holy' (1 Cor. 7:14). We must pause to consider this remarkable statement because of its significance for this one aspect of numerical church growth. In 1 Corinthians 7 Paul is dealing with the problem of Christian marriage in a pagan society. When one member of a pagan couple becomes a Christian, what is the status of each member of the family?

Of the couple themselves Paul says that the unbelieving husband is 'consecrated' through his wife and the unbelieving wife is 'consecrated' through her husband. Of the children of such a marriage he comments that they are 'holy'. In each case Paul is using the Greek *hagiazein*, 'to sanctify', or the adjectival *hagios*. This is Paul's frequent designation for believers: they are the saints, *hagioi*. But quite evidently he does not intend this meaning here, since the 'consecrated' husband or wife is clearly labelled 'unbelieving', and there is an expectation of some future change in that status. Barrett comments:

> The verb 'to sanctify' *(hagiazein),* and the adjective 'holy' *(hagios)*, must therefore be used in this verse in a sense differing from that which is customary in Paul.[27]

What Paul is recognizing here is not an objective change of status of an unbelieving spouse or child Godward, but a definite change of status so far as world powers are concerned. Such powers no longer dominate the family because of the over-riding power of God, brought into the family through just one believing partner. The fear of the Christians at Corinth was that the presence of one unbelieving partner

---

[27] C. K. Barrett, *The First Epistle to the Corinthians (Black's New Testament Commentaries*, A. & C. Black, London, 1968), p. 164.

would infect the other. On the contrary, says Paul, not only is this not so, but the power of God positively counters the power of the world and goes beyond it to place the unbelievers in a special relationship to God. Hans Conzelmann puts it clearly:

> Through the believing partner, the marriage between a pagan and a Christian is withdrawn from the control of the powers of the world. In living together with the world, the 'saints' are the stronger party. The decisive idea lies not in an ontological definition of the state of the non-Christian members of the family, but in the assertion that no alien power plays any part in the Christian's dealings with them.[28]

It is as a consequence of the special conditions obtaining in the 'Christian' home, even when only one spouse is a believer, that biological growth is so regularly observed. Prayer for the unsaved spouse and prayer for the children born to the marriage, the concern of the entire church family, the teaching of the Word as in the case of Timothy, all add up to a special relationship towards God. Although ultimately the children of Christian parents and children who have just one Christian parent, and unbelievers with a Christian spouse, must answer for themselves, still there is an undoubted difference between their position and that of others.

Biological church growth is a reality, it is scriptural, it is to be expected, but still it must be recognized as coming from within the existing Christian community. Such growth is no measure of success in penetrating the hostile world outside. It is restricted to the children of Christian parents, to the parents of Christian children, to brothers and sisters and other close relatives.

Transfer growth is a function of a dynamic society. Christians move into a church catchment area and transfer their membership to the church in that area. No addition is made to the church of God. But there is another aspect of transfer church growth that has, perhaps, a lower level of legitimacy: the transfer of membership from one church to another *within the same catchment area*. Such a transfer of membership may take place for a variety of reasons, but two are very common: the individual has had a disagreement with the membership or leadership of his own church and determines to move, or the individual comes from a small church and is attracted by the large numbers attending another church.

---

[28] Hans Conzelmann, *A Commentary on the First Epistle to the Corinthians* (Fortress Press, Philadelphia, 1975), p. 122. Conzelmann is, perhaps, going beyond Paul's thought which is itself (deliberately) left undefined. Certainly both unconverted spouse and unconverted child are in a special relationship to God, but it is not Paul's purpose to work out the full nature of that relationship. However, it goes beyond Pauline soteriology to suggest that the entire family is withdrawn from worldly powers.

Once again there is no increase in the membership of the church of God. More seriously, there may be no good reason for the transfer; and, more seriously still, there may be very good reason for discouraging it. If a church decides, quite scripturally, to discipline one of its members (Mt. 18:15-20; 1 Cor. 5:1-8; Gal. 6:1-2; 1 Tim. 5:19-20) it is obviously wrong for another congregation to intervene so as to frustrate the purpose of that discipline. And again, it must be questioned whether the development of very large congregations, which gather almost exclusively on Sundays, is to be encouraged at the cost of the development of *churches* which could function right through the week. Large numbers tend to attract more *attenders,* but unless careful provision is made for the congregation to be broken down regularly into smaller groups (house groups, age groups, study groups, purpose groups, pastoral groups) those who attend the Sunday activities will never become truly *discipled* into Christ.

Of course, transfer growth will also include growth that results from the closing of churches and the incorporation of the defunct congregations into other churches. This again is legitimate but there is no net growth taking place.

And finally there is *conversion* growth, which relates to the outreach of the church into the unchurched world. Much of the outreach here will be unstructured, as the church members take their responsibilities and privileges seriously, as they reflect on the great things God has done for them, and as they share their experience of Jesus, their knowledge of him, with others. Especially valuable here is the house group, which can be a clear evidence to neighbours that in *this* house are people who are *Christianoi.* Of course, the house group is effective only where the lives of the people involved are consonant with the claims they make. The difficulty faced by church-centred witness is that even where the outsider comes in he is unable to measure what he sees and hears against the lifestyle of those who speak.

The church that is growing numerically ought to know which of these three types of growth is taking place: biological, transfer or conversion. The implication of each is different. Only in 'conversion' growth is the church reaching out into the unchurched community.

5.4.2 Discipleship growth

Discipleship growth is a measure of the effectiveness of the church in fulfilling the commission to make disciples and to teach them to obey Christ's commandments. It is commonly objected that spirituality cannot be measured, to which it must be replied that if spirituality is properly defined it can be quantified. The difficulty lies in a failure to define.

Spirituality, while not itself discernible, must produce discernible effects in the life of the spiritual person: how else can we know that he is spiritual? It is true that the wind blows where it will and it is itself invisible, but it is not unobservable: we hear the sound of it and we see the force of it. The same must be true of spirituality. If we recognize that *this* individual is spiritual while *that* person is not, we are making an observation based on visible phenomena. The nature of the phenomena adduced for this purpose reveals the concept of spirituality held by the observer.

Discipleship growth could, then, be measured quantitatively by recording the individual's record of church attendance. Does he attend more often or more regularly than before? It could be measured in terms of prayer or Bible study: does he spend more time on it and read more books about it? It could be measured in terms of mission: does he knock at more doors, distribute more tracts than previously? It could be measured in terms of family life: does he argue less with his wife and give more time to his children now? David Wasdell[29] finds that financial giving is a most reliable indicator of spirituality, so that a church's weekly offering might be used as a measure of corporate church growth.

Quite obviously some of the 'indicators' of discipleship growth suggested above may be surrogates. The twin concepts of discipleship and spirituality direct attention to the Christian's responsibility to be a follower of Christ, and to be filled with the Spirit. Both of these requirements suggest that what we are looking for is behavioural: the Christian ought to be living in a way visibly reminiscent of Christ's pattern of living, and clearly consonant with the presence in the Christian's life of the Spirit of holiness. Paul writes to the Corinthian church on the subject, making it quite clear that he could discern the difference between the spiritual man, the *pneumatikos,* and the uncommitted man, the *sarkikos.* He saw jealousy and strife as marks of carnality (1 Cor. 3:1-4). In the same letter Paul equates spirituality with the readiness to recognize and submit to a word from God (1 Cor. 14:37), in direct contrast to those who exercised *charismata* but refused to acknowledge a word from God. In Galatians 6:1 another mark of carnality is sin, *paraptoma,* an act of disobedience. The spiritual man, who has not been guilty of such an act, is encouraged to restore the defaulter, but in the spirit of humility because in that very act he is laying himself open to the temptation to pride, to paternalism, to self-congratulation, to the temptation to harshness — all of them attitudes inimical to spirituality.

The spirit of holiness is set by Paul in opposition to the spirit of the world (1 Cor. 2:12), and Paul is able to assume in writing to the church at Corinth that its members will be ready to act in a way that would be unnatural for the unbeliever. In particular, the Christian does not demand his rights, but prefers to lose financially rather than bring divi-

---

[29]Urban Church Project Workpaper No. 2.

sion and disgrace to the church (1 Cor. 6:7). What must be noted here is that our culturally divergent indicators of holiness ought to be replaced by cross-culturally significant and biblically based indicators of holiness which are still definable and measurable. If a church claims that it is not growing *numerically*, but that it is growing *spiritually*, then it ought to have a biblical understanding of the meaning of spirituality and it ought to have identified quantifiable indicators of that spirituality.

5.4.3 Geographical growth

Geographical growth involves the identification of the actual area within which the church exercises its missiological function. Growth occurs when this area is enlarged. This aspect of growth is important in Third World missions, but of increasing importance in Britain today. For while buildings, termed 'churches', may be said to exist in almost every village and town in Britain, many of them constitute part of the missiological problem, rather than part of the solution. They do not *disciple*, they do not send out witnesses of Jesus, but are restricted to the practice of certain more-or-less religious exercises: the repetition of a liturgy, the hosting of certain social functions, and so on. The active church may find itself inhibited in its planning for mission by the existence of such communities, charitably trying to assume that they represent missiological assets which must be fitted into the outreach programme.

Each local church and each church member should recognize that the commission to be witnesses to the ends of the earth and to make disciples of all the nations is always and everywhere binding. A local church cannot define its catchment area in terms of so many square miles and then abandon the rest of the world to other evangelistic agencies. How this world-wide responsibility is to be implemented is a matter for discussion, but certainly each church should be concerned for geographical growth. This is seriously inhibited when church or minister conceives the immediate task in terms of filling the church. To fill the church building is not consonant with geographical church growth, since the latter regularly implies the planting of new churches, some of them led, at least initially, by members of the evangelizing church.

This raises the question not only of the optimum size of a church congregation, but also of the actual function of the local church.

Group Dynamics indicates that within a group of seventy or so people it is possible for each person to get to know every other individual. In the larger group this is no longer possible, so that where a larger group exists, *either* the concept of the family, of knowing one another, will disappear, *or* some provision will be made for the large group to be split into smaller house groups or fellowship groups. Where this latter provision is made it must be recognized that the central group is not properly speaking a church at all. It becomes an administrative centre, a locus for the sacraments and a focus for formal preaching, all of which may be valuable. But the one centre has become the parent of a number of house churches. There is, of course, no binding reason why a church should be defined, as it often is, as a gathering of God's people under an appointed leadership for worship and the observance of the sacraments. *That* is a definition made out of a historical development, although the definition itself is without scriptural warrant. The New Testament *describes* the church but does not *define* it in such terms.

So then one church, as it grows, may develop daughter churches, and in a sense lose its own identity as a church. But it is very likely that the process will continue and that the daughter churches will, in their turn, grow and give birth to daughter churches, granddaughters of the first church. This has been a very common experience in the Third World, sometimes stimulated by legislation forbidding Christians to make unnecessarily long journeys to church. The Word of Life churches of Ethiopia have frequently ruled that where there are five families in a particular village or locality they *must* form a local church and stop attending any other church. In Ethiopia's Rift Valley, to the east of the Bilate river in Sidamo, twenty-two new churches were planted from Gunde church alone.

5.5 CHURCH GROWTH: AN ASSESSMENT

The chief contribution of the Church Growth movement has been its insistence that the work of mission at home or overseas ought to be subject to scrutiny to ensure that mission is being conducted responsibly and scientifically. It has not attempted to eliminate the dependence of the church on the Holy Spirit, but has suggested that it is wrong to use that ultimate dependance to rid ourselves of any responsibility for the effectiveness of the work we do.

Missions have grown up in a world in which, very largely because of the activities of specialist missionaries, there has been an increasing body of information about the world to which we are sent in mission. But as the academic world has more and more appropriated this wealth of information for itself, so the missions have tended to operate independently of it. Church Growth has reminded us all of the existence of information vital to the responsible exercise of mission, and has gone beyond that in providing facilities where Church Growth studies can be prosecuted and where responsible mission can be planned, implemented and then assessed.

We had thought that spiritual activities could not be quantified; Church Growth has shown us that spirituality is unquantifiable only where it is undefined.

On the negative side it might be urged that Church Growth has failed to provide a biblical basis for itself. And where an attempt has been made to supply a theology of Church Growth it has proved unsatisfactory, a mere running commentary on a catena of texts which have in common the key themes of Church Growth philosophy: 'grow', 'increase', 'added', 'multiplied', and so on. Of course, Church Growth thinking must not run counter to Scripture, but there is a sense in which we do not *need* a biblical basis for Church Growth thinking. What may well be needed is a renewed biblical concept of mission, a concept which will take into account the transformed world situation with churches now planted on every continent and a new phase in world mission opening up before us. Church Growth does not need justification. It calls us to the responsible exercise of mission, and it is for the critics to show that Church Growth concern for the discipling of the nations is unbiblical ... if they can.

6
Confrontation

6.1 INTRODUCTION

In chapter 5 it was observed that the twentieth century, missiologically speaking, has been a century of conferences. This may be traceable to two phenomena: a new emphasis on reflection, and a new experience of confrontation. The second half of the twentieth century has seen the missionary movement, and especially the North American missionary movement, steadily transforming itself from a state of missionary praxis (action, involvement) to a state of reflection, investigation, study, and research. Schools of world mission have proliferated, and hundreds, possibly thousands, of largely ephemeral studies have been published on the theory and history of mission. At the same time, missions have been cruelly short of missionary personnel to maintain existing mission programmes and to develop new ones. Simultaneously, there has developed a confrontation with other religions, religions which some had expected to wither under the impact of a growing western technology. These two phenomena, the urge to reflect and the developing confrontation, may well have been responsible for the multiplication of conferences.

The Christian mission is today necessarily involved in confrontation. The past privileged positions of the Christian missionary is ended. He does not identify with the religious profession of the colonial powers, almost all of which have now been swept away, but finds himself in conflict with the state religions and irreligions of the countries to which he goes. The fact is that the world today is not merely quantitatively different from what it was at the beginning of the twentieth century: it is qualitatively different. The difference may, perhaps, be best illustrated by reference to the Middle East, the heartland of oil power and the cradle of Islam. Sir Winston Churchill describes events in the Middle East in 1921, events in which he was involved on behalf of the British government:

> In the spring of 1921 I was sent to the Colonial Office, to take over our business in the Middle East and bring matters into some kind of order. At that time we had recently suppressed a most dangerous and bloody rebellion in Iraq, and upwards of forty thousand troops ... were required to keep order. In Palestine the strife between the Arabs and the Jews threatened at any moment to take the form of actual violence. The Arab chieftains, driven out of Syria ... lurked furious in the deserts beyond the Jordan ... I therefore convened a conference at Cairo to which practically all the experts and authorities of the Middle East were summoned. Accompanied by Lawrence (of Arabia), Hubert Young and Trenchard from the Air Ministry, I set out for Cairo ... We submitted the following main proposals to the Cabinet. First we would repair the injury done to the Arabs and to the House of the Sherifs of Mecca by placing the Emir Feisal upon the throne of Iraq as King, and by entrusting the Emir Abdulla with the government of Trans-Jordania. Secondly we would remove practically all our troops from Iraq ... All our measures were implemented, one by one.[1]

It is difficult to realize that a handful of western politicians could, within our own lifetime and in so sensitive an area, and without any particular reference to the peoples of the area, define territories and appoint their rulers. Today we see a vastly different world.

Quantitatively we may speak of a world of more independent nations, with more widespread education and a rising Gross International Product and a steadily increasing average life expectation. But qualitatively it is a new world, with the old empires swept away and new empires emerging. The power of the new world lies less in individual nations than in conglomerates: the North Atlantic world of North America and Western Europe, the Soviet bloc countries, China and her satellites, and, of course, the Muslim world. Of these powerful conglomerates, two are of particular importance missiologically: Marxism and Islam.

Both of these worlds, the Marxist and the Muslim, are divided. The Marxist world is divided by the major ideological conflict between Russia and China — between Stalinism and neo-Stalinism on the one hand, and Maoism on the other. A further complication for the missiologist lies in the determined attempt to incorporate Marxist theory and revolutionary practice into Christianity through liberation theology. The Muslim world also is divided, not merely by its major theological disagreements, the Sunni and Shi'a and, more recently, the Ahmadiyya parties, but also between those Muslim nations which are prospering under the accident of oil wealth and those countries which

[1] Winston S. Churchill, *Great Contemporaries* (Fontana, London, 1937), p. 131.

are still struggling with growing populations and shrinking resources.

6.2 THE IMPACT OF MARXISM

Karl Marx was born on 5 May 1818, and died in exile, in London, in 1883. The eschatological overtones of his political theories find their roots in a long line of Jewish rabbi ancestors, while his antipathy to Christianity probably stems from his father's conversion to Christianity when Marx was six years old, and to Marx's subsequent experience of the church. It is impossible to interpret the political movements of the twentieth century adequately without reference to Marxist ideology, since it is out of Marxism that both the extremes of right-wing nationalism, conveniently labelled fascism, and of left-wing radicalism in the broad movement known as communism, have come.

Hunt expounds Marxism in terms of three elements: a dialectical philosophy, a political economy and a theory of state and revolution.[2] For missiological purposes it is more convenient to treat it in terms of an economic, political and religious philosophy.

6.2.1 Marxism as a religion

I take it that Marxism is a religion in the sense in which I have already defined that term: it seeks to provide answers to the fundamental human questions, 'Who am I, where do I come from, where am I going, and why?' As a religion Marxism is essentially materialistic, and in this it differs from Hegelian thinking which was idealistic. As Marx himself put it:

> In Hegel's writings, dialectic stands on its head. You must turn it right way up again if you wish to discover the rational kernel that is hidden away within the wrappings of mystification.[3]

Marxism explicitly claims to be materialistic, and *ultimate* moral values are treated as illusory. Existing moral values were interpreted by Marx and Hegel as being merely the temporary product of the changing social organism. The ethic of any society, then, simply reflects the values of the dominant class, and it is only with the abolition of class through revolution that the classless society might be able to develop a meaningful ethic. In the interim, morality is determined for the Marxist by what serves to destroy the exploiting society.

The ultimate ethic is that of the victorious proletariat which is, inex-

---

[2] R.N.C. Hunt, *The Theory and Practice of Communism* (Pelican, Harmondsworth, [5]1962), p. 39. On Marx's theory of labour see Peter Drucker, *The Practice of Management* (Pan Books, London, 1955), especially chapter 5, and Peter Berger's *Pyramids of Sacrifice* (Pelican, Harmondsworth, 1977), especially chapter 3. On Marx, see David McLellan, *Karl Marx: His Life and Thought* (Macmillan, London, 1973).

[3] *Capital*, in Marx's own preface to the second German edition.

plicably, endowed with something akin to infallibility. But of course morality is the product *not* of mass movements *nor* of societal groups, but of individuals.[4] Marxist morality depends on Marx and not on Marxism. Marx, however, assumed that the proletariat would end the dynamic ebb and flow of society much as a Hindu might end his personal *karma*. But the struggles of society, like *karma,* arise from individuals, not from classes; they are contingent, not inevitable. Marx himself was a contingency creating a new ethic.

Marxism has its ethic, and also has both creed and scripture. *The Communist Manifesto* was first published in 1848, and is the Marxist creed. *Das Kapital* appeared in three volumes, the first in 1867 and the remaining two, posthumously, in 1885 and 1894, and represents the Marxist scriptures. According to the Marxist creed and scripture, salvation history is then the outworking, according to Marx's modified Hegelian dialectic, of the thesis of the capitalists, the antithesis of the proletariat, and the synthesis of Marxist society.

6.2.2 Marxist economic theory

Marx's economic theory focuses on capital and on the use of capital to exploit the working classes. The worker is seen as providing the labour which, for Marx, is the sole source of value. In return for his labour the worker receives wages; not, however, in proportion to the value which his labour has created. Expressed crudely a worker may produce, say, a wheel, to which his labour has given the value of £50, or $100, or whatever unit we may care to use. In return he is given what is necessary to maintain life (since as labour he is essential to his employer), but not the full value of his labour. The difference is the capitalist's profit and the measure of the exploitation of the worker.

Labour, for Marx, is the only source of value. A machine has value only by virtue of the fact that it has been made by workmen and has therefore the value of their stored-up labour. Minerals as such are valueless until they have been extracted by labour, and it is that labour which gives value to the minerals.

The philosophy is increasingly seen to be inadequate as machinery replaces labour, and as minerals, upon which equal amounts of labour have been expended, are recognized to be of differing value, or those on which no labour has been expended to have value. And, of course, the contribution made by those who do not belong to the proletariat is ignored entirely. The prediction, however, is that tensions between capitalist and worker can only increase as the level of exploitation increases, until the inevitable revolution produces the Marxist synthesis.

6.2.3 Marxist political theory

Marx's political theory is essentially revolutionary and focuses on the

[4] Hunt, *op. cit.*, p. 73.

class struggle. We can simplify the dynamic as follows: the initial stage of capitalism in which a feudal relationship exists between capitalist and the proletariat; a second stage in which the proletariat unites with the middle-class bourgeoisie to overthrow the capitalists; and the final stage in which the proletariat disposes of the bourgeoisie. With the disappearance of the classes,[5] the class struggle ends, *karma* is exhausted (as the Hindu might express it), the dialectic has no further material to work on and the eschatological kingdom is realized — without, of course, a king.

This philosophy of revolution may seem attractively simple, but is in fact naive. It does not adequately define the classes of which it speaks with such certainty; and it fails to recognize that human society is not static but dynamic. Initially, Marx, quite pragmatically, defined the industrial labour force of England as his proletariat; but the equally depressed, if not actually oppressed, peasant class was excluded. Here Marx unequivocally displayed his own prejudices. He actually commended the bourgeoisie which, he said, has 'subjected the country to the rule of the towns. It has created enormous cities, has greatly increased the urban population as compared with the rural, and has thus rescued a considerable part of the population from the idiocy of rural life.'[6] But precisely *why* rural life should be idiocy, and *why* the peasant should be excluded from the proletariat, is not clear. It is possibly due to the embarrassing problem of his inability to demonstrate his theory of labour's 'added value' to the peasant worker.

But not only did Marx fail to define his classes reasonably: he failed to take account of society's essential dynamism. However defined, a class of society such as Marx envisaged is dynamic, not static. Members of the proletariat are constantly 'rising' to become part of the petit-bourgeoisie, and at the same time members of the bourgeoisie 'fall' to the level of the proletariat. Since the process is dynamic it is unwise to develop a theory which assumes the permanence of the class systems. Thus when in Britain the trade union movement developed a new social and class structure essentially abolishing the old categories, and effected this through negotiation and not revolution, Marxists found it difficult from their theoretical base to adapt to the new situation. Indeed Marxism has been driven (for example in France and in Ethiopia, to name but two countries) to redefine the proletariat in terms of the student world, of which Marcuse[7] became the unwilling prophet. The brutal fact is that Marxist revolutionary philosophy was based on a

[5] Marx and Engels, *Communist Manifesto*. The first section begins: 'The history of all hitherto existing society is the history of class struggles.' Within classical Communism there was always the expectation that the society which would evolve out of political revolution would be unique because it would be classless.

[6] In the *Communist Manifesto* (Progress Publishers, Moscow, 1965), p. 46.

[7] See L. Kolakowski, *Main Currents of Marxism*, volume 3, *The Breakdown* (OUP, London, 1978), chapter 11. It is certainly worth commenting that in current revolutionary praxis it has been the students who have been identified as the revolutionaries, while the revolt of peasantry or factory

static view of society which has now bypassed it. As a consequence Marxism has been driven to the expedient of espousing revolution merely because it is revolution and with no necessary dialectical basis.

6.2.4 Marxism in Russia
The early history of Marxism is essentially the history of Soviet Russia. There the oppressive regime of the Tsar was first challenged by the abortive revolution of 1905, followed by twelve years of unrest, culminating in the Lenin-led October Revolution. The provisional government was swept away and the promised Constituent Assembly went with it. The theoretical goal of the dictatorship of the proletariat was quietly replaced by the actual dictatorship of the Communist Party, of which Joseph Stalin became Secretary General (on Lenin's nomination) in 1922. Two years later Lenin was dead, and Stalin set about acquiring absolute control over the Party, which in turn was to be given absolute power over the State.

The period from 1934 to 1939 has no parallel in Russian history, and perhaps no parallel in the history of any other great nation. Stalin's potential and actual rivals were eliminated in an extended bloodbath, rendered the more obscene by the readiness of those accused to confess their guilt:

> Millions were arrested, hundreds of thousands executed ... the climate of atrocity brought about a kind of universal paranoia.[8]

The Bolsheviks who had swept Stalin into power disappeared in a welter of blood. Industry heaved its way through the carnage to some kind of progress:

> It did so by methods of mass coercion and complete or partial enslavement, which had as side-effects the ruin of the nation's culture and the perpetuation of a police regime. In these ways Soviet industrialization was probably the most wasteful process of its kind in history.[9]

Marxist theory predicted that the state would wither away. Stalin argued, however, that Marxist dialectic did not operate on the Marxist society. He continued to concentrate power in the hands of the Party over which he had absolute control. He ensured that only Party members were elected to the Congress, and as the state's hold on industry

---

labourers has been suppressed. Even in China, in early 1979, it was the peasantry who revolted against mindless Marxist ideology. Actually, in the *Manifesto*, the bourgeoisie were defined as the owners of the means of production and the employers of wage labour, while the proletariat were defined as the class of wage labourers (p. 39n.) At that time the *students* would probably have been classified with the bourgeoisie.

[8]Kolakowski, *op. cit.*, pp. 81-83.   [9]*Ibid.*, p. 78.

tightened he was able through the Party to control all political and industrial life in the country. The stringencies of the Second World War served to turn what was for him a necessity into a virtue. He emerged into the postwar era a totalitarian dictator.

Thus far the intellectual and cultural world had escaped Stalin's attentions. Now classical Marxist theories were imposed on the intellectuals. Music, art, philosophy and chemistry were particularly brought into question. Modern physics, and especially quantum mechanics, which appeared to endanger the basic *materialistic* presuppositions of Marxism, came under attack. It was bourgeois. Genetics, too, came under survey. Lysenko's quite incorrect theory of the inheritance of acquired characteristics was adopted as Marxist doctrine simply because it appeared to be in agreement with the dialectic. The environment produced moral change, the environment produced genetic change. Stalinization was complete. In Eastern Europe, among the satellite states, independent thought appeared to be dead. Communism was Sovietized and Sovietism was Stalinized.

On 5 March 1953 Stalin died. Almost at once the totalitarian monolith that he alone had held together in sheer ruthlessness began to crumble. In June there was a revolt of the workers in East Germany. The festering sores of the slave-labour camps burst open. Revolt was in the air: the suffering induced by Stalin was too great to be borne. The head of the secret police, Beria, was arrested, and in December he was shot. The process of de-Stalinization began. Three years later there was revolution in Poland. In October 1956 the revolt in Hungary had to be crushed by the Red Army. And it has been impossible for western Communist parties to live down the Soviet invasion of Czechoslovakia in August 1968, and the cynical crushing of the aspirations of the short-lived Dubček government.[10] The tears of helpless rage on the faces of Czech students as they faced Russian tanks with stones in their hands have not been forgotten in the West. Perhaps Latin America is sufficiently far away from these events to enable church leaders seriously to propose revolution as a way to the salvation of the masses. Those who have lived nearer to entrenched Communism know otherwise.

These workers' movements in the Communist satellites were inevitably labelled *reactionary* by Moscow. They shared predictable aims: the re-establishing of civil liberties, the limitation of police powers and the return of a measure of democracy. Conversely the intervention of the Russian power machine aimed at denying civil liberty, at extending the power of the police and their related security services, and at suppressing democratic processes. A significant change in world revolution had taken place: proletarian revolt was now suppressed by the Marxist state.

[10] See Milena Kalinovska, 'Czechoslovakia Ten Years After', *Religion in Communist Lands* VI, 3, 1978.

6.2.5 Maoism

In the early years of the twentieth century, Russia was ripe for revolution, and there were some Communists, Trotsky among them, who mistakenly believed that most of Europe was in a similar situation. Communist parties were formed in several countries; in France as early as 1920. With the exception of Yugoslavia, and later of Albania, all the national Communist parties which eventually formed in Europe were subservient to Russian ideology. But the second half of the twentieth century saw a radical change in the Communist world scene. As a curtain-raiser there was the establishment of the Chinese People's Republic on 1 October 1949, and within a quarter of a century Marxism-Leninism was successfully established in Africa and in Latin America.

Mao Zedong was born in China, in Hunan province, in 1893. Very early on he identified with Marxist-Leninist theory, but even as early as 1942 indicated his individualism by inaugurating the Rectification Campaign, which explicitly set out to adapt Marxist theory to the specific needs of China. In particular he was concerned to relate the concept of the proletariat to the peasant class rather than to the labour work force of industry. With the establishment of the Republic he became both Party Chairman and chairman of the Republic, remaining the cult figure until his death in 1976.

His rule was marked first by the almost total economic collapse which followed on the application of doctrinaire Marxism to the Chinese peasant economy. This was countered in 1957 by his Great Leap Forward, which was more a strategic step backwards, aimed at decentralizing the economy and dismantling at least some of the bureaucracy that burdened it. In 1966-69 Mao returned to centre stage to direct the Cultural Revolution, in many ways reminiscent of Stalin's reign of terror in the late 1930s and postwar anti-intellectualism of Russia. But the excesses of the Red Guard wore themselves out against the patient, stubborn ability of the Chinese to endure.

Chairman Mao was a thorough-going materialist, thus identifying perhaps more with Marx than with Stalin, who was prepared to compromise over theory to gain his ends. Mao rejected any accommodation to western idealism and the Soviet doctrine first of coexistence and then of *détente*. There were direct attacts on Soviet imperialism.[11]

It is, therefore, scarcely surprising that there has been almost continuous tension between Marxism and Maoism. In the conflict between doctrinaire Maoism and the more pragmatic Stalinism (and even the modified form of Stalinism that has followed on the death of Stalin), there has, in fact, been a greater threat to world peace from Stalinism, which remains committed to world revolution, than from Maoism. Mao *was* concerned for the masses of China; Stalin was obsessed with power.

[11]Kolakowski, *op. cit.*, pp. 504-505.

6.2.6 Chinese and Russian influence in the Third World

Any super-power is necessarily involved in the affairs of other nations, and each such power necessarily exports its political ideology, as far as it is able to do so. Russia and China have been exporting Marxism-Leninism into Asia, Latin America and Africa: for convenience we begin with the situation in Tanzania, which has chosen to relate to China rather than to Russia.

In 1965, President Nyerere was able to report a grant of £1 million from China, and credits of ten times that amount. To develop the nation's medical resources Chinese doctors were accepted, and Chinese participation in a scheme to develop the country's external rail links was considerable. But Nyerere was left free to develop his political and economic policies without any particular reference to Maoism. Indeed, he explicitly identified his non-alignment with the Marxist and Maoist exporters of Communism by employing the term *Ujamaa* for his concept of African socialism: 'It is an African word, and thus emphasizes the African-ness of the policies we intend to follow'.[12]

He disassociated himself from naive attemps both inside Africa and outside to replace religion by socialism:

> This attempt to create a new religion out of socialism is absurd. It is not scientific, and it is almost certainly not Marxist, for however combatant and quarrelsome a socialist Marx was, he never claimed to be an infallible divinity ... the years have proved him wrong in certain respects just as they have proved him right in others.[13]

In fact, in the 1967 Arusha Declaration President Nyerere spelled out his version of socialism, its fundamental tenets and its goals. In the Introduction to his *Freedom and Socialism* he clarified the relationship between religion and socialism:

> Once a man has fulfilled his responsibilities to the society, it is nothing to do with socialism whether he spends his spare time painting, dancing, writing poetry, playing football, or just sitting. Nor is it any business of socialism if an individual is, or is not, inspired in his daily life by a belief in God ... a man's relationship with his God is a personal matter for him and him alone ... Socialism is secular. It has nothing to say about whether there is a God.[14]

---

[12] Julius Nyerere, *Freedom and Socialism* (OUP, London and Nairobi, 1968), p. 2.
[13] *Ibid.*, p. 15.
[14] *Ibid.*, p. 12. Commenting on divisions in the Marxist world with respect to the true nature of Marxism, Nyerere comments: 'We are fast getting to the stage where quarrels between different

CONFRONTATION

The Arusha Declaration, which appears in the same work, is clearly a notice of intent to establish a socialist state; it is equally clearly not an attempt to supplant religion.

Turning now to Russian involvement in Africa, we consider the case of Ethiopia. There the position was initially confused by Russia's early commitment to the support of neighbouring Somalia, a country which was claiming the right to large areas of Ethiopia. As a consequence the new military regime in Ethiopia looked initially to China for help. As had happened in Tanzania, China offered medical help and assistance in improving Ethiopia's internal land communications. Politically and militarily, however, China remained uncommitted.

When Russia stopped supporting Somalia, Ethiopia dropped the Chinese and accepted Russian economic, military and political assistance. The Russians quickly attained a good measure of control both militarily and politically. For some two years the regime and its supporters were entirely involved in the fighting on two fronts, with Somalia in the Ogaden and with the Eritrean secessionists in the north.

In 1978 a measure of military and political stability returned to the country with the ending of both of these major conflicts, at least temporarily. Almost at once local action, which was not at the time disowned by the central authorities, was taken against the Christian church in four provinces. Struggle meetings were organized and churches were closed. Christians were imprisoned, and an attempt was begun to discredit Christianity by labelling it non-progressive and counter-revolutionary. The Protestants were contemptuously labelled 'Pentecostals' or 'Penties' and declared unlawful. In an unusual move the Lutheran Makane-Yesus Church appealed for world intervention in the struggle, and some of the prisoners were released, although 1979 saw the execution of the former Patriarch of the Orthodox Church, Theophilus.

True enough, the Party Manifesto in Ethiopia guaranteed religious liberty, but in fact, from the point at which Stalinism was imported into Ethiopia, anti-church propaganda became a part of government policy.

6.2.7 The world church faces Marxism

The world church has reacted diversely to the many varieties of Marxist self-expression. Evangelical North American missionaries have been rather consistently suspicious of and hostile to almost all forms of socialism which many, perhaps through lack of a balanced education in some theological colleges, have failed to differentiate from Marxism. In Latin America and, to a lesser extent, in Africa, there has been a

---

Christian sects about the precise meaning of the Bible fade into insignificance when compared with the quarrels of those who claim to the true interpreters of Marxism-Leninism' (p. 14).

sustained attempt to incorporate Marxist political and revolutionary theory into Christian missiology. As we have suggested in chapter 3, the resultant liberation theology has failed to commend itself to the rest of the world, largely because of the bloody history of Marxist-Leninist praxis in Europe and Asia. In Ethiopia the Protestant church has taken a different position, continuing the position it adopted under the oppressive Haile Selassie regime. The church did not go underground. The church did not join resistance movements and did not plot the overthrow of Colonel Mengistu. Where the claims of Christianity and the demands of the Marxist leadership clashed, they openly followed their Christian principles, and submitted to imprisonment for it.

The confrontation with Marxism will continue, but the fact is increasingly apparent that Marxism cannot credibly maintain itself in an open society. Of course, significant sociological and economic advances have been made under Marxist regimes in some countries. But such advances have too often been paid for by the crushing of the human spirit, by the caging of the human mind.

The Christian church, however, will not overcome Marxism by setting up a straw man and then pushing him over. Marxism thrives on *real* grievances, on situations of exploitation of which too often the church is a part. There is an urgent need for a thorough education of missionaries in particular, but of all Christians in general, in the history and practice and theory of Marxism, to enable us to know the true dimensions of the problem posed by Marxism today.

6.3 THE IMPACT OF ISLAM

It is formally not possible for Islam and Christianity to co-exist through a tacit agreement that each will ignore the presence of the other. The duty of *mission* rests upon the Christian, and the duty of *da'wah*, 'calling',[15] is placed upon the Muslim. The Qur'an commands the Muslim: 'Call men unto the path of your Lord by wisdom and good counsel' (*Sura* 16:125).

There are some 800 million Muslims in the world, considerably fewer than the world's Christian population. The relationship between Christianity and Islam now falls to be considered.

6.3.1 Muhammad

Muhammad was born in Mecca in AD 570 and died in Medina some sixty-two years later. In those years he transformed the life of the entire Arabian peninsula. He was able to overthrow the polydeism which was almost everywhere entrenched. He produced a volume of his sayings which would ultimately become the authoritative scriptures for his millions of followers. He laid the foundations of a political empire

[15]See Isma'l al-Faruqi, 'On the Nature of Islamic Da'wah', *IRM* LXV, 260, October 1976.

which would know only expansion for almost 600 years.

Was Muhammad inspired? Was the Qur'an inspired? In an article in the *International Review of Mission*[16] Mohamed al-Nowaihi claims that two prominent western scholars accept the *divine* inspiration of the Qur'an, W. Cantwell Smith and Bishop Kenneth Cragg. Both these men are unusually sympathetic towards Islam and would probably be prepared to accept the idea of Muhammad as an inspired prophet, but in a lower sense than that asserted by al-Nowaihi. In fact we would be wrong in discussing the *inspiration* of the Qur'an, since to the Muslim the Qur'an is not an *inspired* book but a *revealed* book, owing nothing to its human tansmitter, Muhammad.

In fact the 'miracle' of the Qur'an, the only miracle which Muhammad claimed for himself, lies precisely in the promulgation of a perfect historical, theological and literary document through an illiterate prophet.[17] This concept of inspiration, or more correctly *revelation*, obviously closes the way to serious discussion of the teaching in particular and the contents in general of the Qur'an. The discussion here, therefore, is developed without particular reference to the Muslim concept of inspiration and revelation.

Muhammad grew up in Mecca and acquired first-hand knowledge of the excesses of the capitalistic way of life which had developed there. Muhammad also travelled with his uncle's trading caravans and later with the caravans of Khadijah, who eventually became his wife. He thus encountered the nomadic peoples of Arabia and saw something of the settled communities of Syria to the north. He had contact with Christianity, the more orthodox forms to the north and the diverse heretical forms which flourished in the comparative safety and obscurity of the Arabian deserts. Judaism, too, he would have encountered. His fragmentary knowledge of the Bible is best accounted for by attributing it to the kind of unstructured conversation to be expected of travellers around a fire at night.

His experiences affected Muhammad deeply. He was clearly repelled by the oppression of the poor and the cynical exploitation of religion by the Meccan aristocrats. Although *Al-Ilāh, the* God, Creator of the worlds, was acknowledged in Arabia, the local deities of oasis and mountain, of river and rock, meant far more to the common people. Room for them all was found in the Ka'aba, the cubic structure, one of several similar structures, at Mecca. The Ka'aba became, and remains today, the focus of pilgrimage, and it was out of the exploitation of the pilgrims that the wealth of Mecca largely came.

---

[16]'The Religion of Islam', *IRM* LXV, 258, April 1976.

[17]Muhammad is described in *Sura* 7:157-158 as *al-nabi al-ummi*, which Kenneth Cragg prefers to understand as 'The unlettered prophet', the man who was not a scholastic, of the '*ummi*, the masses; rather than as 'the illiterate prophet'. Obviously the Muslim tradition that Muhammad was illiterate enhances the nature of the 'miracle' of the Qur'an. See particularly the discussion in K. Cragg, *The Event of the Qur'an* (George Allen and Unwin, London, 1971), chapter 3.

Muhammad was able to compare the political and sociological weakness of his people because of their divisions, each clan with its own patch of land, its own leaders, and its own gods, with the inherent strength of the politically and religiously united Christian empire. Only language (Arabic) gave the Arabs any kind of unity.

At first, Islam was essentially a reform movement. Muhammad's concern was to see the end of the oppression of the poor, the protection of the natural rights of women and children. The absurdity of the multiplicity of deities must end, to be replaced by the recognition of Allah, one God. This last was the cornerstone of Muhammad's teaching. Of course, this belief was shared by the Christians and the Jews. Thus in the early, formative, years of Islam the movement might have gone in any one of three ways: absorption into Christianity, perhaps serving to reform the heretical sects of Arabia; absorption into Judaism, with Ishmael reconciled to Isaac; or the formation of a new religion. In the event it was this third option which was taken up.

Obviously we are not to envisage Muhammad as consciously weighing up the options. It was the pressure of events which led him into increasing isolation from Jew and Christian, and the course of these events can readily be traced historically and through the pages of the Qur'an.[18] It was the absence of any precision in Muhammad's knowledge of Old and New Testaments which brought him into conflict first with the Jews and later with the Christians.

With regard to Christianity, Muhammad entirely misunderstood the doctrine of the Trinity, which he saw as tritheism in a nuclear family, Father and Mother to whom a Son was born. His misunderstanding is evident from the Qur'an,[19] and is shared by the majority of Muslims today.[20]

---

[18] The presence of Jews in the Arabian peninsula can be traced to the AD 70 destruction of Jerusalem and to the Bar-Cocheba revolt of AD 136 (article *'al Madina'* in H. A. R. Gibb and J. H. Kramer (eds.), *Shorter Encyclopedia of Islam* (Brill, Leiden, 1974) and P. K. Hitti, *History of the Arabs* (Macmillan, London, 1937), p. 61). A Jewish community comprising more than one clan was established in Yathrib (later to be known as *Madinat al-nabi*, 'The city of the Prophet'). There were Christians even in Muhammad's own family circle: his wife Khadijah's cousin, Waraqah, was a Christian (W. M. Watt, *Muhammad, Prophet and Statesman*, OUP, London, 1961, p. 40). Christian heretical minorities flourished: the Arians and the Sabellian Modalists, the Nestorians and the monophysite Eutychians, the Ebionites, the Mariamites and the Collyridians with their unorthodox Trinity of Father, Son and Mary. These Collyridians are mentioned by Epiphanius (AD 315-403), Bishop of Constantia in Cyprus, in his *Panarion* (*Haereses*). He refers to a sect of women supposed to have reached Arabia from Thrace. They offered a cake (Gk. *kolyris*) to Mary on set days (*Haereses* 78-79), a practice possibly related to Je. 44:19 where Jewish women are described as offering cakes to the Queen of Heaven. There was Christian Ethiopian influence in the peninsula, too. Ethiopian Christianity with its monophysite beliefs and yet strong emphasis on Mary almost certainly provided some part of Muhammad's knowledge.

[19] 'They surely are infidels who say "God is the third of three", for there is no God but one God ... The Messiah, Son of Mary, is but an Apostle; other Apostles have flourished before him: and his mother was a just person: they both ate food' [*i.e.* they were both simply human] (*Sura* 5:77-79). See also *Sura* 4:169.

[20] Mohamed al-Nowaihi in 'The Religion of Islam', *IRM* LXV 258, admits: 'It is true that many Muslims have mistakenly believed that Christians worship three separate Gods and have not paid

CONFRONTATION

The conflict with the Jews appears to have reached its climax after the *hijra,* the withdrawal to Yathrib (Medina). It was in this period that the *qibla,* the direction faced by the Muslim in prayer, was changed from Jerusalem to Mecca.[21] The immediate cause of the conflict was the equivocal conduct of the Jewish community at Medina during the Battle of the Ditch, where they came very close to throwing in their lot with the attacking Meccans. But the more important conflict was religious and concerned the many (though often trivial) differences between Qur'an and Old Testament where they covered the same ground.[22] While the discrepancies are often small, where inspiration is the issue they must prove determinative. Jew and Muslim divided. It has been the consistent teaching of Islam that the admitted discrepancies between Qur'an and Bible are to be attributed to Jews and Christians who either carelessly or deliberately have introduced error into their respective Scriptures.

6.3.2 Islam after Muhammad

Having taken Mecca, Muhammad died at Medina in June 632. He had made no provision for the succession and left no male heir. He was followed by the four 'rightly guided Caliphs' and then by the Umayyad and Abbasid Caliphates. Rapidly the generally high moral tone of early Islam was dissipated as Islam moved from being primarily a religious reform movement to become one more political adventure. The essential unity of Islam was lost in division and schism. Politically, however, Islam was all but irresistible. The advance into Europe through Spain was halted by internal divisions as much as by the army of Charles Martel. As early as 669 the Abbasids reached Constantinople; Persia (modern Iran) and Iraq fell.

But it is particularly to the Muslim occupation of Jerusalem, the city sacred to Muslim, Jew, and Christian, that must be attributed much of the responsibility for the hostility which to the present tends to characterize Muslim-Christian relations. In turn it is scarcely possible to

---

sufficient attention to the latter's protestation that their belief in the Trinity does not imply a multiplicity of Gods, that God is still one with them.'

[21] Montgomery Watt, *Muhammad, Prophet and Statesman*, pp. 112ff. and *Sura* 2:136-147. According to tradition (*hadith*), however, a revelation concerning the change was given to Muhammad while he was at prayer and he at once turned to face the new direction. It appears also that to this point the Helpers had observed the Jewish *yom kippur,* but this was now transformed into the Ramadan fast to mark the beginning of the revelation of the Qur'an to Muhammad.

[22] *Sura* 12; 'Joseph' may be contrasted with Gn. 37 - 50. In the Qur'an Joseph tells his second dream to his father who warns him not to tell it to his brothers: in the Bible he tells his father and his brothers. In the Qur'an the brothers ask for Joseph to go with them whereas in the Bible his father sends him to look for them. In the Qur'an Joseph is placed in a well; in the Bible it is a dry pit. In the Qur'an Joseph is exonerated from the charge of having assaulted Potiphar's wife, but in the Bible he is imprisoned for it. According to the Qur'an he is imprisoned by some unexplained strategem and interprets Pharaoh's dream from his cell and refuses to go before Pharaoh until his innocence is established, while in Gn. 41 Joseph shaves and changes his clothes and comes to Pharaoh to hear and interpret the dream. According to the Qur'an Joseph himself suggests that he be put in charge of the granaries, but in the Bible it is Pharaoh's suggestion. The list could be multiplied.

appreciate the Muslim attitude to the Christian without a sober understanding of the Crusades.

In 1095 Pope Urban II issued the Appeal of Clermont, an appeal to all Christians to unite in ending Muslim occupation of Jerusalem. *'Deus vult'*, 'God wills it!' became the watchword of the church. The first Crusade progressed steadily: in 1097 Nicea fell, the next year Tarsus and Syrian Antioch. In 1099 the Crusaders reached Jerusalem.

After a brief siege Jerusalem was taken. H. Daniel-Rops comments:

> The conquest of Jerusalem was marked with hideous carnage ... at the Mosque of Omar ... there was such a slaughter that the blood ran ankle deep.[23]

Steven Runciman pictures the scene:

> The Crusaders ... rushed through the streets and into the houses and mosques killing all that they met, men, women and children alike. All that afternoon and all through the night the massacre continued ... The Jews of Jerusalem fled in a body to their chief synagogue ... the building was set on fire and they were all burnt within.[24]

The famed Richard Coeur de Lion of England calmly ordered the butchery of 3,000 Saracen prisoners.[25] To quote Daniel-Rops again:

> The history of the Crusades is, indeed, full of episodes that reveal the worst side of human nature: egotism, unbridled lust, frightful cruelty, and rapacity.[26]

It is true that the Crusades were mounted in response to the increasing harassment of Christian pilgrims to the holy places and to the destruction in 1009 of the Church of the Holy Sepulchre in Jerusalem. It is also true that atrocities were not the responsibility of the Crusaders alone. But Runciman rightly recognizes that it has been the memory of the Crusades that has so often poisoned Muslim-Christian relationships at every level.

Viewed politically, the subsequent history of Islam has been one of fragmentation. The Muslim empires have passed away to be replaced by competing nationalistic regimes, in recent years often demonstrating an odd and perplexing admixture of Marxism.

---

[23]*Cathedral and Crusade* (J. M. Dent, London, 1957), p. 446.
[24]*A History of the Crusades* 1 (CUP, London, 1968), pp. 286-287.
[25]*Cathedral and Crusade*, p. 459.
[26]*Ibid.*, p. 437.

6.3.3 Christ and the Qur'an

The traditional Muslim Christology is that Jesus was born of the virgin Mary, but that he is not thereby constituted unique. Indeed he is in a measure less than Adam who had neither human mother nor human father (*Sura* 3:52). He was prophet and Messiah, but precisely *not* Son of God.

In particular Islam denies that Jesus died on the cross. Jesus was a prophet. Jesus prayed to be delivered from the cross (Mt. 26:39). Therefore Jesus *was* delivered from the cross: 'They slew him not and they crucified him not, but they had only his likeness' (*Sura* 4:154). Muslim commentators have uniformly taken this to mean that Jesus did not die on the cross. Another, possibly Judas,[27] was crucified in his place, perhaps in the confusion caused by the unnatural darkness (which is then placed *before* instead of *during* the crucifixion). It is very possible that we have here echoes of Basilides who is represented as teaching that *Simon of Cyrene* was crucified in the place of Jesus.[28]

The Ahmadiyya movement, which originated with Mirza Ghulam Ahmad (1835-1908) in the Punjab, has a different interpretation of the crucifixion. According to Ahmad, Jesus *was* crucified, but did not die on the cross, recovering in the cool of the tomb under the expert ministration of Joseph and Nicodemus (who becomes a skilled doctor).[29] Jesus is supposed to have made a full recovery, and after meeting with his disciples made his way to Kashmir, where he died and was buried at Srinagar.

The intention here is openly polemical. Zafrulla Khan writes:

> Once it is established that Jesus did not die upon the cross, there was no accursed death, no bearing of the sins of mankind, no resurrection, no ascension and no atonement. The entire structure of church theology is thereby demolished.[30]

He is, of course, quite correct in this assertion. Paul makes the centrality of the death of Christ in Christianity clear:

> For I delivered to you as of first importance what I also received, that Christ died for our sins in accordance with the scriptures (1 Cor. 15:3).

---

[27]Detailed support for the view that Judas was crucified in place of Jesus is provided by the sixteenth-century *Gospel of Barnabas*, translated by L. and L. Ragg (OUP, London, 1907), republished in Karachi by Begum Aisha Bawany Wakf. See also my brief article 'The Gospel of Barnabas' in *Vox Evangelica* X, 1977.

[28]See Geoffrey Parrinder, *Jesus in the Qur'an* (Sheldon Press, London, 1976), pp. 109-110, and George Sale, *The Koran* (first published in 1734 and frequently re-issued, for example by F. Warne, London, n.d.), p. 38, footnote u.

[29]Muhammad Zafrulla Khan, *Deliverance from the Cross* (The London Mosque. 1978), p. 33.

[30]*Ibid.*, p. 89. Note also Mohamed al-Nowaihi, 'The Religion of Islam', *IRM* LXV, 258 (April 1976), pp. 216-225: 'Jesus, Muslims believe, was indeed placed on the cross, but he was saved and lifted up from it by divine intervention. Islam rejects the idea that God would allow Jesus to be killed.'

Islam remains a great rebuke to Christianity. In the main we have failed to impress the Muslim with the quality of the life of eternity which we claim to enjoy. Rather we have tended to offer an alternative religion, a comparable system of theology. Christianity ought not to be offered as a mere religion. It is a whole revelation of a new way of life, a total philosophy for the meaning of life, a new *quality* of life made possible through the forgiveness of sin in Christ and the empowering of the Spirit.'

And poignantly, behind the long history of conflict between Christianity and Islam, there lies a great unanswered 'What if?'

During the first five years of Muhammad's preaching in Mecca, the opposition steadily mounted. In 615 the first *hijra,* withdrawal, took place. A total of eighty-three men and eighteen women made their way to Ethiopia to seek refuge. They were well received by the *Negus,* or king. And the very first conversions from Islam to Christianity took place right there.[31] But *what if* the Ethiopian church had been what, in fact, in all its history it never became, a missionary church? *What if* teachers had been sent from Ethiopia to Muhammad in Mecca to expound the orthodox Christology, the accepted trinitarian theology? In fact the opportunity was missed; Ethiopia sent no missionaries to Muhammad, and Muhammad went on to establish an Arab religion with an Arabic scripture.

The twentieth century has brought a new opportunity to the Christian church. In the past we have gone to the Muslim, but we now find the Muslim coming to us. In 1979 there were more than 800,000 Muslims in Britain. The new development has been uncomfortable for both Christians and Muslims.

On the whole the non-professional Christian knew little about the origins or the teaching of Islam, and when the Ahmadis came knocking on Christian doors there was something approaching consternation among the Christians. But the Muslim did not find the transition easy, either. Islam was shaped for a very different setting, and the new setting did not readily receive the old shape. True enough the Sufi mystics could spiritualize and reinterpret the outward forms of Islam. Pilgrimage to Mecca could become for them the mystical search for love-union with God. Mainstream Sunni Muslims had no such recourse.

Muslim mission was not particularly effective in the new world. It was frankly difficult to persuade German industrialists and American

[31] The Muslim historian Ibn Hishām records: 'Ibn Ishaq said, M. b. Ja'far b. az-Zubair told me, "Ubaid Allāh b. Jahsh, after he became a Christian, used to pass by the Companions of the Prophet when they were there in Abyssinia and say to them, 'We now see clearly, but you are still blinking'; that is, we have true sight but you are groping for sight and do not yet see clearly. The word he used is applied to a puppy when it tries to open its eyes to see." '(*Sīra,* Cairo, 1937, iii, 417-418, quoted in J. S. Trimingham, *Islam in Ethiopia,* pp. 45-46). On this period of history Sir William Muir comments: 'If an Arab asylum had not at last offered itself at Medina, the Prophet might haply himself have emigrated to Abyssinia, and Mohammedanism dwindled ... into an ephemeral Christian heresy' (*The Life of Mohammed*, John Grant, Edinburgh, 1923, p. 70).

educators that somehow their salvation could depend on visiting the Ka'aba in Mecca and sharing in what are rather obviously animistic rites. Islam was caught between the need for reform and the fear of the sin of innovation, *bid'a*.

Islam is based essentially on *sunna*, custom, an accepted pattern of conduct. *Hadith* is tradition, tradition concerning the behaviour-patterns of the prophet. The pattern of behaviour observed in Muhammad and recorded in *hadith* is normative for the orthodox Muslim. The opposite of *hadith* is *ahdatha*. The practice of that which is not *hadith* is the sin of innovation.[32]

This concern for *hadith* and conformity with the *sunna* of the prophet is paralleled by the fear of innovation, and permeates every aspect of life. Islam finds it all but impossible to follow the example of Christian missionaries and cross cultural barriers. There can be only one culture for the orthodox Muslim, the seventh-century culture of Muhammad. The proper response to a sneeze is not determined by local culture ('Bless you!') but by what Muhammad said when someone sneezed in his presence.[33] Nor is the paralysing fear of *bid'a* of mere antiquarian interest:

> It is known that the ultra-conservative opposed every novelty, the use of coffee and tobacco, as well as printing, coming under this heading. Muslim theologians even today are not entirely reconciled to the use of knife and fork.[34]

The confrontation with the western world has produced a new challenge for the Muslim world. The present indications are that Islam will choose the road of ultra-conservatism with which to fight western technological development and eastern Marxism. The creation of ultra-conservative Muslim republics and quasi-Muslim republics will continue in an attempt to stem the rising tide of *ahdatha*. The concept of prophetic *sunna* is essentially reactionary and intended to provide Islam with stability. In this case stability has become sterility.

It would be a traumatic time of testing if ever Islam made a serious attempt to rethink the concept of *hadith*, to attempt to interpret Islam for the twentieth century, to grapple with the challenge of *contextualization* which is rightly now the concern of Christian thinkers. Ultimately the Muslim must bring his faith out into the non-conforming, unbelieving world and prove it there. It is not evident that Islam is ready for that test.

---

[32]On *ahdatha* see Ignaz Goldziher, *Muhammedanische Studien*, English translation by C. R. Barber and S. M. Stern (George Allen and Unwin, London, 1967), p. 28, 'The worst things of all are innovations.'
[33]I. Goldziher, *op. cit.*, p. 30.
[34]*Ibid.*, p. 34. *Cf.* also J. S. Pobee (ed.), *Religion in a Pluralistic Society* (Brill, Leiden, 1976).

6.4 CONFRONTATION WITH WORLD RELIGIONS

The two religions which have been discussed in some detail here are chosen because they exhibit both social and political aspects. Hinduism might equally well have been selected, although not Buddhism. It is in part because of the socio-political vectors that these two religions confront Christianity. Alongside the socio-political vectors stands the religious vector, with the call to *da'wah* as the duty of the Muslim, and, as the concern of the Marxist, the labelling of religion (conceived theistically) as the opiate of the people and therefore a proper subject for elimination. Both Hindu and Jew would see Christian mission, as it has been traditionally practised, as an assault on national integrity.

Until comparatively recently the Christian mission has been pursued on the assumption that it is the Christian responsibility to press adherents of other religions to abandon them and to become Christians. In the second half of the present century it has become fashionable to speak of this as religious imperialism, as part of western colonialism. As the latter is seen to be out of date it is tacitly assumed that the former, also, is outdated.

A number of myths are associated with this process of devaluing conversion. There is the myth that the peoples of the world were content with their old ways, with their traditional religions, which have sometimes been painted in idyllic colours which bear little or no resemblance to the sombre hues of the originals. R. de Vaux quotes Plutarch's description of the sacrificial rites of ancient Carthage:

> The Carthaginians were wont to slaughter their own children at the foot of altars. Those who had no children would buy some little ones from poor folk, and slaughter these as one does with lambs or birds. The mother would be present at the sacrifice, never shedding a tear nor uttering a groan. Nevertheless at the base of the statue, the whole arena was filled with flute players and drummers, so that the cries and screams of the victims should not be heard.[35]

Excavations in Carthage have revealed a cemetery containing the ashes of tens of thousands of small children, sacrificed in the name of religion — a realistic picture of religion without revelation. In Nigeria it was once the regular practice to bury twins alive, at birth. It was Christianity that ended the fear of the 'unnatural' birth. In India the practice of *suttee*, the immolation of widows on the funeral pyres of their husbands, was ended through the question mark raised against it by Christian ethics. The hills and the mountains were filled with demons, who were exorcised by the Christian faith.

---

[35] *Studies in Old Testament Sacrifice* (University of Wales Press, Cardiff, 1964), pp. 75-84.

There is the myth that all religions are essentially the same, that all point to the one God. Religion as already defined is any coherent system which attempts to answer the ultimate questions: 'Who am I, where did I come from, where am I going, why?' and the parallel series of questions starting 'Who are you?' and 'What is the world?' Within the sphere of religion so defined we have monotheistic religions such as Islam and Judaism, polytheistic religions such as Hinduism, agnostic religions such as Buddhism and atheistic religions such as Marxism. There is no consensus in the answers these religions provide to the ultimate questions. To the question 'Who am I?' Christianity might reply 'You are a child of God', Hinduism 'You are identical with God', Buddhism 'There is no ultimate reality corresponding to the concept "I"' and Marxism 'You are a cosmic accident'. And to the question 'Where am I going?' the Hindu might respond 'You are caught up in the *samsaric* cycle of birth and rebirth', the Marxist 'When you die that is the end' and the Muslim 'You are going either to one of the seven (or maybe eight) heavens or to one of the seven regions of hell'. Even so simplistic a statement as 'All religions bear witness, at least in some measure, to the presence and activity of God'[36] is inadequate.

The reduced proposition that all theistic religions are essentially the same is even less acceptable. The argument runs:

> The Muslim worships God,
> the Christian worships God,
> therefore Muslim and Christian worship the same Absolute.

In English this appears impressive, but not in those languages which have no generic term for 'God'. The word *god* in English is a common, not a proper noun, and the argument depends on the common noun being slipped in as though it were a proper noun. It is strictly parallel to the following:

> I bought a table yesterday;
> you have a table in your house;
> therefore you have my table in your house,

which would be true were there but one table. Plausible though the concept may seem, the concept that all religions are basically the same, or have the same aims, or share a common 'god', is false. There *is* one God. But there are many gods.

The fact remains that whatever well-meaning attempts are made to nullify the real differences between the world's religions, they stubbornly continue to exist. Nor is there any comfort in a third myth, that

---

[36]Stephen Neill, offering a summary of the principles of ecumenical writers, in his *Salvation Tomorrow* (Lutterworth, London, 1976), p. 28.

the differences, ultimately, are unimportant in comparison with the points of agreement. Religion is of the essence of life, more obviously so if religion is defined as a system which purports to provide the answers to the fundamental questions. In matters of indifference we may afford to be uncommitted. The colour of my bathroom wall (if, indeed, I am fortunate enough to have one), is of supreme indifference to almost everybody. The question on which side of the road I drive my car is of importance to many. But the answer to the question 'Who am I?' is of supreme importance to every person who asks it.

And then, lying behind the three myths, there is the smoke screen of modern theological jargon. The jargon frequently serves to conceal the relativity which has crept into Christian religious thinking. A kind of Christian dialectic is entered upon, where every assertion must die the death of a thousand qualifications. There are no absolutes, only relativistic platitudes. We are often intimidated by the nauseous repetition of the current in-phrases or in-words. 'Pluralistic' is one such word:

> The pressures of our pluralistic societies make necessary a deeper understanding of our relationship as Christians to members of other faiths.[37]

> We are at a time when dialogue is inevitable, urgent and full of opportunity. It is inevitable because everywhere in the world Christians are now living in a pluralistic society.[38]

Translated, these statements mean no more than that since we live in a world in which there are other religions besides Christianity, we need to understand our respective religions and our relationship to one another. There is nothing new or surprising in this. No qualitative change has taken place in this respect. But we are being urged to a new exercise, the exercise of *dialogue,* because of the existence of the pluralistic society in which we live.

6.4.1 The nature of dialogue

Dialogue is communication between at least two people. Communication is not the same as speech, for not all speech communicates. But wherever speech communicates, there dialogue takes place. It is not even necessary for two people to *speak* for there to be dialogue. In all true preaching there is dialogue even when it has traditionally been looked upon as monologue. The congregation *responds* to what is said: it agrees, questions, doubts, applauds, laughs, weeps ... that is dialogue, even though the preacher alone speaks.

---

[37]'The Concern for Dialogue in Asia', *IRM* LIX, 236, p. 427.
[38]'Christians in Dialogue with Men of Other Faiths', *ibid.*, p. 382.

A second concept of dialogue has developed in ecumenical circles. In *Salvation Tomorrow* Stephen Neill summarizes, not unfairly, the ecumenical world's concept of dialogue:

> We must live in a world filled with religions. We have to learn to live at peace with them and this can only be done through discussion.
>
> This situation must be expected to continue indefinitely; the eventual or ultimate triumph of Christianity must not be assumed.
>
> All religions, in some measure, bear witness to the Divine activity in them and in the world.
>
> In dialogue we must hazard all we believe, surrendering any entrenched positions so as to be able to listen to others.
>
> Dialogue starts from the base of equality. Christianity must not be held to be superior to the religions of other peoples.
>
> Dialogue must not be entered into with an eye to conversion.
>
> In dialogue we must expect to receive more than we can give.[39]

A third aspect of dialogue must be differentiated from the preceding two, that level of communication which is necessary to the pupil if he is to learn from his teacher. Dialogue in the Platonic, Socratic and Aristotelian sense involves a precise and even passionate pursuit of truth which may be distinguished from error. It is important here to notice that when I expose myself to the study of mathematics, I am not required to abandon my personal beliefs with regard to biology or theology. Nor, indeed, am I expected to suspend my critical faculties, nor to abandon any insights I may already have on the subject of mathematics.

These three concepts of dialogue — the dialogue of true preaching, the dialogue of surrender and the pedagogical dialogue — must be kept separate from one another. But these uses of the English word *dialogue* (which, of course, we are free to define and redefine as we will provided only that we state our definition clearly and use it consistently) are not to be confused with the New Testament's use of the Greek word *dialegomai* from which English 'dialogue' is formally derived. We may begin our discussion by noting Schrenk's comment on the contrast between the use of the verb in Plato and the other Greek philosophers, as 'debate, discussion', and the New Testament usage:

> In the New Testament there is no instance of the classical use of

[39]Stephen Neill, *Salvation Tomorrow*, pp. 28-29.

dialegomai in the philosophical sense. In the sphere of revelation there is no question of reaching the idea (German *Idee,* better 'concept'?) through dialectic. What is at issue is the obedient and percipient acceptance of the Word spoken by God, which is not an idea, but the comprehensive declaration of the divine will which sets all life in the light of divine truth.[40]

In fact there are thirteen usages of the verb in the New Testament. Two of these refer to argument, but not philosophical dialectic: in Mark 9:34 the disciples argue about who will be the greatest in God's kingdom and in Jude 9 Michael and the devil argue about the body of Moses. In Hebrews 12:5 God exhorts (but does not debate with) his people regarding their sins. All the remaining usages occur in Acts. Four of these might well be taken as determinative of the rest, since they deal with a situation of which we have independent knowledge: preaching in the synagogue (Acts 17:2, 17; 18:4, 19). Such preaching was not debate[41] and most certainly was not an attempt to reach an ultimate truth by means of dialectic:

> And Paul went in, as was his custom, and for three weeks he argued with them from the scriptures (Acts 17:2).

The important point here is that while synagogue preaching might lead to dissension (Lk. 4:28-30) or discussion it did not consist in a dialectical search for consensus. As Stott puts it: 'Paul's dialogue was clearly a part of his proclamation.'[42] Two comments may be made about the Christian's attitude to dialogue. First, we are wrong in exposing ourselves or the gospel to a Platonic dialectic, and still less to a Marxist-type one, in the expectation that truth will be reached by consensus. The extreme view of dialogue is expressed by J. G. Davies in a plea for openness in dialogue: 'Complete openness means that every time we enter into dialogue our faith is at stake.'[43] Such a point of view betrays a total misunderstanding of what it is to be a Christian. It treats being a Christian like being a cultivator of roses. Entering into genuine dialogue with other gardeners might lead to their taking up rose cultivation, or to your transferring your affection to chrysanthemums, or to both of you giving up gardening altogether. Davies continues:

---

[40] Gottlob Schrenk, article *dialegomai* in *TDNT*.

[41] For the synagogue service see S. Safrai and M. Stern (eds.), *The Jewish People in the First Century* (Van Gorcum, Amsterdam, 1976), chapter 18. On p. 921 a midrash on Song 1:15 is quoted: 'When the sage takes his seat to expound doctrine many strangers become proselytes.' In the synagogue the sermon was not mere debate or discussion; it was a call for *decision*.

[42] *Christian Mission in the Modern World* (CPAS, London, ²1977), p. 63.

[43] J. G. Davies, *Dialogue with the World* (SCM, London 1967), quoted by John Stott in *Christian Mission in the Modern World*, p. 60. Stott comments: 'I regard this as an intemperate overstatement.'

CONFRONTATION

If I engage in dialogue with a Buddhist and do so with openness I must recognize that the outcome cannot be predetermined either for him or me. The Buddhist may come to accept Jesus as Lord, but I may come to accept the authority of the Buddha or even both of us may end up as agnostics.[44]

If being a Christian simply means holding a certain academic view of Jesus of Nazareth, this idea of dialogue is tenable. But the biblical teaching is quite different. The Christian is 'born again'. The Christian 'has his mind renewed'. The Christian 'possesses eternal life'. The Christian has been 'incorporated' into the family of God. The Christian is 'a child of God'. These are not theories to be explored, but realities to be expressed. As well tell the Christian that he must be prepared to become a chicken as to suggest that he must be prepared to be un-Christianed.

Secondly, however, we must say that as the Christian enters into dialogue with people of other religions he must be prepared to *hear* what they are saying. It is too easy for us to know already, before we have listened, just what the other person's beliefs are. On the whole, the western world has a better knowledge now of other beliefs than Christians of the nineteenth century had. But still our knowledge is marginal and inadequate. Churches would do well to include in their Christian education programmes adequate and informed teaching on relevant world religions.

Dialogue with the non-Christian world is an urgent necessity; not the philosophical type of dialogue, but proclamation which engages the mind, proclamation which starts from a point of clarity, a clear understanding of the nature of the non-Christian religions. To return to Scripture, the normative assessment occurs in Ephesians 2:11-12:

> You Gentiles ... were ... separated from Christ, alienated from the commonwealth of Israel, and strangers to the covenants of promise, having no hope and without God in the world.

They were — we were — 'without God', *atheoi*. *This* is the biblical view of world religions: they leave man as they find him, without God. In the same vein, Paul speaks of his own attitude towards his former religion: 'We ... put no confidence in the flesh' (Phil. 3:3), a striking statement in view of the fact that he is speaking of circumcision, the essence of external Judaism.

> If any other man thinks he has reason for confidence in the flesh, I have more: circumcised on the eighth day, of the people of Israel, of the tribe of Benjamin, a Hebrew born of Hebrews; as to

[44]*Ibid.*

the law a Pharisee, as to zeal a persecutor of the church, as to righteousness under the law blameless (Phil. 3:4-6).

Paul continues: 'But whatever gain I had, I counted as loss for the sake of Christ' (verse 7).

Paul had to accept Christ's judgment of Judaism. *This* is the reality of Christian mission, that we have been given a commission to proclaim Christ and that wherever he is proclaimed other religious systems necessarily come under judgment. This insistent and authoritative proclamation is not arrogant: the proclamation does not stem from us but from God. Again we quote Paul:

> I delivered to you as of first importance what I also received, that Christ died for our sins in accordance with the scriptures, that he was buried, that he was raised on the third day in accordance with the scriptures, and that he appeared ... (1 Cor.15:3-5).

The content of our preaching refers to historical events allied to revelation. The factual content of our preaching conflicts with the teaching of Islam on the same subject. The resolution of the conflict cannot come through dialogue as it is conceived ecumenically, but through acceptance of the good news or rejection of it.

7
The way ahead

7.1 THE TASK UNCHANGED

Missiologically speaking the principal task of the church is unaffected by the changing world. Always the world challenges the church to abandon the task of mission which, for one reason or another, is termed by the unredeemed world 'anachronistic'. On the contrary, the *chronos* for mission is always *now* and the locus of mission is always *here*. This is necessarily so, since the missiological history of Israel cannot be rewritten, and the missiological charge to the church cannot be abrogated.

Since the missiological commissioning of the church has not been and cannot be withdrawn, mission remains a church priority. But the essential *continuity* of mission also follows because society is dynamic and not static: fresh generations arise and must again be reached for Christ. It is true that there are certain advantages which accrue to a society where the good news is once preached and accepted, and where the church has once been planted. But the new situation gives rise to dangers which did not previously exist. The second-generation syndrome appears, characterized in the churches by a predominance of biological growth (conversions from within the families of church adherents), and a general neglect of evangelism of the unchurched community. Nominal adherents tend to multiply, especially where the early growth of the church has supplied sociological stability and even status to a previously submerged ethnic group. There is a blurring in the differentiation between Christian and non-Christian and new forms of evangelism become relevant to the new situation.

We may, in fact, propound a generalization, that every generation is as lost as was the preceding one. While there is undeniable progress through history in man's understanding of the mechanics of the universe and his ability to manipulate that universe to his own advantage, and while man's knowledge of physics and mathematics and chemistry and biology progresses so that each generation can begin its work from a fresh base, the same is not true morally. Educated man in the twentieth century is as lost, spiritually, as was man in the third century: no more lost, but no less lost. The church must continue to take this lostness, this estrangement from God, this blindness to the real purposes of life, very seriously. For, surprisingly, people who may in other repects appear irreligious will frequently overtly recognize and confess this sense of lostness; 'I can't see any *point* to living.'

Taking this experience of lostness seriously, however, may mean for many of us a fresh appreciation of the nature of the good news. Too often the good news has been limited by our own blindness to our lostness; and emphases, frequently theoretical and theologically formulated, have been allowed to deform the message of Christ. On the one hand the good news is *not* the proclamation of the essential goodness of man, nor is it of the possibility of satisfaction through political liberation. To such aspirations the Christian is essentially a pessimist.[1] But on the other hand the good news is not *only* of life after death, while life in the present must simply be endured. Man's lostness is met, matched and over-matched by the sheer grace of God expressed in his search for man:

> I was ready to be sought by those who did not ask for me;
> I was ready to be found by those who did not seek me.
> I said, 'Here am I, here am I,'
>   to a nation that did not call on my name.
> I spread out my hands all the day to a rebellious people
>   (Is. 65:1-2).

God's seeking and finding, and the restoration of man to a true relationship with himself, however, all take place within time, which is to be viewed merely as a component of eternity. Life *now*[2] is to be changed.

The new quality of life is marked by holiness and righteousness, in Old Testament terms by *qôḏeš* and *ṣ^e ḏāqâ*. Holiness is of the very essence of Old Testament religion[3] while righteousness is its social concomitant. The concept of holiness is determined not so much by the

---

[1] *Cf.* Malcolm Muggeridge's trenchant comment at Lausanne 1974: 'If I ridicule a prospectus for a housing estate to be built on the slopes of Mount Etna, I am not being a pessimist. On the contrary, it is the advocates of so ruinous and ridiculous a project who are the true pessimists. To warn against it and denounce it is optimistic in the sense that it presupposes the possibility of building a house on secure foundations - as it is put in the new New Testament, on a rock, so that when floods arise and streams beat violently against it, it stands firm.' 'Living through an Apocalypse', in J. D. Douglas (ed.), *Let the Earth Hear his Voice* (World Wide Publications, Minneapolis, 1975), p. 449.

[2] Jn. 6:47, 'He who believes *has* eternal life.' Donald (now Lord) Soper expressed the point neatly: 'The Gospel has been called the open secret of victorious living. It is the power to break out of the narrow corner in which we exist and to inherit and enjoy life at its fullest.' *Tower Hill, 12.30* (Epworth, London, 1963), pp. 71-72.

[3] See Alan Unterman, 'Ethical Standards in World Religions, I, Judaism', *Expository Times* LXXV, 2, November 1973.

THE WAY AHEAD

etymology of the word $qād̠ôš$[4] as by the working out of the meaning of the injunction of Leviticus 19:2: 'You shall be holy; for I the Lord your God am holy.'

In the Old Testament record of the outworking of the special relationship between Yahweh and his people, a leading theme is that of Yahweh's *otherness:* his thoughts are not their thoughts and their ways are different from his ways. Yahweh is *different.* The good news carries with it both the possibility of sharing in God's difference, and the expectation of that sharing. The Christian is not to be conformed to the world, but God's action in renewing our minds is to transform us so that we shall be different — different in our thinking and different in our acting, because both thought and action are at one with God's thought and action. Concepts of success and failure will be radically transformed. Attitudes to life and death will be revolutionized. The notion of property will be affected, not to the adopting of humanistic communalism ('What is yours is mine'), but to the practise of biblical *koinōnia* (characterized by 'What is mine is yours'; Mt. 5:40). The good news to be offered, then, provides an end to man's lostness and results in a transformed *now* as well as an asssured future.

The demand for holiness, moreover, may not be taken as an optional extra in the practice of mission. Without it no-one will see God (Heb. 12:14). Now this bald statement cannot be intended to modify the biblical insistence that salvation is God's grace reaching out to the estranged and helpless sinner. The sinner is not expected to acquire holiness before he can see God. But if God is at work in our lives at all, it must necessarily result in *holiness,* in a visibly different way of life. It is in this different style of life that those around us see God. Without holiness of living on my part, the theology I teach or the good news I preach fails to convince. Of course that holiness is always limited, and should be always developing. But if the good news is effective in my life, holiness will result, and will validate the spoken word of the cross.

In the most fundamental respects, then, the twentieth century is no different from any other. The missiological task is the same and man is just as lost. God's claims on his people do not change, and he still demands of us holiness, otherness, without which no-one will be able to see God at work in us.

7.2 THE NEW SITUATION

But obviously there *are* differences between the twentieth century and the nineteenth, and between the second half of the twentieth century and the first half. Mission must be related to the political, sociological

---

[4]But see Norman Snaith's classic *The Distinctive Ideas of the Old Testament* (Epworth, London, 1944), chapter 2, 'The Holiness of God', for a sensitive and balanced interpretation of Hebrew $qôd̠eš$.

and economic changes that have taken place. Inevitably the world will continue to be a divided world, and political action will continue to be divisive and destructive. The world which stands over against the church is characterized by its subjection to ungodly powers, just as the church is characterized by its subjection to Christ. Satanic power is essentially destructive. The demoniac of the tombs (Mk. 5:1-20) illustrates this destructiveness vividly: his social life is disrupted so that he lives in the company of the dead, his mental processes are impaired and his character is marked by unrestrained and unrestrainable violence. Violence will continue to be a feature of the world, and this will ensure a divided world. Dreams of increasing international co-operation will not be realized except where co-operation is imposed by economic necessity.

The new feature will be the *nature* of the division. Already clearly discernible are four competing worlds. First we have the *Communist world*, divided into its Stalinist and Maoist components. Here we may expect Marxism-Leninism to give way to a pragmatic acceptance of a fallen world, abandoning that measure of idealism, still surviving in Marxist theory, that confidently expects the revolutionary masses to relinquish self-interest for the common good. A new synthesis is already emerging, with only a token indebtedness to classical Marxism. Pragmatically the acceptance of the realities of life is to be seen in the Berlin wall, in the machinery of the secret police, in the labour camps, in the consigning of dissidents to mental institutions, in the total and cynical denial of freedom in the name of the enslaved people themselves. But theory has not caught up with practice. It may yet do so.

The second world division embraces the Arab nations, the *world of Islam*, allied to the financial resources of oil wealth. This second world is of obvious importance, since we should expect world events to centre not on London or Washington, but on the Near East. The world of Islam tends to be out of step with the developed world, and the consequent tensions consistently give rise to revolutionary movements of the right and the left. Thus, on the one hand, Muslim lands tend to isolationism, Islamic states throwing out the baby with the bathwater in a total rejection of even the real advantages of technological society; while on the other hand the students of such lands, and more especially the women of such lands, tend to a left-wing radicalism which sets Communism in conflict with Islam. Somalia, Egypt, the Yemen, Iran, Pakistan, Indonesia and Malaysia all face the conflict. In the 1970s, right-wing Saudi Arabia was progressively encircled by countries either openly Marxist (the Yemen, Ethiopia) or under imminent threat by Marxism (Iran, Iraq). The world of Islam, in fact, offers fertile ground for Communist subversion, and the years ahead will demonstrate the outworking of the inevitable confrontation. Somalia was far enough away from Russia, geographically, to throw off Russian domination. Other nations will be less fortunate.

The Third World will continue with us. The helplessness even of the world's philanthropists will not avail to bring any real improvement in the lot of the majority of Third World nations during the present century. People there will continue to live in squalor and to die, often unnecessarily, in pain. They will spend the larger part of their lives hungry. These words must be written down because they are true, and yet one burns with shame even as they are written. Surely there is some way in which the church in the developed world can be persuaded to release its wealth to succour the hungry world? If anything meaningful is to be done a lead must come from the leaders of the church. Cannot our bishops and moderators and presidents lead us into a new and radical caring and giving?

The economic situation of the Third World will be adversely affected by the inevitable world-wide energy crisis. The world at the end of the seventies already stood in the penumbra of the crisis: the deep shadows cannot be far away. The world stands, with regard to energy, much as the astronomists stood immediately before the first moon landing. Then there were proponents of the dusty-moon-surface theory and proponents of the rock-moon-surface theory, and the argument was abruptly ended by the return to earth of samples of the moon's rocks. The likelihood of an energy crisis is flatly denied by some and presented as a certainty by others. In a few years we shall know. It is almost certain that there will be a fundamental crisis, and this will hit the Third World just as it is beginning on the pathway of industrialization.

Whether this energy crisis will prove to be another blow at Third World aspirations, or its deliverance from a potentially disastrous pathway leading to the same inhumane mechanization that has blighted life in the rest of the world, is not yet clear. Having myself worked in the 8.30 to 5.30 industrial world of Britain, and having lived for almost twenty years in Third World Ethiopia, one of the world's poorest nations, I would still deeply regret the imposing on Third World nations of the dehumanization apparently inseparable from industrialization, the surrender of the birthright of freedom in exchange for the dubious mess of pottage misleadingly called development. Dr Edward Norman, commenting on the possible effect of the energy crisis on the Third World, asked:

> Will that give the inherent religious instincts of the peoples of those vast regions the opportunity to avoid the processes of secularisation and perhaps to teach the world the basic nature of spirituality once more?[5]

[5] Dr Norman was commenting on the 1978 Lambeth Conference in his article 'Crisis of belief' in the London *Sunday Telegraph*, 23 July 1978.

Industrialization, with its concomitant of 'development', continues to be one of the unquestioned axioms for progress in society. But it is necessary only to examine the *quality* of life in the developed world, the desperate lack of any ultimate purpose, the collapse of any ultimately significant code of moral imperatives, and the disappearance of *society,* to be forced at least to the recognition that so-called progress carries with it some very unexpected and potentially destructive forces.

It is, of course, too easy to dismiss these observations by a simplistic reduction of the options to two: industrialization (and 'progress') and the pastoral life (and Marx's 'idiocy of rural life'). It is equally possible to think of a third way out of the obscenity of a profits-dominated industrialization without losing the very real benefits of industrialization — medical care, education, adequate housing and so on. The Third World may, then, retain its present concern for spiritual values and may lead the developed world back from its ruthless and suicidal secularization of society into an acceptance of at least some spiritual values again.

The fourth area embraces *the developed world* other than the Communist powers. This division includes North America, Western Europe and Australasia. Its present characteristic is loss of purpose. With the collapse of the old British Empire and the gradual withdrawal of the USA from its own Empire-building, mere continuance, existence, has replaced any genuine long-term goals. Apathy towards politics and even towards business is only too apparent. It cannot, therefore, reasonably be supposed that this part of the world will take any *decisive* part in over-all developments.

Over against these four great world divisions is *the church,* present in differing measure in each of the four. The church is theoretically one, but it is not demonstrably so. Practical unity appears to be brought into the church not through the political negotiations of a hierarchy which happens to have the leisure to debate, but through the desperate confrontation between the church and the hostile world, often in the context of persecution where the luxury of denominational rivalries can no longer be afforded.

Although it has not been demonstrated that the persecution of the church causes the church to grow, there is some evidence to suggest that when the church begins to grow it attracts persecution.[6] And it is when the church begins to grow and then experiences persecution that the church recognizes its need of a unity which, in more peaceful times, it could afford to be without. Denominational rivalry is a luxury of the developed world and it ought not to be exported to countries which cannot afford the luxury.

The church faces the Communist world. Here nothing is so neces-

[6] See my *Born at Midnight* (Moody Press, Chicago, 1973), chapter 15, 'The Role of Persecution'.

sary as instruction. Theological colleges the world over need to search their curricula to ensure that all who train at the college study the theories and practices and dogmas of world Communism. Communism is humanistic and the church is supernatural, and it is inevitable that the two must clash. It is possible that America has passed through a McCarthy era of over-reaction to Communism, and it is equally probable that Britain has hopelessly underestimated its threat. Tragically, very few Christian Bible colleges established by the missionary societies ever included the serious study of Communism in their curricula. Islam will not conquer Communism. Communism will not conquer the church. But the church must use the present to prepare for the inevitable future conflict with Communism.

The church faces Islam. Islam, indeed, is threatened from all directions, by its irrelevance to a world of industrialization, unable to change because of its reactionary leadership, by its geographical closeness to Communism and the development of revolutionary structures for the advancement of Islam, structures which are then open to manipulation by Communism. Here again Christians need to learn the nature of Islam, its history and its teachings, and especially its attitudes to Christ. But in the confrontation with Islam little will result unless the church can demonstrate a quality of life consonant with the promises of the New Testament, the life of eternity brought into time, to demonstrate irrefutably the transforming power of the risen Christ.

The church faces the Third World. As we have seen, it remains for the church to demonstrate the real compassion of Christ in a relevant and significant sharing of its material resources with the peoples of the Third World, *and* more especially with the churches of the Third World. It is too easy to criticize the Third World church's use of money, and too easy to forget that our missionary societies, too, have often proved irresponsible in financial matters. Every large missionary society has projects which it would like to forget, projects which proved to be impressive failures. We have made our mistakes and we must not be surprised if others make theirs. True love will not rejoice when things go wrong (1 Cor. 13:6) but will show trust. It would be a wonderful thing if the wealthy churches of the developed world could abandon the role of auditor and arbiter of the church accounts world wide, and could be humble enough to become simply a purse.

The church faces the developed world. Here as everywhere else the message of the church is challenged, her credentials scrutinized. It is not Christ who is examined: his credentials are not at issue, but it is the credentials of his people that are so ruthlessly examined. As we face an essentially naturalistic world, it is vital for the church to demonstrate to that world a frankly supernatural life. Too often splendid Christian doctrine stands in marked contrast to the poverty of our Christian living. A new spirit of community is developing in the church, and our ability to transcend the natural barriers of race and social class may well determine the impact of our mission. Pragmatism, that encourages the perpetuation of class distinctions on the plea that they promote church growth, must, in the long term, be self-destructive.

7.3 MISSIONARY SOCIETIES

Over against the contention of Ralph Winter and others, Costas is surely right in saying, 'There is no ground in the New Testament for a concept of mission apart from the church.'[7] Commenting on the emergence of missionary societies as a response to the failure of the *church* to engage in mission, Costas adds:

> When in her missionary endeavour she fails to make adequate room for the legitimate expression of God's multiple gifts, mission sodalities emerge spontaneously. Such a phenomenon, however, ought not to be seen as representing God's *perfect* will.[8]

If Costas is right (and it is apparent that Winter promotes the mission sodality pragmatically and not from Scripture), then a mission *society* has no permanent validity. If and where the church becomes structured for mission, there the mission society as a non-church sodality becomes anomalous. The observation necessarily raises two questions: are the churches prepared to change their structures in the interest of world mission, and are mission societies prepared to hand back their mission task if the churches so act?

The alternative to this revolutionary change is the continuance of the present unscriptural situation, in which churches abdicate their responsibility for world mission in favour of the non-church sodalities — goal-oriented mission societies. This in turn means that potential missionaries grow up in churches which tacitly accept a modality role concerned primarily with their own continuing existence. If the potential missionary ever advances to a church-planting role he will inevitably plant modality churches. By a further extension the modality church in the receiving country will necessitate the formation there of a non-church mission sodality, so perpetuating the unbiblical cycle. As Stephen Neill cogently summarizes:

> Once this fatal dichotomy of church and nation has been established, it is very difficult to correct it and to bring the church back to a true understanding of its nature.[9]

---

[7]*The Church and its Mission* (Tyndale House, Wheaton, 1974), p. 168.
[8]*Ibid.*, p. 169.
[9]*Salvation Tomorrow* (Lutterworth, London, 1970), p. 55.

As a historical fact it is readily demonstrable that God has used the mission sodality as an instrument for the planting of the world church. But a pragmatic observation of this kind ought not to be used to develop an axiom of mission. A historical necessity, consequent upon the failure of the church to engage in mission, cannot convincingly be transformed into a biblical virtue.

It is, in fact, difficult to avoid the conclusion that much of the argument for the preservation, the continuance and even the extension of the multiplicity of mission sodalities may be attributed to vested interests. Here, certainly, is an area for repentance on the part of missionary societies and an opportunity for the societies actively to encourage the world church to take up the task of world mission again.

Missions might also need to consider the consequences of the rivalries which have too often characterized their operations. It is surely wrong to find no fewer than sixty distinct missionary societies from North America listed as 'Baptist'.[10] Fragmentation on such a scale wastes personnel, is irresponsible in its financing, divides the world church, is abhorrent to God, and makes the church's claim to brotherhood patently untenable.

Missions which fail to take seriously either the responsibility of the *church* for mission, or the essential unity of the church (to be carefully distinguished from a merely external, formal and organizational unity), ought not to be accorded the support of the church. Here again is a way forward: let the missionary societies actively seek to come together, abandoning all worry about their own individual survival, and concerned solely that the unending task of world mission should be prosecuted vigorously, effectively and biblically. The traditional divisions within missions and the traditional dichotomy between church and mission should end, and end now.

7.4 THEOLOGICAL TRAINING

The content of a course of study fitted to the realities of modern mission has yet to be agreed. Indeed, in the United Kingdom, the content of theological studies curricula in general owes more to the vagaries of history than to any conscious assessment of the tasks to be undertaken by the students when they have completed their studies. There are faculties of theology in the universities, there are Bible colleges and there are seminaries. Stephen Neill warns:

> Seminaries may be a necessary part of the apparatus of the churches. It can hardly be denied that they are dangerous places...it

[10] In the 11th edition of the MARC production *Mission Handbook*. Of the sixty mission organizations listed as Baptist, twenty-nine include the name Baptist in their designation. The multiplication of mission structures may indicate burgeoning life or strangling bureaucracy or fragmentation and competition. But it always requires justification.

is not long before the question forces itself upon the attention as to precisely why these students are being trained.[11]

The answer *ought* to be elicited by a study of the syllabus being followed. Too often the answer so elicited does not coincide with the anticipated tasks of the potential graduates.

There is, quite obviously, a direct link *implied* between any course of training and the use to which that training is to be put. Expressed crudely, the would-be historian is not expected to study the flute, and the would-be physicist is not expected to master economics. Furthermore, it is generally accepted that within any one discipline there is far too much information for any one student to master, and specialization ensures that a student is exposed only to such areas of the subject as provide an adequate training in a relevant but limited field.

In some universities it has been possible for lecturers to ignore the immediate needs of their students and to design their courses of lectures in accord with their own special interests. But theological training ought not to be so. Here the lecturer must be prepared to abandon his own predilections to become the master of such aspects of theological training as are consonant with the ultimate needs of the students. For here we are not involved in a more-or-less relevant discipline, but with the transmission of an eternally relevant and utterly essential message.

In terms of communication theory, this last observation would lead to the recognition that missions training all over the world should leave the graduate competent in three areas:

1. He should understand the message that is to be communicated.
2. He should know enough about himself and his resources to enable him to transmit the message effectively.
3. He should know enough about his potential auditors to enable him to formulate the message and transmit it effectively.

7.4.1 The nature of the message

Although the actual formulation of the message may be determined by cultural factors, so that drama, poetry, prose, parable, and allegory are employed appropriately, the content of the message is not culturally determined. To use the categories of Bible translation, in order to preserve the *content* of the message, the *form* of the message may have to be altered.[12] The good news is not difficult to define succinctly:

[11] *Salvation Tomorrow*, p. 104.
[12] E. A. Nida and C. R. Tabor, *The Theory and Practise of Translation* (Brill, Leiden, 1969), p. 5.

Christ died for our sins in accordance with the scriptures ... he was buried ... he was raised on the third day in accordance with the scriptures (1 Cor. 15:3-4).

This historico-theological core does not require contextualization,[13] precisely because the core deals with *event* and not with abstract propositions arising out of the event. The process of contextualization can only mean providing a context for that which has been deprived of one. As Neill puts it: 'there would be no need to contextualize unless we ourselves had first taken theological education out of context.' [14]

Where theological education is removed from the context appropriate to it—the context of fallen society—and isolated in the context of an antiquated, obscurantist and totally academic community, then theological education becomes necessarily isolated, antiquated, obscurantist and academic. It would be wrong to deny it a *context*, but it is not the context appropriate to it. It is scarcely surprising, then, if the ordinand, confronted with a congregation of which he knows little, should revert to preaching the comfortingly familiar irrelevancies which were the focus of his training.[15]

In fact it is only too possible that missiological investigation effected in an isolated academic community may be counterproductive so far as the possibility of any real communication beyond that community is concerned. It is commonplace to observe that ordinary people fail to understand the theologian. And yet it was the very simplicity of the good news that led Mark to comment concerning the teaching of Christ that the 'common people', the *polys*, the 'toiling masses' as Marxism might express it, heard him gladly (Mk. 12:37).

On the other hand it remains true that within the Christian good news there is a depth and breadth and height and length which even the most profound of thinkers has failed to exhaust. It is the continuing and prayerful study of these deep things of God which may give to the Christian witness so *profound* an understanding of the ramifications of the good news as will enable him to express it *simply*.

A perception of the nature of the message will come primarily through an acquaintance with the text of the Bible, if in the original languages so much the better. But it is vital here that the medium of

---

[13]The word *contextualization* signifies yet one more ephemeral 'in' subject for theologians: I must confess that it was with some difficulty that I restrained myself from bowing to the tradition of the day and including some modest treatise of my own on the subject.
[14]*Salvation Tomorrow*, p. 109.
[15]Perhaps the most startlingly irrelevant sermon I ever suffered was delivered in an Anglican church situated in a working-class suburb of Birmingham. The curate introduced it at Evensong as 'The significance for modern thought of recent theories concerning the inter-Testamental period'!

instruction should be the learner's own language. Still today Third World seminaries and Bible colleges tend to use English or French as the medium of instruction despite the fact that the majority of the students speak English or French only as a second or even as a third language.[16] The reasons for this anomaly are apparent: first, many of the instructors cannot adequately speak the relevant local languages; secondly, it is not possible to translate the necessary textbooks into the local languages, or, if they can be translated, it is not possible to finance their publication; and, thirdly, a certain prestige often attaches to instruction in the international languages, more especially in the many situations where the Bible school is merely a convenient rung on the ladder of academic self-advancement. At least part of the answer must lie in the steady replacing of expatriate teachers by adequately trained local Christians.

Since the area of study must necessarily be selective, it would seem best to omit the traditional study of the history of the missionary societies, since the world in which they were relevant has long since passed away (and this despite the fact that we are still too close to that world to enable us to write a balanced assessment of the modern missionary movement). Similarly the study of European church history, so much of it a painful account of schism, division and disorder, could safely be passed over. The study of the first five centuries of the history of the church, however, is another matter, for in those years all the classical heresies in Christology arose and since then have simply been repeated. Ecclesiology and missiology should be taught in the context of the local church, and not in the isolation of a centralized educational institution. In the interplay between the New Testament and the theologians of the early church may be seen the necessary outworking of the implications of trinitarian theology.

The study of the *history* of the church must necessarily be accompanied by a study of ecclesiology, for without it the student lacks any authoritative criterion for his assessment of the church. At once we are confronted with the problem of acculturation, so that it must be our concern to decentralize the teaching of ecclesiology as rapidly as possible. The same must be true of missiology, which should certainly form part of any training programme.

Mission practice becomes missiological when it is accompanied by the process of formal reasoning, of logical analysis. Missiology will involve the study of at least five distinct areas of study: the purpose of God in constituting a church, the concept of lostness which underlies the search aspect of mission, the relationship which obtains between the believer and God, the history of missiological practice and the existing socio-political context within which mission is to be exercised.

---

[16]See in particular Stephen Neill's comments on the role of language in theological education in *Salvation Tomorrow*, pp. 105-109.

This last can, of course, be realized to any meaningful extent only when theological education is radically decentralized.

It is, perhaps, worth indicating that decentralization is not difficult to institute. In Ethiopia we were able to develop a quite remarkably comprehensive scheme of theological education using Bible schools at four levels, the first three of which were all localized, situated within walking distance of the homes of the students. The four levels were Basic (assuming no full-time basic education at all), Ordinary (assuming three or four years of basic education), Advanced (assuming seven or eight years of education), and College (assuming completed secondary education). Thus any Christian who wanted to study was able to find a Bible school suited to his ability. The system was instituted in 1963, and in 1970 there was a total of 3,165 students in eighty Bible schools.[17]

7.4.2 The role of the messenger

Ultimately it is the Holy Spirit who is the true Communicator, taking what is said or written and from it revealing Christ. The human messenger, however, is of course also active: there is a factual, historical core to what is preached that must be expressed with clarity. The Holy Spirit may then make effective in new life what is already known as historical fact or theoretical proposition. The missionary needs to understand himself in his role of communicator, and needs to understand both his own strengths and his weaknesses. A useful training will, therefore, include at least three elements related to the transmission stage of mission: linguistics, communications and homiletics.

The study of *linguistics* is a salutary discipline in that it makes possible a deep understanding of the true complexity of language, and of the diversities in structure which are to be found in language. Such a course of instruction should be distinguished from the in-depth study of descriptive linguistics required of the professional linguist or translator, although it would include at least an introduction to descriptive linguistics. At a more general level the course would include a study of language learning in the child and in the adult, the basic principles of literacy, and the fundamentals of Bible translation.[18]

The process of *communication* is dealt with by David J. Hesselgrave in his classic *Communicating Christ Cross-culturally*.[19] He deals realistically with the conception, encoding and decoding processes inherent in all forms of communication, and also considers the role of culture in enhancing or inhibiting perception. The diversity of learning processes is explored with an unprejudiced recognition of the diversity in those

---

[17] Statistics from an unpublished statistical report from the Sudan Interior Mission, *Current Facts and Figures*, April 1970.
[18] See my *Language and the Christian* (Bagster, London, 1978).
[19] (Zondervan, Grand Rapids, 1978.)

processes, a diversity which is accepted as representing alternative, but not mutually exclusive, means of processing knowledge. These more theoretical aspects of communication would need to be supplemented by some exposure to the practical use of the media: the role of audio-visual aids, the effective use of radio, cassette, television and the video-recorder, literature and camera.

The third element is *homiletics*. Oddly, the student always resists any training in homiletics. James Black encountered it in students in his day,[20] and the resistance continues. But homiletics has little to do with cultivating rhetoric and a great deal to do with voice production and the organization of material. It is at once apparent that if a speaker cannot conveniently be heard, or if, having been heard, what he says is unintelligible, the listener will abandon the unprofitable task of listening. In the development of any course of homiletics care is needed in relating the course to the anticipated task of the student: as a person-to-person communicator, as the leader of small-group discussions, as a committee chairman, or as preacher, teacher or lecturer. Each of these roles will necessarily require a different approach homiletically.

7.4.3 The role of the listener

The third aspect of missionary training involves understanding the listener. The listener exists as an individual who is part of a specific culture, as a member of a number of inter-related groups, and potentially as a member of the family of God, the church. The analysis would again suggest three areas of study, anthropology, group dynamics and Church Growth.

Anthropology is here conceived in its widest sense, the study of the entire life of man, his society and his history. It will be concerned with an examination of family life and inter-family relationships, of systems of government, of selection processes, and of decision-making norms; with the study of music, art, and, of course, religion. We must make a much more determined and honest attempt to understand religion in all its forms, but for many this may mean an emphasis on the two great polarities, Islam and Marxism. History must mean the history of peoples and the history of the *local* and national church. We desperately need church histories of Africa and Asia and Latin America, written by and for the indigenous church.

The study of *group dynamics* has been inhibited by fears that the discipline implies the mere manipulation of groups through learnt techniques. Of course, it *is* possible to manipulate groups, and such manipulation *may* be facilitated by an awareness of the principles of

---

[20]James Black, *The Mystery of Preaching* (Marshall, Morgan and Scott, London, ²1977), p. 106. See also C. H. Spurgeon, *Lectures to my Students* (Marshall, Morgan and Scott, London, 1954), especially chapter 8. Although obviously dated and with some typically Spurgeonic idiosyncrasies, this book has still to be equalled, far less surpassed, in the field of homiletics.

group dynamics. The word *manipulate,* however, is unnecessarily pejorative. All communication is in some sense manipulative, in that communication is intended to secure some response to the communication. A baby 'manipulates' its parents when it cries, the student 'manipulates' his teacher when he asks a question. Group dynamics is not intended to extend the inevitable process of manipulation in some illegitimate way, but to make the communicator aware of the effect, for example, of group *size* on group *conduct,* and to enable him to present what he has to say in a manner appropriate to the particular group he is confronted with. One may 'orate' to a group of two hundred, but not to a group of seven; one may converse with a group of twelve, but it is unrealistic to expect conversation, *vocal* dialogue, with a congregation of a thousand. Discussion time with a large group of five hundred may see participation by only five or so people, while the same congregation, divided into small groups of six or seven people, will make it possible for as many as two hundred people to speak. The Christian communicator needs to know this.

Of course there is no guarantee at all that the basic principles of group dynamics as they have been worked out in the West are cross-culturally transferable. Thus there is a need for group dynamics to be investigated from the detached viewpoint of anthropology, before statements appropriate to one culture are unthinkingly applied to another. The study of group dynamics should serve to make the missionary of any culture aware of the immense diversity of relationship patterns, communication systems and societal norms that he may encounter. He needs to be rid of the innate belief that his own patterns of relationships and his own societal *mores* are somehow the ideal from which all others diverge.

And finally there is the study of Church Growth. I would not expect this to be a permanent feature of a missionary study curriculum simply because it has been necessitated by a particularly dangerous phase in the life of the church, a phase in which the churches of the West lost sight of their primary task of mission. A monumental sociological study of the church has led to the propounding of a five-phase model of church development. A situation of *depression* is followed by *activation* and *revival.* These three phases then lead to complacency, a sense of security, and so to the fourth phase, *de-activation,* and finally to *declension* and a return to the initial state of depression.[21] If this model is reliable then we would identify the situation in the western church as being now between the first two stages, moving out of depression and into activation. Church Growth thinking depends, for its importance, on the contingency of precisely such a phase situation. And when the phase has passed, the centrality (although not the validity) of Church

---

[21] R. Currie, A. Gilbert and L. Horsley, *Church and Churchgoers: Patterns of Church Growth in the British Isles since 1700* (OUP, London, 1977).

Growth thinking will also pass. There can be little doubt that for at least a decade Church Growth teaching and thinking will remain dominant.

The training programme outlined here is not intended to enable the western missionary to move into the Third World with the confidence that he now understands how 'they' think. On the contrary, it represents the basic training needed by all missionaries engaged in mission in the six continents. It is as true that Americans do not understand African culture as that Africans do not understand American culture. Linguistic incompetence is not restricted to the missionaries of the West. Few Christians *anywhere* really get to grips with the heart of the good news, and fewer still know how to communicate it. We need to abandon on the one hand the denunciation of the follies of the missionaries of the past and on the other hand the luxury of wallowing in an interminable orgy of repentance. Instead we need to apply ourselves to a relevant programme of training for mission and then on to the practice of mission in obedience to the Commission.

We all need training. But this training must, like mission itself, be co-operative and not competitive; we must all learn and we can all teach. It may be that for a time the North Atlantic churches have something to offer in training leaders for the Third World churches simply because of the impressive facilities available and the gathered expertise of their faculties. But such a position must inevitably be short-term, and such training ought on principle to lead to the development of training colleges in the Third World, with the initial capital freely given by the developed churches.

7.5 REPENTANCE AND RENEWAL

There is a place for repentance by the world church. Some of us have practised mission as a form of neo-imperialism and others have used their financial resources to recolonize the peoples to whom they have gone. Cultural aggression has marked much of our work.[22] On the other hand some have refused to engage in mission at all. In an excess of humility which does little to honour God they have surrendered the uniqueness of the gospel or have adopted the policy of *laissez-faire*: 'Our church is built; let's look after it and leave the world to look after itself.' Others have dissipated their energies in a biting and carping criticism of what has been done in the name of Christ. It has been so easy to lose sight of the missiological imperative: the lostness of man and the grace of God shown in Christ on the cross.

We all need to repent. But there comes a point when there has been

[22] But of course the gospel will always challenge culture, and the missionary cannot be faulted for his opposition to much of what he found in the world's religion-without-revelation: see Stephen Neill, *Salvation Tomorrow*, p. 73.

enough repentance. It can become stultifying, unedifying, unproductive. Enough is enough. As an Englishman I would say to North Americans that it is time to stop bewailing your manifold missiological sins and wickedness, to stop grovelling, and to stand up and to recognize soberly the great things accomplished in the world largely through North American missionaries and with North American money and resources. It is time to thank God for what has been done, and to move on in world mission.

It is time for the churches of the United Kingdom to move again into mission, to look on the needs of Europe, to see again the peoples still not reached for Christ, to hear the challenge of Islam, to reach out to the million Muslims in Britain and to the bewildered multitude of the immigrant peoples, and to the humanistic masses who have already found that life without God is unsupportable because, however affluent, it is still meaningless.

It is time, too, for the mission societies to face the church at home and overseas and to seek together a clearer revelation of God's purposes for them, without any particular concern for their own continuing existence at all. Let the missions come together; let the worldwide church come together, not, in a spurious organizational unity, but practically, recognizing the marvellous diversity of the many members which together constitute the one body of Christ.

I do not believe that the crucial issue for the church today is the doctrine of Scripture. I believe it to be the battle between naturalistic religion and a frankly supernatural faith. The Christian may be as fundamental in his beliefs and as orthodox in his beliefs as it is possible to be, and yet never experience the supernatural dynamic of the good news. It will be as we all submit ourselves to the authority of Scripture and the unifying Spirit that we shall be empowered to live together and to work together in world mission.

Bibliography

Ali, Syed Ameer, *The Spirit of Islam* (Chatto and Windus, London, 1964).
Allen, Roland, *Missionary Methods: St Paul's or Ours?* (Eerdmans, Grand Rapids, 1963).
Atkinson, James, *The Great Light* (Paternoster, Exeter, 1968).

Barr, James, *The Semantics of Biblical Language* (OUP, London, 1961).
Barraclough, Geoffrey, *The Medieval Papacy* (Thames and Hudson, London, 1968).
Barrett, C. K., *The First Epistle to the Corinthians* (A. and C. Black, London, 1968).
The Gospel according to Saint John (SPCK, London, ²1978).
Beekman, J. and Callow, J., *Translating the Word of God* (Zondervan, Grand Rapids, 1974).
Berger, Peter L., *Pyramids of Sacrifice* (Pelican, Harmondsworth, 1976).
A Rumour of Angels (Penguin, Harmondsworth, 1970).
Bion, W. R., *Experiences in Groups* (Tavistock Publications, London, 1961).
Black, James, *The Mystery of Preaching* (Marshall, Morgan and Scott, London, ²1977).
Boer, Harry R., *Pentecost and Missions* (Lutterworth, London, 1961).
Bockmuehl, Klaus, *The Challenge of Marxism* (IVP, Downers Grove and Leicester, 1980).
Bonino, José M., *Revolutionary Theology Comes of Age* (SPCK, London, 1975).
Brierley, Peter, *UK Protestant Missions Handbook* (Evangelical Alliance, London, 1977).
Bright, John, *A History of Israel* (SCM, London, ³1981).
Bultmann, R., *The History of the Synoptic Tradition* (Blackwell, Oxford, 1963).

Bush, R. C., *Religion in Communist China* (Abingdon Press, New York, 1970).

Carey, S. P., *William Carey* (Hodder and Stoughton, London, 1924).
Cone, James, *A Black Theology of Liberation* (Lippincott, Philadelphia, 1970).
Conzelmann, Hans, *A Commentary on the First Epistle to the Corinthians* (Fortress Press, Philadelphia, 1975).
Costas, Orlando E., *The Church and its Mission* (Tyndale House, Wheaton, 1974).
Cotterell, F. P., *Born at Midnight* (Moody, Chicago, 1973).
Language and the Christian (Bagster, London, 1978).
Currie, R., Gilbert, A., and Horsley, L., *Church and Churchgoers* (OUP, London, 1977).

Daniel-Rops, H., *Cathedral and Crusade* (J. M. Dent, London, 1957).
Davies, J. G., *Dialogue with the World* (SCM, London, 1967).
Drucker, Peter F., *The Practice of Management* (Heinemann, London, 1955).
Douglas, J. D. (ed.), *Let the Earth Hear his Voice* (World Wide Publications, Minneapolis, 1975).

Gibbard, G. S., Hartman, J. J., Mann, R. D. (eds.), *Analysis of Groups* (Jossey-Bass Publishers, Washington, 1974).
Goldziher, Ignaz, *Muslim Studies* (English translation by C. R. Barber and S. M. Stern. George Allen and Unwin, London, 1971).
Green, Michael, *Evangelism in the Early Church* (Hodder and Stoughton, London, 1970).
Gutiérrez, Gustavo, *A Theology of Liberation* (SCM, London, 1974).

Haenchen, E., *The Acts of the Apostles* (OUP, London, 1971).
Hastings, Adrian, *African Christianity* (Geoffrey Chapman, London, 1976).
Hayward, Victor, *Christians and China* (Christian Journals, Belfast, 1974).
Hebblethwaite, P., *The Christian-Marxist Dialogue and Beyond* (Darton, Longman and Todd, London, 1979).
Hesselgrave, D. J., *Communicating Christ Cross-culturally* (Zondervan, Grand Rapids, 1978).
Hick, J., and Hebblethwaite, B., *Christianity and Other Religions* (Collins, Glasgow, 1980).
Hitti, P. K., *History of the Arabs* (Macmillan, London, 1970).
Hollenweger, W. J., *The Pentecostals* (Augsburg, Minneapolis, and SCM, London, 1972).

Holt, P. M., Lambton, A. K. S., and Lewis, Bernard (eds.), *The Cambridge History of Islam* (CUP, London, 1970).
Hoskyns, Sir Edwyn, *The Fourth Gospel* (Faber and Faber, London, ²1956).
Hunt, R. N. C., *The Theory and Practice of Communism* (Pelican, London, 1950).

Jay, E. G., *The Church, its Changing Image through Twenty Centuries* (SPCK, London, 1977).

Khan, Sir M. Zafrulla, *Deliverance from the Cross* (The London Mosque, London, 1978).
Kirk, Andrew, *Liberation Theology* (Marshall, Morgan and Scott, London, 1979).
  Theology Encounters Revolution (IVP, Leicester, 1980).
Kolakowski, L., *Main Currents of Marxism* (OUP, London, 1978).
Kreeger, L., *The Large Group* (Constable, London, 1975).
Küng, Hans, *The Church* (Search Press, London, 1968).

Larson, P., Pentecost, E., and Wong, J., *Missions from the Third World* (Church Growth Study Centre, Singapore, 1973).
Latourette, K. S., *A History of the Expansion of Christianity* (Paternoster, Exeter, 1971).
Lyon, David, *Karl Marx* (Lion Publishing, Tring, and IVP, Leicester, 1979).

McGavran, D. A., *Crucial Issues in Missions Tomorrow* (Moody, Chicago, 1972).
  The Eye of the Storm (Word Books, Waco, 1972).
  The Bridges of God (World Dominion Press, London, 1955).
  Understanding Church Growth (Eerdmans, Grand Rapids, 1970).
MacGregor, Geddes, *Corpus Christi* (Macmillan, London, 1959).
McLellan, David, *Karl Marx: his Life and Thought* (Macmillan, London, 1973).
Macquarrie, J., *Principles of Christian Theology* (SCM, London 1966).
Marshall, I. H. (ed.), *New Testament Interpretation* (Paternoster, Exeter, 1977).
Marx, Karl, *Capital* (Everyman edition, Dent, London, 1930).
Marx, Karl, and Engels, Friedrich, *Communist Manifesto* (Progress Publishers, Moscow, 1965).
Mechan, J. L., *Church and State in Latin America* (University of North Carolina Press, Chapel Hill, ²1966).
Minear, Paul S., *Images of the Church in the New Testament* (Lutterworth, London, 1961).

Moltmann, Jürgen, *Theology of Hope* (SCM, London, 1967).
  The Crucified God (SCM, London, 1963).
Moorhouse, Geoffrey, *The Missionaries* (Eyre-Methuen, London, 1973).
Morris, Leon, *The Apostolic Preaching of the Cross* (Tyndale, London, ³1965).

Neill, Stephen, *Christian Faith and Other Faiths* (OUP, London, ²1970).
  A History of Christian Missions (Pelican, Harmondsworth, 1964).
  Salvation Tomorrow (Lutterworth, London, 1976).
Neill, Stephen, Anderson, G. H., and Goodwin, J. (eds.) *Concise Dictionary of the Christian World Mission* (Lutterworth, London, 1970).
Newbigin, Lesslie, *The Open Secret* (SPCK, London, 1979).
Nida, E. A., and Taber, C. R., *The Theory and Practice of Translation* (Brill, Leiden, 1969).
Norman, Edward, *Christianity and the World Order* (OUP, London, 1979).
Nyerere, Julius, *Freedom and Socialism* (OUP, London and Nairobi, 1968).

Oliver, Roland, *The Missionary Factor in East Africa* (Longmans, London, ²1965).
Oussoron, A. H., *William Carey, Especially his Missionary Principles* (Suthoff, Leiden, 1945).

Parrinder, G., *Jesus in the Qur'an* (Sheldon Press, London, 1965).
Peers, E. A., *Fool of Love* (SCM, London, 1946).
  Ramon Lull (SPCK, London, 1929).
Perham, Margery, *The Government of Ethiopia* (Faber and Faber, London, 1948).
Peters, George, *A Biblical Theology of Missions* (Moody Press, Chicago, 1972).
Pickett, J. W., Warnshuis, A. L., Singh, G. H., and McGavran, D. A., *Church Growth and Group Conversion* (William Carey Library, Pasadena, 1973).
Pobee, J. S. (ed.), *Religion in a Pluralistic Society* (Brill, Leiden, 1976).

Ragg, L. and L., *The Gospel of Barnabas* (OUP, London, 1907).
Rahner, Karl, *Theological Investigations* (Darton, Longman and Todd, London, 1954 and onwards).
Read, W. R., Monterroso, V. M., and Johnson, H. A., *Latin American Church Growth* (Eerdmans, Grand Rapids, 1969).

Riesenfeld, Harald, *The Gospel Tradition and its Beginning* (Mowbray, London, 1957).
Rodinson, Maxime, *Marxism and the Muslim World* (Zed Press, London, 1979).
Runciman, S., *A History of the Crusades* (CUP, London, 1951-54).

Safrai, S., and Stern M., (eds.), *The Jewish People in the First Century* (Van Gorcum, Amsterdam, 1976).
Sale, George, *The Koran* (Warne, London, n.d.).
Schweizer, Eduard, *The Church as the Body of Christ* (John Knox Press, Atlanta, 1964).
Snaith, Norman, *The Distinctive Ideas of the Old Testament* (Epworth, London, 1944).
Sookhdeo, P. (ed.), *Jesus Christ the Only Way* (Paternoster, Exeter, 1978).
Stott, John, *Christian Mission in the Modern World* (CPAS, London, ²1977).
The Preacher's Portrait (Tyndale, London, 1961).

Temple, William, *Readings in St John's Gospel* (Macmillan, London, 1955).
Tippett, Alan, *Church Growth and the Word of God* (Eerdmans, Grand Rapids, 1970).
Religious Group Conversions in Non-western Society (School of World Mission, Pasadena, 1967).
Solomon Islands Christianity (William Carey Library, Pasadena, 1967).
Trimingham, J. S., *Islam in Ethiopia* (OUP, London, 1952).
Turquet, P. M., *Leadership: the Individual and the Group* (Tavistock Publications, London, 1967).

Ullendorff, E., *The Ethiopians* (OUP, London, ³1973).
Ullmann, W., *The Growth of Papal Government in the Middle Ages* (Methuen, London, ²1965).
A Short History of the Papacy (Methuen, London, 1972).

de Vaux, R., *Studies in Old Testament Sacrifice* (University of Wales Press, Cardiff, 1964).
Ancient Israel: its Life and Institutions (Darton, Longman and Todd, London, 1961).

Warren, Max, *I Believe in the Great Commission* (Hodder and Stoughton, London, 1976).

Watt, W. Montgomery, *Bell's Introduction to the Qur'an* (Edinburgh University Press, Edinburgh, 1960).
Muhammad, Prophet and Statesman (OUP, London, 1961).
Winter, Ralph, and Beaver, R. Pierce (eds.), *The Warp and the Woof* (William Carey Library, Pasadena, 1970).
Wilson, S. G., *The Gentiles and the Gentile Mission* (CUP, London, 1973).

Index

AACC, *23*
Abyssinian Frontiers Mission, *83*n.
Acts of Thomas, *76*
African traditional religion, *11*n.
ageing problem, *85*
ahdatha, *141*
Ahmadiyya movement, *139*f.
Allen, R., *52*
al-Nowaihi, M., *135*, *137*n., *139*n.
Alves, Rubem, *62*n.
anonymous Christianity, *10*, *13*
anthropology, *107*, *162*f.
apolytrōsis, *45*ff.
apostle, *72*f.
Apostles' Creed, *39*
apostolic, *25*f.
Arusha Declaration, *132*f.
Atete cult, *102*f.
Atkinson, J., *78*n.

Babel, *54*ff.
Barnabas, Gospel of, *139*n.
Barraclough, G., *77*n.
Barrett, D., *24*n.
Barrett, C. K., *51*n., *54*, *117*
Basilides, *139*
Bavinck, J. H., *16*n.
Beekman, J., *31*n., *47*n.
Berger, P., *101*n.
biological growth, *117*-*118*
Bion, W. R., *50*n.
Black theology, *68*
Body of Christ, *29*-*32*
Boer, H., *52*
Bonino, J. M., *63*, *65*, *66*
Booth, General, *62*
Brierley, P. W., *85*
Bryant, Arthur, *22*
Büchsel, F., *16*n., *46*
Buddhism, *9*, *143*, *147*

Bultmann, R., *46*n., *54*n.

Callow, J., *31*n., *47*n.
Canaanite religion, *12*
canonical mission, *18*
Carey, W., *22*-*23*, *78*, *79*
Carthage, religion of, *142*
charismata, *11*
Chile, *23*
China, *131*-*133*
Chinese Congress on World Evangelization, *87*
Christian Witness to Israel, *86*
Chua Wee Hian, *86*
Church, the, *24*-*41*, *52*-*54*, *73*, *154*
  apostolic, *25*-*26*
  body of Christ, *29*-*31*, *40*
  its task, *42*-*74*
Church Growth, *92*, *93*-*122*, *162*-*164*
  axioms of, *95*-*109*
  types of growth, *116*-*122*
Church of England, *113*-*114*
Churchill, Sir Winston, *124*-*125*
CIDA, *84*
CLAME, *87*
Clermont, Appeal of, *138*
CNEC, *91*
Collyridians, *136*n.
Communism, *126*-*134*, *152*, *154*-*155*
Communist Manifesto, *127*
community, *35*-*37*
complexity of mission work, *89*-*92*
Cone, J., *68*
conferences, mission, *93*, *124*
confrontation in mission, *124*-*148*
conscientization, *67*
contextualization, *19*, *159*
Conzelmann, H., *118*

Costas, O. E., *19*, *28*, *41*, *62*n., *63*, *94*, *156*
Cragg, K., *135*
Cranfield, C. E. B., *70*
Crusades, *137*-*139*
crux decision, *104*-*105*
cultural barriers, *20*, *102*-*107*
Czechoslovakia, *66*, *130*

Daniel-Rops, H., *138*
Davies, J. G., *56*f., *95*, *146*f.
da'wah, *134*
Delitzsch, F., *33*
dialegomai, *145*-*148*
dialogue, *144*-*148*
Dictatus Papae, *77*
disciple, *49*-*51*
discipleship growth, *119*-*121*
Drucker, P., *126*
dynamis, *52*

ecclesiology, *19*-*20*, *110*-*111*
ECWA, *87*
Edinburgh Conference, *93*
ekklēsia, *28*-*29*, *97*, *103*
elenctics, *16*-*18*
elenchus of the Spirit, *17*-*18*
Epiphanius, *136*n.
Ethiopia, *23*, *66*, *98*-*99*, *102*-*103*, *107*-*108*, *133*, *134*, *140*, *153*, *161*
ethnology, *109*-*110*
euangelizomai, *59*-*61*
Eusebius, *50*
Evangelical Alliance, *75*
Evangelical Missionary Society, *87*
evangelism, *20*, *79*-*80*
evangelist, *72*, *79*
exclusivism, *21*, *39*-*40*
exodus, *53*, *64*

Franciscans, *77*
Freire, P., *67*

furlough system, *84*

Gerhardsson, B., *49* n.
Gibbs, E., *80* n.
glossolalia, *55 - 56*, *57*
goals of the church, *95*
Goldziher, I., *141* nn.
Gotch, F. W., *22 - 23*
Great Commission, *53*, *56*
Green, Michael, *60*
group conversion, *100*
group dynamics, *50*, *121 - 122*, *162 - 163*
gunboat diplomacy, *78*
Gutiérrez, G., *62* nn.

hadith, *141*
Haenchen, E., *32*
hamartiosphere, *62*
Hebblethwaite, B., *10* n.
Heilsgeschichte, *19*
hermeneutics, *19*
Hesselgrave, D. J., *16* n., *161*
Hick, J., *10* n.
Hinduism, *9*, *11*, *142*, *143*
holistic, *20*, *21*, *75*
Holy Spirit, *18*, *40*, *47*, *51*, *73*, *96*, *97*, *106 - 107*
  Rahner's concept, *14*
homogeneous unit, *39*, *99*
Hoskyns, Sir Edwyn, *54*
Houston, T., *88*
Humphreys, Christmas, *14*
Hunt, R. N. C., *126* n., *127* n.

India, *23*, *82*
Inflation, *85*
Innocent, Pope, *77*
insufflation, *52 - 54*
International Ecumenical Congress of Theology, *63*
International Needs, *91*
International Review of Mission(s), *75*
Irenaeus, *57*
Islam, *9*, *77*, *134 - 141*, *152 - 153*, *155*

Jerusalem, *137 - 138*
Jesus in the Qur'an, *139 - 140*
Judaism, *9*, *69 - 70*, *136*, *137*, *148*, *150*

Ka'aba, *135 - 136*
Kalinovska, M., *130*
karma, *127*, *128*
Kealy, S. P., *39*
kēryssō, *60 - 61*
kingdom and church, *34*
Kinshasa Declaration, *24*
Kirk, J. A., *63*
Koehler, J., *54*

koinōnia, *36 - 37*, *151*
Kolakowski, L., *128* n., *129* n.
Kreeger, L., *50*
Küng, H., *25* f., *41*

Lambeth Conference, *39*
Lambie, T., *98 - 99*
Latourette, K. S., *76* ff., *100* f.
Lausanne Congress, *59*, *93*
Lausanne Covenant, *21*
Lenin, *129*
liberation theology, *61 - 67*
linguistics, *107*, *161 - 162*
Livingstone, D., *23*
London Missionary Society, *82*
lostness of man, *150*
Lull, R., *77 - 78*
Luther, M., *78*
Lysenko, *130*

McGavran, D. A., *19*, *94*
Macquarrie, J., *34*, *39*
man, doctrine of, *42 - 47*
Maoism, *131 - 133*, *152*
Marcuse, H., *63*
Mar Thoma church, *23*
Marsh, J., *51*
Martyn, H., *81*
Marx, K., *126 - 127*, *128*, *132*, *154*
Marxism, *63*, *66*, *125*, *126 - 133*, *152*, *159*
mathētēs, *49 - 51*
Mecca, *105*, *134*, *135*, *137*, *140*
MECO, *86*
medical missions, *79 - 80*
Melanesian Brotherhood, *75*
Memorbuch, *70*
Mengo, Battle of, *78* n.
Messiah, *33*
Metzger, B. M., *50*
Michaelis, W., *32*
Minear, P. S., *26*
missionary,
  as church planter, *24*
  definition of, *20*, *72 - 74*
  societies, *76*, *80 - 85*, *88 - 91*
  training of, *82 - 83*, *157 - 161*
Missionary Aviation Fellowship, *109*
modalities, *156 - 157*
Moltmann, J., *41*, *66* n.
Moorhouse, G., *78* n.
Morris, L., *46* n., *54* n.
Mott, J., *94*
Muggeridge, M., *150* n.
Muhammad, *52*, *134 - 137*, *140*
Muir, Sir William, *140*
Murray, J., *69*
Muslim, *14*, *70*, *77*, *99*, *103*, *125*, *134 - 141*

Neill, Stephen, *23* n., *24* n., *66*, *81*, *83*, *93*, *143*, *145*, *156*, *157*, *159*, *160* n.
nepotism, *91*
Newbigin, L., *15*, *63* n., *65* n.
Nicene Creed, *25*, *39*
Nicholls, B. J., *19*
Nida, E. A., *31* n., *48* n., *159* n.
nihilism, *43*, *44*
nirvana, *42*
Norman, E., *66 - 67*, *153*
North Atlantic churches, *20*, *67*, *73*
Northampton Baptist Association, *22*
notae of the church, *40*
Nyerere, J., *132 - 133*
Nygren, A., *70* n.

Oliver, R., *78* n.
Origen, *50*
Oussoren, A. H., *22* n., *79* n.
Overseas Missionary Fellowship, *85*

paraclete, *17*
parousia, *32*
Parrinder, G., *139* n.
Passover, *52 - 53*
Peers, E. A., *77* n.
Pentecost *50*, *52 - 58*
people movements, *100 - 102*
persecution, *24*
persuasion evangelism, *59 - 61*
Peters, G., *72*, *76* n.
philanthropy, *36 - 37*
pleroō, *71 - 72*
Plummer, A., *50* n.
pluralism, religions, *14 - 16*, *143 - 144*
Plutarch, *142*
praxis, *26*, *64 - 67*, *124*
proactive interference, *106*
proclamation evangelism, *59 - 61*

qādôš, *151*
qāhāl, *26 - 29*, *49*
qôdeš, *150*
Quadrilateral, Chicago-Lambeth, *39*
Quito Consultations, *87*, *89*
Qur'an, *134*, *135 - 136*

Ragg, L., *139*
Rahner, K., *9*
  his theses, *10 - 15*
ransom, *45 - 46*, *73*
redemption, *44 - 47*
relativism, *9*
religion, definition of, *42*
Rengstorf, K. H., *49*, *51*

173

responsive peoples, *98 - 100*
resurrection of Christ, *106*
retroactive interference, *106*
Richardson, A., *28*
Riesenfeld, H., *51*
Runciman, S., *138*

Sadducees, *48*
Sahel, *81*
Sale, G., *139*
salvation, definition of, *42 - 43*
samsara, *42*
Sartre, J.-P., *43*
Schrenk, G., *146*
s^{e}dāqă, *150*
self-destruct programmes, *79 - 81*
Septuagint, *35 - 36*, *46*
Servant of the Lord, *33 - 34*
Seventy, the, *50*
slave, *34 - 35*
Snaith, N., *62*, *151*
social action, *83 - 84*
sodalities, *156 - 157*
Soper, Lord, *150*
South American Missionary Society, *80*, *86*
Spurgeon, C. H., *82*, *162*
Stalin, J., *129 - 130*
Stott, J. R. W., *16*n., *21*, *59*, *61*, *146*
Sudan Interior Mission, *24*, *80 - 81*, *86*
Sufi, *140*
sunna, *141*
suttee, *142*

Tabor, C. R., 1n., *159*n.
talmîd, *49 - 51*
Tanzania, *132 - 133*
Tear Fund, *75*
Temple, W., *17*, *24*
Third World, *100*, *153*, *155*, *160*
 missions, *75*, *80*, *86 - 88*
 churches, *91*
Tippett, A. R., *75*n., *94*n., *97*, *104*
Townsend, W. Cameron, *81*
transfer growth, *118*
translation, of Bible, *81*
Trimingham, J. S., *140*n.
Trinity, *18*
Turquet, P. M., *95*n.

ujamaa, *132*
Ullmann, W., *77*n.
uniflow mission, *88*
Unterman, A., *150*n.
USAID, *84*

de Vaux, R., *28*, *142*

Vriezen, Th. C., *27*

wage differentials, *68*
Warren, M., *72*, *94*
Wasdell, D., *114*nn., *120*
Watt, W. M., *137*n.
way, the, *32 - 34*
Wieser, T., *25*n.
Wilson, S. G., *50*n.
Winter, R. D., *79*, *156*
World Council of Churches, *93*, *94*
World Vision International, *75*
worship, *34 - 35*, *37 - 38*
Wycliffe Bible Translators, *81*

Zafrulla Khan, M., *139*